# Balanced Asset Allocation

The Wiley Finance series contains books written specifically for finance and investment professionals as well as sophisticated individual investors and their financial advisors. Book topics range from portfolio management to e-commerce, risk management, financial engineering, valuation and financial instrument analysis, as well as much more. For a list of available titles, visit our Web site at www.WileyFinance.com.

Founded in 1807, John Wiley & Sons is the oldest independent publishing company in the United States. With offices in North America, Europe, Australia, and Asia, Wiley is globally committed to developing and marketing print and electronic products and services for our customers' professional and personal knowledge and understanding.

# Balanced Asset Allocation

## How to Profit in Any Economic Climate

ALEX SHAHIDI

WILEY

*Library of Congress Cataloging-in-Publication Data*

Shahidi, Alex.
  Balanced asset allocation : how to profit in any economic climate / Alex Shahidi ; [foreword by] Ray Dalio.
    pages cm. – (Wiley finance)
  ISBN 978-1-118-71194-1 (hardback) – ISBN 978-1-118-71217-7 (ePDF) – ISBN 978-1-118-71202-3 (ePub)
  1. Finance, Personal. 2. Investments. 3. Portfolio management. I. Title.
  HG179.S42577 2014
  332.6–dc23

                                                                  2014029359

Printed in the United States of America

10  9  8  7  6  5  4  3  2  1

# Contents

Foreword    Bill Lee    ix

Acknowledgments    xi

About the Author    xiii

Introduction    1

**CHAPTER 1**
The Economic Machine: Why Being Balanced Is So Important Today    5

**CHAPTER 2**
Your Portfolio Is *Not* Well Balanced    19

**CHAPTER 3**
The Fundamental Drivers of Asset Class Returns    29

**CHAPTER 4**
Viewing Stocks through a Balanced Portfolio Lens    49

**CHAPTER 5**
The High Value of Low-Yielding Treasuries within the Balanced Portfolio Framework    69

**CHAPTER 6**
Why TIPS Are Critical to Maintaining Balance (Despite Their Low Yield)    89

**CHAPTER 7**
Owning Commodities in a Balanced Portfolio    101

**CHAPTER 8**
Even More Balance: Introduction to Other Asset Classes    115

**CHAPTER 9**
How to Build a Balanced Portfolio: Conceptual Framework 127

**CHAPTER 10**
How to Build a Balanced Portfolio: The Step-by-Step Process 143

**CHAPTER 11**
The Balanced Portfolio: Historical Returns 155

**CHAPTER 12**
Implementation Strategies: Putting Theory into Practice 181

**CHAPTER 13**
Conclusion 195

**About the Website** 197

**Index** 199

# Foreword

et's face it—everyone needs a catalyst now and then. For me, this book has been a wake-up call; it has heightened my awareness of the risks in the portfolios I manage, and reminded me that managing money is as much art as it is science. Reading *Balanced Asset Allocation* has both reinvigorated my perspective related to constructing portfolios, but also given me valuable insights into how the portfolios could react under different economic conditions. Balancing risks and diversifying is what my job is all about. As an institutional investor, I have put the concepts of this book to work in the portfolios I manage. But as the saying goes, the cobbler's children have poor shoes, and I need to do a better job in my personal portfolios.

By explaining how to balance the risks in a portfolio, Alex has written a book that is completely accessible and useful across a wide spectrum of investors. Both the institutional investor managing billions and the average investor saving for retirement over a long time horizon can benefit. You don't need a lot of math skill to implement a balanced portfolio. The recipe is right here in the book. Alex does a wonderful job explaining why the economic machine works the way it does. You don't have to know the volatility of the stock market or the bond market, although the book spends time showing the reader how the numbers work if they are so inclined. The problem with the way we currently invest our portfolios is that they are too dependent on stock market risk. This book shows us a different path. We can construct portfolios with less stock market risk and over time, be fairly confident of achieving similar returns with fewer ups and downs.

What I like about the risk parity concept, pioneered by Bridgewater Associates, is that it explicitly addresses the real world economic events that impact our portfolios, and gives us options when traditional diversification efforts may not always work. The economic machine that produces rising and falling growth and rising and falling inflation, are the big four scenarios that our portfolios should be built to withstand. By balancing risks to these four economic scenarios and rebalancing as necessary, we don't have to worry so much about which stocks are correlated and which bonds are correlated. Correlation is one of the most difficult statistics to rely upon—especially in times of market stress. A balanced portfolio is a different and vitally important way to look at investing. Reading this book will open your eyes to a new perspective. I found it to be a useful and enjoyable read.

—Bill Lee
CIO, Kaiser Permanente

# Acknowledgments

I wrote this book with the intention of sharing core investment concepts that I thought might be informative for the majority of investors. My target audience was anyone interested in a thoughtful analysis of asset allocation. This applies to the entire spectrum, from novice to expert. Consequently, an indispensable part of the process was to seek honest feedback from a wide range of people.

The first thank-you goes to my friends at Bridgewater, the organization that pioneered many of the core concepts presented in this book. Ray Dalio, Seth Birnbaum, David Gordon, and Parag Shah were invaluable supporters. I am grateful to each of them for introducing me to these ideas and providing essential feedback. This group of special individuals ultimately inspired me to accept the challenge of writing this book and publicly sharing these important concepts.

I am grateful to Bill Lee, a true expert in the balanced portfolio concepts, for writing the foreword and taking the time to discuss these ideas with me. We share a similar passion for investing, and I am so fortunate to have met him through this process.

Charles de Vaulx, one of the most successful investors in the world, has expressed particular interest in these topics. He and I have spent countless hours debating the merits and potential flaws of the approach. He offers a unique assessment because of his financial expertise, and perhaps even more importantly, his intellectually curious and naturally skeptical nature.

Sam Lee from Morningstar offered suggestions that incorporated his experience with many of the concepts presented here. I am appreciative that he took the effort to share detailed, thoughtful comments that materially enhanced the final manuscript.

I would also like to acknowledge Fran Kinniry (Vanguard), Rob Arnott (Research Affiliates), and Dr. Vineer Bhansali (PIMCO), three investment industry giants, for reading through the manuscript and taking the time to provide insightful input.

Other financial experts, who I also consider good friends, were kind enough to dive into the manuscript and provide an indispensable peer review. David Hou, Ben Inker, Wendy Malaspina, Nick Nanda, Larry Kim, and Ron Kutak enthusiastically pored over the manuscript and gave advice that made the final book a clearer communication of the core concepts. Peter Joers, a founding partner at Greenline Partners and a former senior professional at Bridgewater, took the time to read every word and make valuable suggestions. I must thank Damien Bisserier, my trusted friend and business partner, for all his support and feedback from the very beginning of this prolonged journey until the final review.

I would like to express my gratitude to the many colleagues in the industry who also read the manuscript and offered comments. Each was successful in pointing out ways that I could more effectively convey the message. John Ebey, my longtime friend and mentor, graciously guided me through this book as he has throughout my career. My colleagues of more than a decade, Len Brisco, Sergio Villavicencio, and Michael Tidik, eagerly reviewed what I had written and assisted in making needed improvements. My uncle, Clayton Benner, has a remarkable ability to review all my writings with a fine-tooth comb to uncover and correct oversights. Thank you all.

Above all I wish to recognize my wife of 16 years, Danielle Shahidi, who offered a nonfinancial professional perspective and, most impressively, read the original manuscript multiple times cover to cover. I will forever be thankful for her candid remarks and for helping make the final product so much better than what I had originally put on paper. I must also acknowledge her undying support through this long process, which helped me build momentum at each trough.

Likewise, I appreciate the genuine understanding of my wonderful children, Michael and Bella, on all of those late nights and weekends when I was occupied with this project. Of course, my parents, without whom no opportunities at all would exist, are owed most of the credit for this work as well as any other contribution that I have made. Without the full backing of my family, there simply would be no book.

Finally, my team at Wiley deserves recognition for their patience, direction, and extraordinary efforts throughout this endeavor. I would like to express my deepest gratitude to Bill Falloon for giving a new author a chance. Meg Freeborn, Helen Cho, and Susan Cerra are extremely talented editors and were an integral part of helping me bring this project to fruition.

It has been a very long road from when I had an idea about this book until the time it was actually completed. I feel so fortunate to have had so much encouragement and help throughout this prolonged process and will remain immeasurably appreciative to everyone involved.

# About the Author

Alex Shahidi has over 15 years' experience as an investment consultant. He has worked for one of the largest financial firms in the world his entire career. Alex focuses on advising large pension funds, foundations, endowments, and ultrahigh-net-worth families. He currently advises on over $13 billion in assets, including several portfolios that are in excess of $1 billion. His average client portfolio is over $300 million.

Prior to beginning his career in investments, Alex graduated with honors from University of California, Santa Barbara, with degrees in business economics and law. He earned his JD from the University of California, Hastings Law School, and is a licensed attorney in California.

Alex is a Chartered Financial Analyst (CFA) Charterholder, Certified Investment Management Analyst (CIMA), and a Certified Financial Planner (CFP). Alex was designated one of the 250 best financial advisors in America by *Worth* magazine in 2008. He was also ranked as one of the top 40 advisors in the country under the age of 40 by *On Wall Street Magazine* in 2008, 2009, and 2010. *Barron's*, a Dow Jones publication, designated him one of the top 1,000 financial advisors in America in 2010, 2011, 2012, and 2013. In 2014, *Barron's* listed him among the top 1,200 financial advisors in the country.

Alex has published articles on asset allocation and long-term equity market cycles in the *Investments and Wealth Monitor*, a national publication offered by the Investment Management Consultants Association (IMCA). Alex has also been published by Advisor Perspectives, a leading publisher for financial professionals. His piece on building balanced portfolios, which was the basis for this book, was recognized with the IMCA 2012 Stephen L. Kessler Writing Award. The article was also recognized by the *Wall Street Journal*, *Market Watch*, *Moneynews*, Fidelity Investments, and *Wall Street Daily*.

# Introduction

Sitting in my seat as an investment consultant to institutional investors, I get to meet the best investment managers in the world and glean from them the best concepts. The purpose of this book is to share with you the concepts I consider to be the most important for investors. Most of the concepts in this book were originally conceived of by Ray Dalio and Bridgewater Associates, with whom I have had an invaluable relationship for the past 10 years.

First and foremost, I want to alert you to the most common and costly mistake investors make: having a poor asset allocation. Portfolios are simply not well balanced. In fact, most portfolios are so inadequately balanced that the risks of underperformance are much greater than investors realize. Even the most sophisticated investors are guilty of this oversight, which means that you are most likely exposed as well.

The good news is that this mistake is easy to fix. Big mistake, easy solution—why do we need an entire book to cover this topic? Portfolios have been imbalanced for so long that such a state has become the convention. *Poor balance is normal.* Consequently, I first want to convince you that your existing portfolio and strategy need fixing. I also should explain why keeping a balanced mix is especially important in the uncertain economic climate of the present decade. Finally, I wish to provide compelling support for the characteristics of a truly balanced portfolio, and most importantly, introduce you to a unique way of thinking about portfolio construction.

The idea here is not to present another purported winning portfolio tactic that happened to work well in the past. This solution is neither a trading strategy nor a super sophisticated way to capture returns that are not available to others. In fact, much of what you are going to read should sound extremely obvious and rational. I strive to appeal to your common sense by explaining the logic from a conceptual, sensible perspective rather than by attempting to convince you of the merits by backfilling historical data. My goal is to engage you in an intellectual exercise to help you see investing from a fresh viewpoint. In the end, you control your destiny and get to decide what makes most sense. I simply want to contribute to the process of helping you make an informed decision.

Throughout this process the greatest challenge will be to help you unlearn what you are confident is true about investing and retrain your

1

mind to think in a way that others simply don't. This renewed perspective will ultimately enable you to make your own decisions about the most logical thought process for developing a balanced portfolio. My responsibility is to help you make an informed decision. Your responsibility is to approach what you are about to read with a blank slate and an objective mind-set. In other words, forget all your assumptions about investing and let us start from the very beginning.

What is the main objective of building a portfolio? The goal is to try to make money in the markets. More specifically, you want to achieve a good rate of return with as little risk of loss as possible. Everyone knows that the markets go up and down; you just don't want to take a big hit. There are essentially only two ways to make money in the markets. You can trade investments (repeatedly trying to buy low and sell high) or you can simply hold investments (buying and holding for the long run). The first approach is risky because you might guess wrong and buy too high or sell too low. The second also has downside because you may choose to invest in the wrong markets at the wrong time. Trading securities is a zero sum game because for every winner there has to be a loser, since the market as a whole is made up of all the buyers and sellers. Moreover, with trading, time is not on your side. You can trade for a long period of time and earn nothing (or less than nothing after fees, taxes, and headaches). Holding markets, on the other hand, is not a zero sum game and time is your friend. You have a high likelihood of success if you wait long enough, particularly if you are invested in a well-balanced portfolio. Most importantly, holding markets is far easier to do and anyone can be successful doing it. For this reason, *the focus of this book is efficient asset allocation.*

What makes picking the correct allocation an onerous task is the fact that guessing what will happen next in the market is inherently difficult, if not impossible. This is particularly true when you consider that even if you think you know for a fact what the future economic environment holds (which you never do, regardless of what you may think), it does not necessarily mean that you will profit from this prescience. Markets are discounting machines. Current prices reflect expectations of the future. Thus, *you must not only accurately guess what the future holds, but your guess must be different from the majority view* (which set the price in the first place). In other words, be very careful about being too confident about your ability to consistently pick tops and bottoms in markets. Very few market participants have demonstrated success doing so, and even those who have cannot easily prove that their success is due more to skill than luck.

One of the key messages in this book is the notion that you should have *greater confidence in the benefits of diversification than in your investment convictions.* Even if you strongly believe that you know what the future holds, you should always trust that a well-diversified portfolio will provide greater benefits over time. In fact, the most dangerous scenario is when you are highly confident of future events that never transpire. The greatest losses generally occur not only when they are least expected, but when investors are most confident that the catastrophic loss is a nearly impossible outcome. For it is during these periods that investors are most apt to maximize their bets.

The answer, then, is to develop a *truly balanced portfolio*. A balanced asset allocation can help you profit during various economic environments and is *not dependent on successful forecasting of future conditions*. As you read this book, my hope is that you will better appreciate the appropriate context in which to analyze portfolios. You will gain a viewpoint that will make it obvious that the approach taken by most (likely including you) completely misses the mark and exposes portfolios to major, unanticipated risks. You will learn how to effectively construct a well-balanced portfolio that is less vulnerable to economic shocks. And best of all, the concepts that I will share are extremely simple, intuitive, and easy to implement. Although the logical sequence may make sense to you, the makeup of the truly balanced portfolio will undoubtedly surprise you. The simplicity of the thought process and the asset allocation outcome is the most compelling feature. As is often the case, simple is more sophisticated.

This book is divided into the following sections:

- Chapter 1 will establish the foundation for understanding how the economic machine functions. Viewing today's unique climate within this context will explain why maintaining a well-balanced portfolio is even more important than usual.
- Chapter 2 will demonstrate just how rare it is to find true balance in portfolios despite the great need. Many think their portfolios are well balanced and will be surprised to discover the reality of significant imbalance in the conventional asset allocation.
- In Chapter 3 I will explain what fundamentally drives asset class returns. The insights shared in this chapter will set the stage for how you should think about asset classes and balanced portfolio construction.
- Chapters 4–8 will analyze the major asset classes through the newly introduced balanced portfolio lens. By viewing stocks, bonds, commodities, and other market segments through this new perspective, you will likely reach a different, unconventional conclusion about the role of each asset class within the context of a truly balanced portfolio.
- Chapters 9 and 10 will help you apply the lessons in practice. Specific steps to build a balanced portfolio will be described. The rationale for a sample balanced portfolio, as listed below, will be provided.

**The Balanced Portfolio**

20% Equities

20% Commodities

30% Long-Term Treasuries

30% Long-Term TIPS

- Chapter 11 will demonstrate the benefits of a truly balanced portfolio by providing long-term historical returns to support the core concepts.
- To round out the discussion, Chapter 12 will provide implementation strategies to help you put into practice the concepts you learn in this book.

# CHAPTER 1

# The Economic Machine

## Why Being Balanced Is So Important Today

**B**ridgewater Associates, the largest and most successful hedge fund manager in the world, pioneered most of the concepts that I will present in this book more than 20 years ago. Bridgewater is at the forefront of economic and investment research and has been refining and testing its concepts over the past two decades. The company has a great understanding of what drives economic shifts and how those shifts affect asset class returns. The first chapter is effectively my summary of its unique template for understanding how the economic machine functions. Bridgewater has released a short animated video that explains their template and related research at www.economicprinciples.org, and I encourage you to visit the site. The core principles presented throughout the rest of the book were also developed by this remarkable organization over the past couple of decades. I know of no one in the industry that has a better command of this subject.

In order to fully recognize today's unique economic climate, you first need to better comprehend how the economic machine generally functions. The goal of this first chapter is to arm you with a command of the basic inner workings of this machine to enable a deeper appreciation of why this topic of building a balanced portfolio is so *timely*. Insight into the economic machine will also lay the required foundation for an improved understanding of the *key drivers of asset class returns*. I will refer back to this opening chapter throughout the book because it introduces *core, fundamental concepts that impact markets, and therefore portfolio returns.*

## HOW THE ECONOMY FUNCTIONS

Constructing the appropriate asset allocation is always a challenge, but it is particularly difficult in the current economic environment. The reason is simple: The United States and many other developed world economies are fighting through a deleveraging process that is likely to last for a decade or longer. Deleveraging is a fancy term for debt reduction or lowering leverage. When the amount of debt in any economy gets too high relative to the ability to pay it back, then the debt burden must be reduced. But what does this really mean and why is it so important? To effectively answer this central question, I will start at the most basic level.

The economy functions like a machine. Money flows through the machine from buyers to sellers. Buyers exchange their money for goods, services, and financial assets. This is what money is used for, and it is only worth something because you can exchange it for goods, services, and financial assets. Sellers sell these items because they want money. Buyers buy these things to fill a need. Goods and services help support their lifestyles while financial assets are used to preserve and increase wealth over time. An economy is simply the sum of billions of transactions between buyers and sellers. An economy grows when there are a lot of such transactions and it stagnates when the flow of money slows. At a fundamental level it really is that simple.

## THE SHORT-TERM BUSINESS CYCLE

The ability to borrow money slightly complicates the mechanics of the machine. If borrowing were not allowed in the system, then buyers would only buy what they could afford to pay using existing money. There would be no deleveraging because leverage would not exist. The economy could be more stable, although it may operate below its potential because capital would not flow as efficiently. With borrowing, a buyer is able to spend tomorrow's income today. If I want to buy a good, service, or financial asset and do not wish to (or cannot) pay with cash, then I can simply promise to pay for it in the future. I have created credit. This is what typically happens when you buy a house, swipe your credit card at the grocery store, or promise to pay your friend back if he buys you lunch. In each case you have created credit. Your balance sheet has been leveraged, and the amount of debt you owe and your debt service have just increased. A simple way to summarize these concepts is to say spending must be financed either from money or credit (so spending = money + credit).

With leverage an economy can grow more than it would otherwise because buyers can use both money and credit to make purchases. If they don't have enough money, they can use credit to buy what they couldn't afford to pay for with current funds. Because your spending is someone else's income, when you buy more using credit, then others earn more than

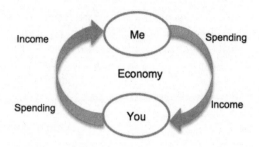

**FIGURE 1.1**   Basic Cycle of Economic Growth

they would otherwise. Then their increased earnings lead to increased spending and so on. The economy grows because it is simply the sum of all the transactions. Figure 1.1 displays this general cycle.

The central bank plays a key role in managing this process. The Federal Reserve (known as the *Fed*) is the central bank of the United States; other major economies around the globe have their own central banks. The objective of the central bank is to try to smooth out fluctuations in the economy. Fluctuations can be measured in terms of both economic growth and price stability or inflation. The Fed does not want the economy to weaken too much because reduced spending feeds into falling incomes, which begets more spending cuts. The Fed also does not want prices to rise too quickly. If there is too much money chasing too few goods, services, and financial assets, then upward pressure is exerted on prices, which can be harmful to an economy if it goes too far. In short, the Fed seeks the goldilocks economy (moderate growth and low inflation—not too hot, not too cold, just right).

How does the Fed try to maintain economic and price stability? The main policy tool the Fed uses is to control short-term interest rates. Whenever the economy is weakening or inflation is too low, the Fed can stimulate more borrowing by lowering short-term interest rates. When inflation is too high or the economy is growing faster than desired, then the Fed can raise interest rates to curtail borrowing. Recall that total spending must be financed by money or credit. The supply of money is relatively fixed most of the time. However, the supply of credit constantly changes and is largely influenced by interest rates. All else being equal, the lower the interest rate you are being charged the more money you would borrow and the higher the rate the less you would borrow. When credit is cheaper, the growth of credit typically increases and vice versa. When the Fed wants to stimulate more borrowing to support the economy or to increase inflation, it lowers rates to a level that encourages sufficient borrowing to achieve the desired outcome.

This interrelationship is why we have the familiar business cycle: The economy weakens, the Fed lowers rates, credit expands, spending picks up,

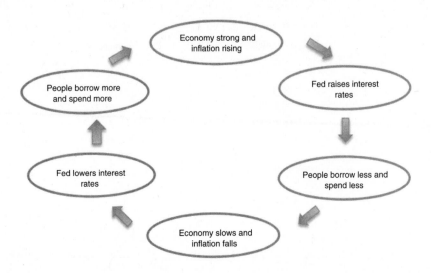

**FIGURE 1.2**   The Normal Business Cycle

and the economy improves. Eventually inflation pressures may build and the cycle reverses: The Fed raises rates, credit contracts, spending declines, the economy weakens, and inflation subsides. These cycles typically last three to seven years and are easily recognizable because of both their frequency and the relatively short time frame between inflection points. Investors have seen these cycles so many times that they have a good understanding of the pattern and how they work. Few are surprised when the cycle turns because they have firsthand experience with this dynamic. Figure 1.2 displays the normal business cycle.

Most investors, economists, and even lay people are probably familiar with the above-described parts of the economic machine. What follows next is much less understood, and in fact the concepts that will be presented have been completely missed by many economists and certainly by most investors.

## THE LONG-TERM DEBT CYCLE

There is another cycle that is working in the background of the economic machine just described. Most people are completely unaware of its existence because the cycle only hits its inflection point once or twice in a lifetime. By comparison, the business cycle covered earlier turns every three to seven years, on average. This longer-term cycle, often referred to as the long-term debt cycle, may last many decades before it changes direction. The only time it really matters and is worth paying attention to is near those critical inflection points. It is at those rare moments that no one can continue to ignore the powerful forces that ensue.

As covered above, the short-term business cycle exists because the Fed moves short-term interest rates in response to economic conditions. Over time, whenever the Fed lowers rates, increased borrowing adds to debt levels on balance sheets. Debt *levels* can continue to rise for a long period of time due to the *self-reinforcing* dynamic that is involved. The dynamic is self-reinforcing because the creditworthiness of a borrower is based largely on the value of his assets and income. Lenders want to make sure that they can be paid back. The higher the borrower's income and collateral, the higher are the odds of repayment. Going back to economic machine basics, when I borrow and spend, then the economy grows because that spending is some-one else's income. In sum, when we borrow to spend, our collective incomes rise. Rising incomes further support debt accumulation. Additionally, the value of our assets increases through this leveraging phase of the cycle because we have a greater ability to spend on assets such as stocks and real estate. The boosted spending on assets pushes their prices higher. The cycle is virtuous in nature: More borrowing leads to increased spending, which improves incomes and asset values, which are the key factors used by lenders to assess creditworthiness of borrowers.

Therefore, the short-term business cycle (three- to seven-year boom-bust economic cycles) operates within this longer-term debt cycle (50- to 75-year leveraging-deleveraging cycles). Each time the Fed lowers rates, the amount of debt in the economy increases; when it raises rates, debt *growth* slows. The level of debt generally does not materially decline during this phase; the growth of the debt merely pauses temporarily. Then the economy requires additional stimulus and debt levels go up once again. This continues until the total amount of debt in the system is too high and can no longer rise. In other words, balance sheets go through a long period of leverag-ing as they are constantly supported by higher asset values and incomes. This cannot continue forever as the cycle ends when *debt limits are reached*. We collectively hit our debt ceiling when we can no longer make interest payments on our debt and our assets have become impaired. At that point, we are no longer creditworthy and have difficulty refinancing our debt and increasing our borrowing. Our aggregate balance sheet is too highly levered relative to our assets and income and must be repaired over time. The typical dynamic is illustrated in Figure 1.3.

## The Deleveraging Process

The virtuous cycle continues until the system collapses under its own weight. Bad loans are made to bad borrowers; defaults pick up and the cycle finally turns. The Fed, in its normal response to weakening growth, predictably

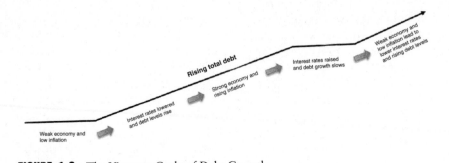

Weak economy and
low inflation

Interest rates lowered
and debt levels rise

Rising total debt

Strong economy and
rising inflation

Interest rates raised
and debt growth slows

Weak economy and
low inflation lead to
lower interest rates
and rising debt levels

**FIGURE 1.3**   The Virtuous Cycle of Debt Growth

lowers interest rates to stimulate more borrowing. *This time it does not work*. More borrowing is not possible simply because the borrowers are no longer creditworthy and the lenders, after recently being burned with massive defaults, have stopped lending. Rates fall to zero and the business cycle unexpectedly does not revert this time. The market is stunned and the economic machine literally stalls. Since total spending must come from money plus credit, and credit growth has reversed, total spending falls precipitously. This surprise creates fear, and those with money significantly cut their spending, which further exacerbates the problem. The cycle reverses after decades of going in one direction and the deleveraging process begins. It's akin to a speeding car on a crowded freeway suddenly shifting into reverse. Horrific accidents are inevitable. This is exactly what happened to the U.S. economic machine in 2008, and it is the exact same experience that captured the nation in 1929 at the onset of the Great Depression. These periods are normal responses, but they just don't repeat frequently enough for people to fully recognize and understand them.

The deleveraging process is just that: a process. It is inescapable and will repeat over and over again. The process is a largely unavoidable part of the economic machine because it is fundamental to how the machine is built. A credit-based economic system like ours is dependent on increased borrowing to finance spending, and there is great incentive to keep the cycle going as long as possible. It works well for a long time until the debt cycle reverses. When the cycle changes course, the process is *self-reinforcing*, just as it was during the upswing. In contrast, the normal business cycle is *self-correcting*. When the economy is too strong, tight policy causes it to slow, and when it is too weak, loose policy promotes an improvement. The long-term debt cycle feeds off of itself, however. I have already covered how this is the case on the way up. The opposite set of conditions drives the self-reinforcing process on the way down. I can't borrow any more so I spend less than I spent before. My reduced spending brings down your income so you spend less and that in turn negatively impacts someone else's income. The reduced overall spending and selling of assets to pay down debt also drives down asset prices, which hurts the value of borrowers' collateral, further degrading their ability to borrow. I spend less because I am earning less but also because I recognize that I have too much debt and want to take some of my income and pay down debt to gradually repair my balance sheet. This self-feeding dynamic causes a severe economic contraction in the beginning stages of the deleveraging process. The weak economic climate exacerbates conditions and confidence and can quickly lead to an economic depression. This is why a depression is not simply another variant of the normal business cycle recession. It is caused by a reversal of the debt cycle, not by the Fed tightening interest rates too much, which is precisely what causes normal recessions. Most people fail to appreciate this critical distinction because of a general misunderstanding of the mechanics of the economic machine and a lack of appreciation of the difference between the short-term business cycle and the long-term debt cycle.

How does all this relate to where we are in the cycle currently? The simplest way to measure the total debt to income ratio of a country is by taking all the debt in the economy and dividing it by the country's income, called the gross domestic product (GDP). This is a very basic measure of how indebted a nation is. You would follow the same logic to assess whether you personally have too much debt relative to your income. The country as a whole is merely a sum of its parts and is no different.

Figure 1.4 illustrates the debt level of the United States over the past century. The last deleveraging process in the United States took about 20 years to run its course. The country reached its debt ceiling in 1929 (after the Roaring

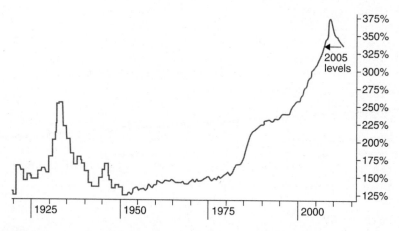

**FIGURE 1.4** U.S. Total Debt as a Percentage of GDP (1900–2013)
*Source*: Bridgewater Associates.

Twenties) and deleveraged until around 1950. It subsequently enjoyed the tailwinds of the leveraging cycle from the early 1950s until 2008 and is likely now once again saddled with the headwinds of the deleveraging process, and will likely be for a decade or two. The ratio of debt to GDP in 1929 was about 175 percent (it jumped to 250 percent during the Great Depression because GDP fell faster than total debt). In 2008 the ratio hit 350 percent, twice the level that caused the Great Depression! It took about 60 years of leveraging to achieve such a high ratio. Last time it took 20 years to bring the debt-to-GDP ratio back to a normal level; how long will it take this time, given the more extreme starting point? It certainly will not happen in a few years.

In most cases throughout history, economies live through a painful depression during the deleveraging process as the self-reinforcing negative feedback plays out. This process produced Japan's so-called lost decade, which began in the early 1990s. Europe is suffering through the same fate today, and even countries like Australia and Canada remain vulnerable to that critical inflection point, given their high debt levels.

Given this discouraging backdrop, why has the U.S. economy not fallen into a depression during the present deleveraging process? What makes the current period seem not as bad as the Great Depression or other similar depressionary environments? Deleveraging produces a persistent headwind for the economic machine and prevents it from functioning in its normal fashion. This force is exceptionally powerful and *if left alone to run its course, extreme economic and social hardship is a near certainty*. Fortunately the central bank has the tools to manufacture a smooth deleveraging, one in which the debt ratio gradually declines over time, but with positive growth through the process. Recall that the Fed's main policy tool is having control of short-term interest rates. Thus, their first step is to lower rates to zero. Normally during the deleveraging process this does not work because high debt levels prevent the normal leveraging response to lower rates. People can't borrow more, even though rates are extremely low, because they already have too much debt and are no longer creditworthy.

Recall that spending must be financed by money or credit. The credit pipelines have been impaired so the Fed is not able to increase spending by stimulating borrowing. Therefore, it must create money to make up for the spending falloff from declining credit. If spending must be financed by money or credit, and credit is constrained, then the only tool left to stimulate more spending is to manufacture more money as shown in Figure 1.5.

## Printing Money

The Fed has the unique ability to print money and buy assets. It can essentially create more money and inject it into the economic machine. Normally

# Spending = Money + Credit

Fed tries to increase this

Constrained during
deleveraging process;
Fed can't increase this

**FIGURE 1.5** The Source of Spending

the Fed prints money to buy government bonds, which has the dual effect of lowering long-term interest rates and pushing money into the economy. Lower long-term rates along with already low short-term rates help reduce debt service and leaves more money to be spent.

Many argue that printing money is irresponsible and will ultimately create more problems than it solves (including hyperinflation). Proponents of this perspective may not recognize that nearly every deleveraging in history has ended with printing of currency. The reason is straightforward within the context of the economic machine: The negative feedback loop of the deleveraging process will continue until the cycle is broken with the printing of more money. Spending will continue to decline as credit contracts (remember that spending = money + credit). *The debt-to-GDP ratio will get worse because the debt is falling slower than asset values and incomes.* This is exactly what happened during the first few years of the Great Depression and in the United States in 2008, and is what Japan has been living through since the early 1990s. In all three cases conditions degraded until the printing of currency ensued. The same process has been repeated across countries over time.

Along the same lines, a common question is why the printing of trillions of dollars does not automatically result in high inflation. The answer is that the printing of more money replaces the decline in credit to the degree that total spending does not increase enough to cause inflation. Money plus credit equals total spending, and the decline in credit is roughly offset by the increase in money. If there were no printing of currency, then total spending would likely fall significantly (because the quantity of money would not have grown), and deflation would be the most probable outcome. In other words, *the printing of money—which is normally inflationary on its own—merely offsets the deflationary conditions that exist at the time.* That is why we have yet to see inflation from the 2008 crisis and why printing money may never lead to inflation. The result is entirely dependent on whether too much money is printed. Printing money alone is not a sufficient prerequisite for higher inflation. In fact, printing currency is necessary to keep spending positive while the debt-to-GDP ratio is simultaneously reduced over time. By pumping more money into the economic machine the resulting increase in spending can generate positive growth rates while credit—the normal tool used to prop up the economy—is healing itself from high debt levels.

## THE IMPORTANCE OF BALANCE ALWAYS, BUT PARTICULARLY TODAY

Today's environment should be observed within this understanding of how the economic machine operates. Prudent portfolio construction should thoughtfully consider the wide range of potential economic outcomes. In a nutshell, the headwinds of deleveraging constrain economic growth and inflation. Unprecedented levels of money printing that aim to produce a tailwind of strong growth and rising inflation are meeting this negative force. Deleveraging versus the printing of currency: these two powerful forces are going head to head. Which will win? We are in uncharted waters and the potential range of economic outcomes is extremely wide. If there is too much printing of money, inflation becomes a high risk; but if there is not enough, deflation may result. More printing of currency is positive for economic growth; however, an insufficient level will be overcome by the deleveraging process and result in low or negative growth. How this dynamic plays out is a crucial input for developing the appropriate portfolio mix for the foreseeable future because of its impact on the economy.

Investors may be blindsided if they are positioned for one specific economic environment and experience another. For example, if one expects strong growth and weak inflation (as we experienced for much of the 1980s and 1990s) and instead experiences weak growth and strong inflation, then significant portfolio underperformance is likely. This is because the type of portfolio that does well during one economic environment is very different from the allocation that outperforms during the opposite environment.

Given the broad range of economic outcomes in the current market environment, maintaining an economically balanced portfolio is prudent. That is, rather than aggressively betting on one economic outcome, you may be better served by balancing the risks across multiple economic environments. *Balance is always important, but especially so when the range of potential economic outcomes is so wide.*

What do economic outcomes have to do with asset allocation? The fact is that the future returns of asset classes are largely dependent on what transpires in the economic environment relative to what was expected. These foundations will be more fully explored throughout this book, but for now a simple summary should suffice. If growth is stronger than expected, then certain asset classes are biased to do better in that environment. If inflation is rising faster than what had been anticipated, then certain asset classes will benefit from such a scenario. What really matters is how the future plays out in relation to what was expected. Therefore, about half the time the economy is growing faster than expected, and half the time it underperforms expectations. The same holds true for inflation. This is a critical point that will be repeated and reinforced.

A corollary to this fact is that the bigger the difference between the discounted economic environment and actual results, the bigger the market response. For instance, if the market is expecting (and pricing in) 3 percent growth and the economy ends up growing by 3.2 percent, then assets that benefit from rising growth will probably outperform a little bit because the environment was slightly better than what was expected. This is a logical outcome. If I buy stocks and pay a price that assumes 3 percent growth and actually get 3.2 percent economic growth, then the price should rise to reflect this new reality. I received a benefit and am rewarded for the foresight. This example can be repeated for a single company as well. If I want to buy company X, a big factor in the price that I will pay depends on how much I think this company will earn in the future (since the return of my investment is ultimately based on the company's future earnings). I would expect to earn more if the economy is doing well versus if the economy is doing poorly, all else being equal. If I calculate that a fair price would be $10 per share if the economy grows 3 percent, then I would certainly be willing to pay more if I knew for a fact that the economy would deliver a little more than that (again, all else being equal). For one company, *all else being equal* is a less likely reality as the idiosyncrasies of individual units become bigger factors in the analysis. But if we are talking about hundreds or thousands of big public companies, then how the economy performs becomes a much more reliable factor.

Conversely, if the market prices in 3 percent *growth* and the economy actually *contracts* 3 percent, then the prices of these stocks are likely to fall drastically. If I paid for growth and the companies actually lost money, then I must have really overpaid. Public markets reflect changed conditions and shifts in future expectations (which are often a reflection of recent trends) by adjusting today's prices. As −3 percent growth becomes recognized, prices will reflect the deteriorating conditions.

In the current period, we are experiencing not only a massive deleveraging process, but also a policy response of printing an unprecedented amount of money. The natural consequence of such conditions is an extremely wide range of potential economic outcomes. In other words, the range of outcomes is always unknown because the odds of guessing right are about fifty-fifty during all periods. However, the likelihood of *extreme* outcomes today are even greater because of the significant forces of the deleveraging process and of printing trillions of dollars. In short, we live in times of great uncertainty both in terms of *direction* and *magnitude.*

## SUMMARY

The following summarizes the key points thus far:

- An appreciation of how the economic machine works and the current deleveraging cycle suggests that we live in a challenging environment that may last as long as a decade or two.
- Asset class returns are highly dependent on how economic growth and inflation transpire relative to what was expected. These outcomes are inherently unpredictable, particularly relative to anticipated conditions.
- The bigger the difference between growth and inflation expectations and actual conditions, the bigger the price changes in asset classes.
- Given the economic backdrop and policy response to such conditions, the odds of extreme outcomes have been heightened.

The natural conclusion from this analysis is that the importance of constructing a portfolio that is very well balanced is paramount. By balance, I mean a portfolio whose success is not overly dependent on one economic outcome. This may sound obvious. However, the reality is that nearly every portfolio fails this simple test and in most cases the portfolio owner is completely unaware of this crucial oversight. The main reason for this oversight is that investors do not think of portfolios within this context. There is a lack of appreciation of the fact that every asset class is merely a package of economic biases. Most do not construct portfolios with this perspective and therefore do not realize the inherent biases, exposures, and risks that exist. I will cover this topic in greater detail in the chapters ahead.

Since economic outcomes (relative to expectations) largely drive asset-class returns and more extreme outcomes lead to wider ranges of returns, the most prudent investment approach is to build a portfolio that is positioned to perform well regardless of the future economic environment—that is, one that is well balanced across economic environments so that whether inflation or growth is rising or falling the portfolio's result will not be materially impacted. Good balance is always important because the future is always uncertain; however, because of the *greater likelihood of extreme outcomes* in the current period, *balance is even more critical today.* It is one thing to get the direction of outcomes wrong, but completely another when the *consequences of being wrong are severe.*

One final warning before you proceed to the next chapter. You should never be too confident that you know what will happen next. This is especially true today. Look at all the major inflection points in history and honestly ask yourself whether you would have been able to accurately predict the next economic environment. How many people accurately forecasted the current period 10 years ago? The next 10 years will be equally difficult to foretell. If we know that we don't know the future, then we shouldn't invest as if we do. Simply stated, the reason to keep good portfolio balance is to minimize the risk and impact of guessing wrong.

In investing you cannot control the outcome, so your goal should be to put yourself in the best possible position to achieve the highest probability of success. The thought process behind developing such a strategy as described in this book is key because it provides the tools to help you create the conditions to increase your odds of achieving your long-term portfolio objectives. Even if you do not agree with everything you read, my hope is to introduce you to a different way of thinking so that you can make your own informed decisions about the most rational approach to balancing your portfolio.

# CHAPTER 2

# Your Portfolio Is *Not* Well Balanced

**G**ood balance is particularly important in today's uncertain economic climate given the wide range of potential outcomes. Most investors probably agree with this argument, considering the current atypical economic environment and the considerable central bank response. Indeed, printing massive amounts of money and resorting to other unusual stimulative measures are not activities that we are used to seeing. Both the state of the economy and the reaction to conditions are undeniable signs that we do not live in normal times.

Consequently, most investors would reasonably wish to hold a well-balanced mix of asset classes. In fact, most investors (including you, most likely) feel that they already do own a well-balanced portfolio and are appropriately positioned for the present uncertainty. That disconnect is the topic of this chapter. *You think your portfolio is well balanced, but it is not.*

## WHAT IS GOOD BALANCE?

Let's begin with the definition of good portfolio balance. What does it mean to be well balanced? Most significantly, you should consider the return pattern of the portfolio over a very long time period. The return stream should be as steady as possible and should certainly not fluctuate considerably through time. Consider two portfolios that have achieved the same returns over a 30-year time frame: Portfolio A and Portfolio B, as depicted in Figure 2.1.

Portfolio A performed very strongly during the first 15 years and was roughly flat the ensuing 15-year period. In contrast, Portfolio B ultimately earned the same return but through a far more consistent path by delivering a similar return in both halves of the 30-year time frame.

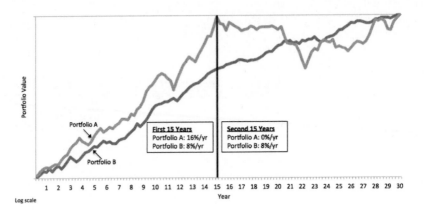

**FIGURE 2.1**　What Is Good Balance?

If the two portfolios produced the same returns over the 30-year period, why should you care which you own? The reason has to do with the stability of long-term returns and the risk that you enter at an inopportune time. Let's take a 15-year investment time frame, which most would agree is long term. If you happened to invest during the right 15-year period, then you would have been very happy with Portfolio A. However, if you were unfortunate enough to have guessed wrong and had bought that portfolio during the wrong 15-year period, then you would have been quite disappointed with the outcome.

Compare the timing risk involved with Portfolio A to that of Portfolio B, which achieved the same average annual return over the same 30 years. However, this mix was able to maintain tighter dispersion from the average over time. Clearly, this is a more desirable allocation since the odds of earning close to the average are substantially improved. Even if you guess wrong and buy at the worst time, you still achieve success with Portfolio B. In this example, Portfolio A is clearly poorly balanced, whereas Portfolio B is well balanced.

These two examples may sound extreme and you may feel that they are an unrealistic comparison. You might contend that in real life the outcomes can't be that spread out. After all, 15 years is a long enough time frame to smooth out the short-term volatilities of markets and the economic climate. Favorable periods are followed by bad spells, and the cycle is repeated multiple times throughout a 15-year history such that more normal results are far more likely with any portfolio. Although this widely held viewpoint sounds reasonable, it is not reality and is not supported by actual historical results. In fact, the so-called extreme examples I provided above are far more realistic and representative of past returns and future probable outcomes. The main point to remember is that you should strive to build an asset allocation that is positioned to achieve relatively stable returns through time rather than one that is highly dependent on picking the right period in which to invest. When I encourage investors to hold well-balanced portfolios, this is the ultimate objective to which I am referring. Stable returns through all long-term time periods is what we should all strive to achieve.

## THE CONVENTIONAL PORTFOLIO IS NOT BALANCED

If your objective is to construct a portfolio mix that is expected to earn steady returns over time, then the next logical discussion point is an analysis of how the conventional portfolio fits within this context. Is the conventional portfolio well balanced? A 60/40 asset allocation (60 percent stocks and 40 percent bonds) has long been considered a balanced portfolio by most investors, professional advisors, and other experts. This mix sounds balanced because it invests in both stocks and bonds, two asset classes that are materially different from one another. One is highly volatile (stocks) and offers attractive long-term expected returns, while the other (bonds) provides stability and lowers the volatility of the total portfolio. Conventional theory posits that bonds earn less but are needed to lessen variability in returns, and stocks earn more but are far too volatile to be held alone. The balance comes from owning both. Further, since stocks earn more than bonds—the theory continues—investors should own more stocks than bonds if they have the luxury and patience to hold on for the long run. The more risk they want to take, the more stocks they should own. This is the normal thought process that has led to a conventional asset allocation mix of 60/40.

The problem with this conclusion is that a 60/40 portfolio is not only imbalanced, but it is exceedingly out of balance and much more akin to the extreme example described above. Table 2.1 lists the returns of the 60/40 asset allocation over long-term bull and bear market cycles since 1929. The return is broken down into two parts: the return of cash and the excess return above cash. Combining the two provides the total return, which is

**TABLE 2.1** Annualized Return by Long-Term Cycle

| Period | 60/40 Portfolio Excess Return | Cash | Total Return |
|---|---|---|---|
| 1929–1948 | 2.2% | 0.5% | 2.7% |
| 1948–1965 | 8.4% | 2.3% | 10.8% |
| 1965–1982 | −2.3% | 7.5% | 5.2% |
| 1982–2000 | 9.2% | 6.5% | 15.6% |
| 2000–2013 | 2.7% | 2.1% | 4.8% |
| Avg. All Periods | 4.1% | 3.8% | 7.8% |

*Source*: Bloomberg and Bridgewater Associates.

**TABLE 2.2**    Annualized Return by Decade

| Period | 60/40 Portfolio Excess Return | Cash | Total Return |
|---|---|---|---|
| 1970–1980 | −0.9% | 6.8% | 5.8% |
| 1980–1990 | 5.3% | 9.6% | 14.9% |
| 1990–2000 | 8.9% | 5.3% | 14.2% |
| 2000–2010 | −0.5% | 2.9% | 2.4% |
| Avg. Four Decades | 3.1% | 6.1% | 9.2% |

the actual return you would have experienced. Your focus should be on the excess returns above cash because that is the return you earned for taking risk. You could have just held cash and received the yield without taking any risk. The average excess return above cash of this allocation has been 4.1 percent per year since 1929, but actual experience is highly dependent on picking the right long-term period in which to invest. You would have performed much better than 4.1 percent less than half the time and much worse during the other periods.

Further observe returns for the past four decades as shown in Table 2.2. During the 1970s, and from 2000 to 2010, the 60/40 portfolio performed miserably, returning less than cash. This represents a period covering roughly half of the past four decades! I am not referring to short time periods, but rather considerable lengths of time that are certain to leave lasting adverse consequences if mismanaged. Conversely, the 1980s and 1990s produced outsized returns in the completely opposite direction as both stocks and bonds earned strong results. It should be clear at this point that the example offered at the outset of this chapter was not merely an attempt to make a point by resorting to hyperbole. It was a statement of fact that should be taken very seriously and not quickly dismissed as an unlikely scenario.

From a simple review of historical results, it is obvious that a conventional asset allocation is not well balanced. I have already established that the key attribute of good balance is the achievement of stable returns over time. Clearly, the 60/40 mix has not passed this simple test, as it has delivered great returns for long periods and terrible results over other extended time frames. Putting it all together, about half the time you'll love it and half the time you'll hate it. This bipolar set of outcomes is hardly representative of good balance.

## WHY IS IT NOT BALANCED?

An asset allocation of 60/40 is not balanced largely because of the particular characteristics of the two asset classes used. Stocks are highly volatile, whereas bonds are not. This may not seem like a big problem, particularly since according to traditional methodologies that is the precise reason for the inclusion of these two asset classes. The total return of the portfolio is dependent on the returns of the two asset classes during each period. For instance, if stocks earn 10 percent and bonds earn 5 percent in one year, then the total portfolio that has allocated 60 percent to stocks and 40 percent to bonds will achieve an 8 percent return during that year. If stocks earn 20 percent and bonds earn 0 percent, then the total return will be 12 percent. If stocks lose 20 percent and bonds earn 5 percent, then the portfolio's value will decline by 10 percent. Table 2.3 lists the excess return of the 60/40 portfolio for each calendar year since 2000. The returns of the stock and the bond component are provided as well.

Notice that the returns of stocks are all over the place, as can be expected. This is what it means to say that this asset class is highly volatile. It can do very well or extremely poorly and tends to produce returns year-over-year far away from its long run averages. Bonds, on the other hand, are much less volatile. Thus, their return stream ends up much closer to their long run average over shorter time frames. This is why the average return is lower than it is for stocks. If that were not the case, then investors would opt to own bonds over stocks since they could get the same return for less risk.

The key observation that should be drawn from Table 2.3 is that the total return of the portfolio is almost entirely dependent on whether stocks

**TABLE 2.3** Calendar-Year Excess Returns 2000–2013

| Year | Equities | Bonds | Total 60/40 Portfolio |
|---|---|---|---|
| 2000 | −17.8% | 5.0% | −8.7% |
| 2001 | −15.3% | 4.4% | −7.4% |
| 2002 | −24.0% | 8.5% | −11.0% |
| 2003 | 27.8% | 3.0% | 17.9% |
| 2004 | 9.2% | 2.9% | 6.7% |
| 2005 | 2.4% | −0.8% | 1.1% |
| 2006 | 9.9% | −0.7% | 5.7% |
| 2007 | 1.0% | 1.9% | 1.4% |
| 2008 | −38.3% | 3.3% | −21.7% |
| 2009 | 26.9% | 5.8% | 18.5% |
| 2010 | 15.3% | 6.4% | 11.8% |
| 2011 | 1.9% | 7.8% | 4.2% |
| 2012 | 16.0% | 4.1% | 11.2% |
| 2013 | 32.2% | −2.1% | 18.4% |

*Periods of underperformance for equities and 60/40 asset allocation are **bolded**.

have performed above or below their average return. Since bonds are not very volatile, their results have little impact on the total portfolio. A bad period for bonds is not far from its average, just as a good period is not that far above it. Since stocks are so much more volatile than traditional bonds used in conventional portfolios, the total portfolio's success is highly correlated to the returns of stocks. When stocks do well, the total portfolio outperforms its average and when stocks suffer through downturns (highlighted in bold in Table 2.3), the total portfolio experiences underperformance.

To make matters worse, investors own more of the highly volatile asset class—stocks—relative to less volatile bonds. This results in poor balance because the impact of an asset class on the total portfolio is only dependent on two factors: (1) how volatile the asset class is, and (2) how much of the total portfolio is weighted toward it. For example, a portfolio that is 90 percent allocated to stocks and only 10 percent to bonds is obviously poorly balanced. This is because the 90 percent is very volatile and the 10 percent is not. However, a 60/40 mix is not much better. By overweighting stocks relative to bonds (60/40 still has 50 percent more stocks than bonds), investors are effectively and unknowingly putting all their eggs in one basket. It should actually go the other way. The more volatile asset class should get a lesser weight to make up for the fact that it is more volatile. The less volatile segment should receive a higher allocation so that its impact on the portfolio matches that of the higher-volatility asset class. At this point, I just want to introduce this sort of thinking for portfolio construction. In later chapters I will discuss this crucial concept in much greater detail. For now, you might consider adjusting the way you think about the portfolio construction process to one that incorporates an understanding of the importance of asset class volatility on portfolio balance. Most critically, this insight is often missing in the conventional approach to asset allocation.

Although most investors mistakenly believe 60/40 is well balanced, the reality is that *the traditional 60/40 allocation is 99 percent correlated to the stock market*! This is a fact that has been observed since 1927 over short and long time periods. This means that the success of the 60/40 portfolio is nearly entirely reliant on how the stock market performs. You can clearly see this in Table 2.3 by comparing the success of 60/40 year by year to outperformance and underperformance of equities during the same periods. This basic, undeniable attribute of the 60/40 portfolio is perhaps the *single biggest oversight in investing* today. Indeed, most professional investors are not aware of the extremely high correlation between a portfolio that is widely considered to be balanced and the stock market.

This imbalance is why a 60/40 portfolio can go through very long periods of underperformance, as exhibited in Table 2.1. The stock market can experience long stretches of severe underperformance, which directly leads to poor results for the 60/40 mix (which is 99 percent dependent on a good stock market return). This obvious observation has existed for nearly 100 years and will likely continue to hold true in the future.

Another important reason that the conventional 60/40 allocation is imbalanced is because its construction completely ignores the economic bias inherent in each asset class. As it turns out, both stocks and bonds are biased to do well during falling inflation climates. Therefore, 60/40 predictably does well when inflation is falling and poorly in the opposite environment. This topic will be covered at great depth later in the book.

## THE FLAW IN CONVENTIONAL THINKING

The historical results make it obvious that 60/40 is imbalanced. However, the key takeaway should be to recognize that the core issue is that the traditional *thought process* used to develop the conventional asset allocation is highly flawed. This is the key oversight. After all, the historical results could certainly have been different and will undoubtedly vary in the future. You can, however, learn about the issues with the thought process that led to the conventional allocation and emphasize less the actual results. Such an analysis is more likely to lead you to make improvements in how you build portfolios to give yourself a better chance to achieve long-term success.

The *flawed conventional thought process* is as follows: Stocks offer a higher expected return than bonds. Because they are riskier, it is reasonable to expect that the relationship between higher returns and risk will hold over time. According to the theory, it follows that the longer the time horizon investors have, the more they should allocate to the higher returning asset class (stocks). Bonds are only there to provide stability, since their returns are inferior to those of stocks over the long run. Thus, the longer the investment period, the more the investor can afford to live with ups and downs. Assessment of the appropriate asset allocation ratio is often based on factors such as the investor's age, cash flow needs, and emotional risk tolerance. Are you someone who can ride the roller coaster without emotion or are you more prone to selling at the first downturn? This combination of factors results in a portfolio that scales up and down from a starting point as low as perhaps 30 percent stocks for conservative investors, to as much as 75 percent stocks for those with more aggressive temperaments.

You should note that nowhere in the aforementioned traditional thought process is there a thought to how the *volatility* of the asset classes impacts the total portfolio's return stream. Moreover, there is no attention paid to the *economic bias* of the asset classes in the conventional approach. The emphasis is entirely on the *returns* of the asset classes. The only consideration of volatility is the fact that bonds are less volatile than stocks and so have a place in a portfolio merely to help achieve a lower total portfolio volatility than that of one with 100 percent stocks.

This distinction is critical. If your thinking follows conventional logic, then you are likely to end up with a portfolio as imbalanced as the traditional 60/40 mix. However, if you are trying to construct an asset allocation that is more balanced and less dependent on the success of the stock market, then you should contemplate adopting a different mind-set.

## A NEW LENS

Instead of automatically following others, first consider viewing the crucial asset allocation decision through a new lens. Stocks have a higher return than traditional bonds because they are prepackaged to contain higher risk. You do not have to accept this prepackaged product, as you have the ability to make modifications. For instance, you can simply add leverage to a low-risk, low-return asset class such as bonds to achieve a similar return as that from stocks. This is available to you because the risk-to-return ratio for most asset classes is roughly similar. If it were not, you could simply use leverage to achieve a superior risk-return ratio. For example, if stocks offered an average return above cash of 6 percent with 20 percent volatility, and bonds provided a 3 percent return with 10 percent volatility, then you could simply double your bet on bonds by using leverage to create a similar risk-return tradeoff as stocks. You may not want to do this because of your views on the future of bond returns today, but the opportunity exists nonetheless and should be part of the analysis.

Alternatively, you can simply own twice as many bonds as stocks to neutralize the impact of volatility in the portfolio. If bonds earn half as much as stocks, then you can own twice the allocation to equalize the net effect. Finally, with bonds in particular, you can simply lengthen the duration in order to increase volatility. Longer-dated bonds are more volatile than shorter-dated debt securities and can help better balance the portfolio. I will dig into much deeper detail on these topics in later chapters. At this point, the key insight you should understand is that there are easy fixes to the prepackaged asset class limitation. Before moving to the next chapter, try to start thinking about constructing a balanced portfolio using this different perspective.

The new lens involves thinking about an asset class *not as something that offers returns*, but as *something that offers different exposures to various economic climates*. Each asset class reacts in a predictable and logical manner to various economic environments. Each asset class offers a bias to different *economic conditions* and each is predisposed to contain a certain level of *volatility*. It is these characteristics that you can emphasize in your attempt to construct a well-balanced portfolio.

## SUMMARY

Given today's unique economic climate, there is great need for strong balance in portfolios. However, the vast majority of portfolios are not well balanced. This can be seen by simply observing the makeup and long-term history of the conventional 60/40 allocation, which many investors and professionals consider to be balanced. The assumption that 60/40 is well balanced, when deeply analyzed and when incorporating a longer-term data set that includes various economic climates, is clearly not supported by history. Perhaps most believe that there is nothing that you can do to minimize exposure to the markets' inevitable ups and downs. This conclusion is simply misplaced.

In the next chapter, I discuss what truly drives asset class returns over time. The concepts that will be introduced next are designed to set the core fundamental underpinnings to help you see investing through a new lens. Through this new viewpoint, the flaws in conventional logic will become much more apparent and a novel approach to building a truly balanced portfolio will appear more logical.

# CHAPTER 3

# The Fundamental Drivers of Asset Class Returns

**R**ay Dalio took his understanding of the relationships that exist between economic and market shifts to create a revolutionary new and better way to structure a portfolio. He called it All Weather because it is designed to perform well across economic environments. Those investment firms that adopted the concepts (and could not use the All Weather name because it was Bridgewater's) call their products *risk parity*. Regardless of what we call it, it is a simple and effective way to balance your portfolio so that it lowers risk without lowering returns, and I want you to understand it. It is an elegantly simple solution to an important problem.

My goal in this book is to describe this framework for building a mix of asset classes that can reasonably be expected to deliver stable returns through time. Volatility is obviously unavoidable, but an asset allocation that has a decent probability of experiencing an extended period of significant under-performance is unacceptable. A necessary prerequisite to constructing such an efficient allocation is an understanding of the key fundamental drivers that result in the returns that you see. A better appreciation of the *source* of asset class returns will provide the needed insight for assembling an optimal asset allocation and minimizing volatility over time. If you understand the source of returns and what factors make them volatile, you will be better positioned to appreciate how to neutralize the risk as much as possible. In this chapter I share with you a very effective methodology that I learned from Bridgewater.

The fundamental reasons asset class returns are volatile can be classified into three broad categories: (1) shifts in the economic environment, (2) shifts in risk appetite, and (3) shifts in expectations of future cash rates. The latter two sources of volatility are unavoidable if you invest in risky asset classes. These risks are inherent and necessary. You can understand them, but you can't do much to protect yourself against these two factors.

Fortunately, these two infrequently result in big losses in asset class returns, and the pain generally only lasts for a short time when losses do occur. The first risk—shifts in the economic environment—that impacts returns occurs all the time and can persist for long stretches. The good news is this risk is diversifiable. That is, you have the opportunity to build an appropriately balanced asset allocation that is targeted to minimize the volatility associated with this risk. That, in a sense, is the entire purpose of this book: to introduce you to a methodology to *balance your portfolio by diversifying against the risk that is diversifiable.*

Although you can't protect yourself against all three risks, it is crucial to appreciate where they all come from. A comprehensive understanding of the fundamental drivers of asset class returns will help establish context for the discussion that follows in later chapters. Furthermore, the insight will better prepare you for actual experience. The dominant source of volatility in asset class returns—shifting economic climates—can largely be neutralized with the methodology introduced in this book. That still leaves the other two that will inevitably cause a well-balanced portfolio to still experience some volatility and losses over shorter time frames. By understanding the core causes of this volatility in advance and by being equipped to explain why returns fluctuate, you are more likely to make prudent investment choices during challenging periods. For this reason, this chapter will begin by breaking down asset class returns into their core components.

## BREAKING DOWN RETURNS INTO CASH PLUS EXCESS RETURN

The first step in isolating the underlying source of volatility is to break down the return of an asset class into its two most basic components. Previously I mentioned three key sources of returns and volatility. Before discussing these factors in more detail, I would like to begin at an even more basic level.

The return of any asset class can be broken down into two parts:

1. The return of cash
2. The excess return above cash

Why is this? When you make an investment you are effectively exchanging cash for an asset with the objective of exchanging it back for cash at some point in the future (because you can only spend cash). For you to make this exchange requires that the asset offer an *expected* return above the rate for cash to adequately compensate you for taking the risk of loss with your money. Another way to think of this is any asset class (such as stocks, bonds, commodities, real estate, etc.) offers a return that is cash plus some excess return. This excess return above cash is often termed the *risk premium*. It is the premium you receive for taking risk.

In fact, the excess return above cash you receive for taking risk is the return that really matters. For example, if stocks earned 10 percent per year for 10 years, but cash earned 8 percent per year during the same time frame, then it is the 2 percent *excess return* above cash that is significant. You could have earned 8 percent without taking any risk, which makes the 10 percent stock return much less impressive. Conversely, if cash had only earned 1 percent per annum during that time, then the 10 percent stock return becomes more meaningful. For this simple reason, most of the focus in this book will be on the excess returns above cash rather than total returns (which includes the embedded cash return). Most investors mistakenly overemphasize total returns in their analysis and therefore fail to appropriately break down returns into their fundamental components.

To summarize, the total return of an asset class is merely the sum of its core parts:

Asset class total return = Return of cash + Excess return above cash

Looking at these two parts separately will reveal some interesting facts about the true source of risk in asset class returns. The return of cash has very low volatility. However, the excess return above cash is highly volatile and therefore explains nearly all the volatility that is embedded in asset class total returns. Excess returns above cash can be further subdivided into three components. It is these three fundamental drivers of asset class returns that explain why asset classes are volatile.

I will begin with a detailed walkthrough on the return of cash, followed by a deep dive into excess returns above cash. The final section of the chapter will bring the two together to leave you with a good understanding of the main drivers of asset class returns and the key implications for prudent portfolio construction. The main idea here is to get you to start thinking about *where* returns come from and *why* they fluctuate. This core understanding will set the foundation for a new way to *think* about the entire asset allocation construction process. With a fresh perspective, the methodology for building a well-balanced portfolio should make more sense.

## THE RETURN OF CASH

The simplest asset to understand is cash. Cash earns an interest rate that is, by and large, set by the Fed. The first chapter explained that the Fed controls this rate and adjusts the levels to help stabilize the economy. When growth or inflation is too strong, the Fed raises the rate to slow an over-heated economy and get it back on a more sustainable track. When growth or inflation is too weak, then the Fed takes the opposite approach by low-ering rates to stimulate more borrowing to help engineer a rebound. These conditions normally do not change rapidly and instead gradually shift over time. Consequently, the return of cash is predictably constant during most environments. Wild swings in the rate of cash would result in significant volatility in the economic environment. Since the Fed is commonsensically trying to maintain economic stability, it is incented to keep cash rates as steady as possible.

As a result, the interest rate for cash is fairly stable nearly all the time. If the Fed sets short-term rates at 5 percent, then you earn about 5 percent per year on your cash. This investment is the safest way to earn a return on your money. There is essentially no risk of loss, and as a result the cash rate is widely considered to be the risk-free rate. The only volatility you will experience is the change in the interest rate. It could be 15 or 5 or even 0 percent. However, it has never been negative in absolute terms (although it can be negative in *real* terms, meaning that the interest rate may be less than the rate of inflation).

Figure 3.1 displays the average return of cash over every 10-year period since 1927. Ten-year average *rolling returns* are used to smooth out shorter-term fluctuations and to demonstrate that over a long time period, cash returns have been extremely reliable. The average return of cash since 1927 has been 3.8 percent per year. You will notice that over every 10-year period the return of cash has, by and large, not materially fluctuated from its long-term average, and it has never been negative. This is exactly why cash is considered the risk-free asset.

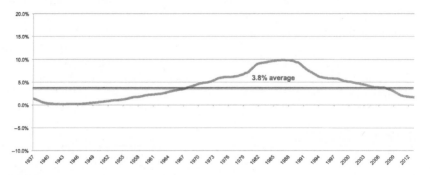

**FIGURE 3.1**   10-Year Rolling Cash Returns
*Source*: Bloomberg and Bridgewater.

## EXCESS RETURNS ABOVE CASH

You may not be satisfied with just holding cash. The rate may be too low or you may simply wish to try to achieve higher returns by increasing the risk that you take. If you want to take more risk, then you can do so by investing in other asset classes (such as stocks, bonds, commodities, and so on). By risk, I am referring both to the risk of loss of capital and the volatility of returns. The more volatile the returns of an investment are, the greater the risk of losing money. This is true because the return may be negative when you sell. The higher the volatility, the greater is the likelihood that you could earn a return less than cash offers (which, again, is the return you would have had without taking any risk). Generally speaking, the more risk you take, the higher the *expected* return. This relationship should hold over time; otherwise investors would not be willing to take the added risk. Note that this does not mean that you will automatically earn higher returns simply by taking more risk. *If returns were guaranteed, then these investments would not be risky.* This highlights a very common, unwarranted assumption and oversight. More risk means the *expected* return is higher, but the *actual* results may be lower. The key insight to appreciate is what may *cause* the actual results to fall below the expected returns. If you can understand the *causes*, then you will be more fully informed to protect yourself against the impact of some of these occurrences.

Different asset classes offer various excess returns above cash. The goal is to capture these excess returns over time and to do so with as little risk as possible. The problem is that the excess returns fluctuate over time and are not stable like cash. The excess returns are roughly commensurate with the level of risk taken. The higher the level of risk, the higher the expected excess return will be. This relationship makes sense because if it were not true, then investors would choose to take less risk for a similar expected excess return. Stocks are riskier than bonds and therefore enjoy higher expected excess returns over time. Long-term historical excess returns support this assumption.

Since 1927, the four asset classes on which I will focus—stocks, long-term Treasury bonds, long-term Treasury Inflation-Protected Securities (TIPS), and commodities—have provided excess returns above cash, as listed in Table 3.1.

These figures represent average excess returns over 86 years. (I am able to show TIPS returns since 1927, even though TIPS were created in 1997, by using Bridgewater's data that is based on their proprietary methodology to simulate a long-term historical return series. See also the explanation accompanying Table 6.1 in Chapter 6.) During this time, significant volatility in returns was experienced. One way to observe the volatility in

**TABLE 3.1**   Average Excess Returns for Four Asset Classes
(1927–2013)

| Asset Class | Average Excess Return |
|---|---|
| Equities | 5.6% |
| Long-Term Treasuries | 1.4% |
| Long-Term TIPS | 4.6% |
| Commodities | 2.0% |

*Source*: Throughout this book the following indexes were used to calculate returns for the various asset classes:
U.S. equities: S&P 500 Index. Data provided by Bloomberg.
Long-term Treasuries: constant 30-year maturity Treasury index. Data provided by Bloomberg and Bridgewater Associates.
Core bonds (for the bond component of the 60/40 portfolio): 1976–2013 Barclays U.S. Aggregate Bond Index. 1927–1975 U.S. Treasury constant 10-year maturity index. Data provided by Bloomberg and Bridgewater.
Commodities: 1970–2013 Goldman Sachs Commodity Index. 1934–1969 Dow Jones Futures Index. 1927–1933 Reuters/Jeffries-CRB Total Return Index. Data provided by Bloomberg and Bridgewater.
Long-term TIPS: 1997–2013 constant 20-year duration US TIPS index. For periods prior to TIPS inception in 1997, Bridgewater simulated TIPS returns using actual Treasury returns, actual inflation rates, and Bridgewater's proprietary methodology.

historical returns is to analyze *excess returns above cash* over longer time frames. A long time horizon may consist of 10 years (and probably even shorter than that for most investors). A helpful way to see the volatility that comes from investing in these asset classes is to strip out the relatively stable return of cash and isolate the volatility in excess returns above cash. This is the volatility that is associated with unexpected shifts in the three key sources of returns that will be covered in this chapter. Figures 3.2a–3.2d show the rolling 10-year historical excess returns above cash for the four asset classes.

Notice how volatile the excess returns of each individual asset class have been when compared to their average excess returns. Most asset classes rarely returned the average even over a 10-year period, which is a long time for most investors. You are more likely to earn a return either far above or far below the average long-term expected return—even over a long time frame (such as 10 years)—when investing in any individual asset class. Other asset classes are similarly volatile. The key insight is that the excess returns above cash can be far above and far below the average for long periods of time.

What causes this volatility? There are three ways to separate the fundamental drivers of excess returns above cash. Two are nondiversifiable; the

**FIGURE 3.2a**  10-Year Rolling Equity Excess Returns

**FIGURE 3.2b**  10-Year Rolling Long-Term Treasuries Excess Returns

**FIGURE 3.2c**  10-Year Rolling Long-Term TIPS Excess Returns

**FIGURE 3.2d**   10-Year Rolling Commodities Excess Returns

other can be mostly neutralized and is therefore the main subject of this book. The following three key factors impact the excess returns above cash:

1. Shifts in the economic environment (unexpected changes in growth and inflation). This risk is diversifiable.
2. Shifts in risk appetite, or the general market willingness to take risk. This risk is not diversifiable.
3. Shifts in expectations of future cash rates. This risk is not diversifiable.

### Shifts in the Economic Environment (a Risk You *Can* Diversify Against)

It is important to understand what you are really doing when you exchange cash for an asset class. This trade is largely a bet on shifts in the future economic environment. I am referring to changes in economic growth and inflation when describing the overall economic climate. In the first chapter I emphasized that the Fed tries to minimize the volatility of the economy in terms of growth and inflation by controlling interest rates and printing money, as necessitated by prevailing conditions. These are also the key forces that impact asset class returns because they are fundamental to what makes an investment.

When you decide to convert your safe cash into an asset class, you do so with the expectation that at some point in the future you will be able to convert it back to cash at a profit. If you did not expect this, then you would not accept the risk of losing money. More precisely, you convert cash into another asset with some expectation about the future economic climate. You have this expectation because in order to profit from the exchange, you factor in what future growth and inflation will be. Your expectation of inflation matters because you want to be compensated in real terms for the risk that you are taking. You need the return achieved from taking risk to exceed the rate of inflation in order for you to improve your purchasing power. After all, you can only spend cash, and the main reason you exchange cash for another asset class is because you expect to improve your purchasing power in the future. Thus, your expectation about the rate of inflation—or general increase in future prices of goods and services—is a critical factor.

Economic growth also influences your decision. If you anticipate strong economic growth, then you would be willing to accept a smaller piece of the future (if you are buying equities) or ask for a higher yield (if you are buying bonds), all else being equal. If you feel that growth is going to be very weak, then you would demand a bigger cushion in the price paid for equities in order to give you added protection. In this scenario you would be willing to accept a lower yield from bonds because of the safety it provides.

In diving a little deeper into why it is that changes in the economic environment impact asset class returns, I will use examples that feature the two most familiar asset classes, bonds and stocks.

## Bonds: Why Shifts in the Economic Environment Impact Returns

If I exchange my cash for an investment in U.S. government-guaranteed Treasury bonds, then I am in effect making a bet that I will earn more with this investment than I would by simply holding cash over the same time frame. Since Treasury bonds held to maturity have very little risk of loss due to credit impairment, they are effectively a longer-duration version of the risk-free cash rate. I have a choice of low-risk investments: (1) hold cash and earn the variable interest rate over time, or (2) lock in a fixed rate by investing in a bond and take the risk that I would have done better holding cash. You make a similar decision when you are deciding on a home loan. You would select a variable rate loan if you wanted to take the risk that short-term rates will average less than the fixed rate you can guarantee today. In the case of buying a bond, you essentially are taking the other side of the transaction. Instead of being the borrower you become the lender, and the choice between a fixed or floating rate is a similar decision and is based on your expectation of future cash rates.

The key insight is to appreciate what would *cause* cash rates to shift over time. Changes in economic growth and inflation result in a reaction by the Fed to adjust interest rates (as was discussed in the first chapter). Thus, the price of the Treasury bond will change between now and maturity based on what transpires in the economic environment relative to what was expected at the time you purchased the bond. As the Fed lowers rates in response to falling growth or weak inflation, then the price of the bond rises. More precisely, what really matters is how cash rates shift relative to the path that was reflected in the price when you bought the bond. If cash is yielding 3 percent and the bond 6 percent, then rising interest rates are already discounted in the price. The fact that they rise is not necessarily a negative for the price of your bond because that eventuality was already factored in the price. That is exactly why you got 6 percent instead of 3 percent for your investment. The key is how the future path of cash varies relative to the path that had been priced in at the time you made your initial investment, which was based on a certain expectation of future growth and inflation outcomes.

## Stocks: Why Shifts in the Economic Environment Impact Returns

I now turn to another example of the same dynamic to further clarify why shifts in the economic environment affect asset class returns. When you decide to invest in a broad portfolio of stocks, you are also making a statement about future economic growth and inflation. If you get 5 percent per year economic growth over time and the market was only pricing in 2 percent growth, then you are likely to do well with your stock investment. Companies generally earn more money when the economy is growing faster, and when they earn more the performance for shareholders normally improves. That is, you might expect higher than the average excess return during these periods. Logically, the opposite also holds true. If the market discounts 5 percent growth and only 1 percent growth actually transpires, then there is a good chance that stocks will underperform their average return as companies earn less than expected.

Likewise, shifts in inflation impact returns. Rising costs negatively affect stock prices because of the inability to pass on the entire cost increase to customers, resulting in lower profits. Again, this is all versus what was expected at the time the price was set. If high inflation was already priced in and we experience low inflation, then that is a huge positive for stock prices. Putting shifts in inflation and growth together and how both relate to prior expectations will provide you with a better sense of the key drivers of returns over time.

Perhaps a helpful way to better appreciate the impact of shifts in the economic environment on the returns of stocks is to review U.S. stock market history. I will begin with a memorable time period for many of today's investors. The greatest bull market in the history of U.S. stocks took place from 1982 to 1999. The market averaged about 13 percent excess returns per year during that stretch (cash also earned about 5 percent per year for a total return of around 18 percent per year!). It was an age in which vast fortunes were created. The unforgettable events that defined this extraordinary run included the curbing of the runaway inflation that had plagued the nation the previous decade, interest rates that fell from the highest levels in history, sustained economic growth for nearly two decades and, to top it all, an Internet bubble that far exceeded expectations.

The more precise reason the stock market performed so well was because the U.S. economy grew faster than most people had expected, and inflation declined much more than anticipated. In short, investors were expecting a much worse economic scenario than what actually transpired. *Given these sets of conditions*, which represent the ultimate tailwind for equities, it should be no surprise that stocks fared so well.

The previous two decades had effectively set the stage for the success of the 1980s and 1990s. A completely different experience plagued investors from 1963 to 1981. During this 18-year phase the United States suffered through the worst increase in inflation in its history. Interest rates rose more than ever before (surging from 4 percent to 15 percent) and inflation peaked at nearly 15 percent. All of this occurred concurrently with slower than discounted growth. The economic scenario of high inflation and low growth tends to be a terrible backdrop for equities. Predictably, risky stocks earned the same return as risk-free cash for over 18 years! Imagine the investors who had bought stocks for the long run, lived through all the ups and downs of the 1960s and 1970s, and had nothing to show for it. Certainly such an experience would dampen future expectations. Such widespread pessimism was captured on the cover of *Business Week* in 1979 as it infamously proclaimed "The Death of Equities." Of course, these low expectations sowed the seeds for the great run during the aforementioned 1980s and 1990s.

The stagflation (a period of high inflation and weak growth) of the 1970s was nothing when compared to the devastation that had roiled the economy and markets several decades earlier. From 1929 to 1949, the U.S. economy suffered through one of its worst periods in history. These 20 years were characterized by a major depression and deflation—a completely different set of conditions when compared to the 1982 to 1999 environment. Thus, stocks performed dreadfully as should be anticipated given these difficult conditions. During one 33-month run the stock market fell 84 percent! Those who lived through the Great Depression and much of the 1930s and 1940s never were the same again. The horrors of the severe market and economic downturn had scarred them for life.

Sadly, the recent environment from 2000 to 2013 is not much different from the experience of the 1930s and 1940s. Growth severely underperformed expectations and has caused equities to do much worse than many had thought possible 13 years earlier. The past decade included two periods in which the value of the stock market fell by half (2000–2002 and 2008–2009). The bursting of the Internet bubble, an extraordinary housing collapse, and the 2008 credit crisis that pushed the economy to the brink of another great depression caused devastating market downturns. Consequently, stocks barely outperformed cash for the first 13 years of the new century, a reality that extremely few market experts had predicted at the height of the Internet bubble.

The lesson from these historical experiences is clear: *The economic environment by and large drives the returns of stocks.* The market outperforms during better times and underperforms during periods dominated by weaker economic conditions. More succinctly, when growth outpaces market expectations and when inflation comes in lower than discounted, the stage has been set for significant upside in equities and vice versa.

**All Asset Classes: Why Shifts in the Economic Environment Impact Returns**
The same logic that applies to stocks holds true for every asset class. Each market segment, whether we are talking about stocks, bonds, commodities, inflation-hedged assets, or just about any other asset contains inherent biases to various economic environments. Rising growth tends to be favorable for stocks and commodities, whereas falling growth is generally better for bonds. Rising inflation benefits inflation-hedged assets like TIPS and commodities, just as falling inflation helps stocks and traditional bonds. Much greater detail about the impact of the economic environment on these asset classes and others will be provided in later chapters. For now, you should appreciate that each asset class is simply a package of changes in the future economic environment and a risk premium level above cash.

Importantly, the reason that the risk of changes in the economic environment can be neutralized is logical and intuitive. This source of risk does not impact every asset class similarly. *The impact is simultaneous, but each asset class has different inherent biases to each economic environment, so the resulting returns may be positive or negative. One particular economic climate may be negative for one asset class and simultaneously positive for another due to a perfectly reasonable and predictable explanation.*

The critical insight here is that there always will be the risk that the economic environment will drastically and unexpectedly change. However, the key distinction between shifts in the economic environment and the other two risks—shifts in risk appetite and shifts in expectations of future cash rates—is the impact of shifts in the economic environment is *different* toward various asset classes. Moreover, these relationships, as will be discussed later, are *highly reliable and logical*. That is, *while the outcome is always uncertain, the cause-effect relationships between shifts in the economic environment and various asset class returns are far more predictable.* You don't have to know what the future holds, but you should know how different asset classes will react to different economic conditions. *And it is the reliability in the relationships that provides the opportunity to diversify against the risk of adverse economic outcomes.*

## Shifts in Risk Appetite (Not a Diversifiable Risk)

Shifting risk appetite represents the second fundamental driver of excess returns. Think of risk appetite as the amount of excess return above cash you would be willing to accept to take the risk of investing your cash in asset classes. If you are feeling optimistic and your animal spirits are stirring, then you may be willing to accept a lower expected return for a certain level of risk than during more normal times. Alternatively, if you are really concerned about the future and think we may be headed for challenging and uncertain times, then you may require a higher expected return to part with your cash. The fact that you may demand a different level of excess return above cash depending on the environment should sound intuitive. Imagine if I approached you at the depths of the 2008 crisis and asked you to invest in my company at a price that offered a return of 4 percent above cash over time. Compare that to considering the same offer in the early 1990s as the momentum of strong economic growth was in its early stages. You would certainly reject my proposal in the first case and may seriously consider accepting it in the second. After all, both offers come with uncertainty, but you may reasonably conclude that the first has much greater downside risk. Your general fear about the uncertainty in the global economy would likely cause you to demand a higher excess return to part with your safe cash.

You are only one investor; however, the truth is that the majority of market participants use the same logic that supports your instinct in this example (probably more so than you realize). And it is the majority that sets the consensus view, which in turn establishes the market price. The consensus, by definition, is the market. The pendulum swings to extremes over time. When the majority is fearful, the demand for higher excess returns dominates, and when it is popular to be more aggressive, then lower expected excess returns exist. Fear and greed are another way to view these changes. At times, we are greedy for a higher return than cash offers and are willing to accept less for the same amount of risk. At other points in time we are fearful of losses and will only take risk if outsized returns are offered. Interestingly, greed often *follows* good periods and fear comes *after* severe downturns. That is, emotion tends to be a reactive rather than a proactive phenomenon.

How do changes in risk appetite affect prices and returns? What does it mean when the appetite for risk goes up or down? In simple terms, your return for an investment is the price you get when you sell (Y) minus the price you paid when you bought (X). The higher price X is, the lower your return, all else being equal, because of the less attractive entry point. When the appetite for risk declines, then the price falls to compensate you for taking risk. The lower the current price, the higher the potential forward-looking return if you buy. This is how shifts in risk appetite add to volatility in asset class prices.

The impact to asset classes is most visible during extreme periods. You may know that there exist rare environments when investors are terrified of taking any risk and sell all risky asset classes in favor of cash. Two stark examples of this environment include the Great Depression and the 2008–2009 crisis. During those two periods the markets were characterized by fear and the focus shifted to return *of* capital rather than return *on* capital. There was no desire to lend during these climates, so there was little access to credit. Forced sales of assets and heightened demand for cash caused risk premiums of all risky asset classes to concurrently skyrocket.

These severe cases help demonstrate why shifts in risk premiums, or risk appetite, are not diversifiable risks. As an investor in asset classes, this is a risk you are constantly subject to and there is no way to minimize it. *Shifts in risk appetite understandably and simultaneously impact all asset classes.* Therefore, there is no magic combination of asset classes that will help insulate you, since they are all affected in the same direction. That is, all asset classes are negatively impacted as risk appetite falls and risk premiums rise (or positively impacted as risk appetite rises and risk premiums fall).

The final important point about shifting risk appetite is the difficulty in avoiding this risk entirely. You might argue that investors can simply own cash when risk premiums are low and wait for risk premiums to rise before reallocating into riskier asset classes. However, you should keep in mind that your future appetite for risk is highly dependent on the state of the economy, your personal financial situation, the general momentum at the time, and many other factors. Most of these important inputs cannot be known because they have yet to occur. *You don't even know how you are going to feel in the future, so how can you presume to know the collective mind-set of everyone else?*

### Shifts in Expectations of Future Cash Rates (Not a Diversifiable Risk)

The third and final fundamental driver of excess returns is shifts in expectations of future cash rates. Earlier I explained that the rate of cash is relatively stable. The steadiness of cash returns can, however, be misleading. *Although current cash rates are not highly volatile, shifts in expectations of future cash rates contribute to volatility of* asset class *excess returns.* The reason this is true is related to a central theme that will be repeated throughout this book. With any return series, *what really matters is how the future transpires relative to what was expected.* This guiding principle applies to cash, stocks, bonds, and every other asset class. The *volatility of returns* is driven by how the future plays out versus what had been discounted to occur. If the market expected something to happen (for example, rising interest rates, a strengthening economy, or falling inflation), then that outcome is already reflected in today's price. The price will shift if and when the future does not follow the path that had been anticipated.

I will now address how shifts in expected future cash rates produce volatility in asset class excess returns. Recall that cash represents the risk-free rate. All asset classes compete with the risk-free rate since you, as a rational investor, always have the option to accept the guaranteed return offered by cash. As the rate of cash changes through time, there is a direct impact on all asset class prices for this simple reason. More technically, the yield on cash sets the discount rate used to calculate the present value of future cash flows provided by other asset classes. You invest in an asset class because you expect higher returns than cash (called excess returns) over time. Those future cash flows that you will receive for your investment can be valued at current levels by using current cash rates. The lower the cash rates, the higher the present value and vice versa. This is because a lower interest rate results in less compounding over time. Thus, as cash rates change, there is a direct impact on asset class pricing. This logic is merely the corollary of the fact that the cash rate is the risk-free rate and represents an investment option for those who wish to take no risk of loss.

When cash rates surprise the market with a sudden increase, such an event has a negative impact on *all asset classes*. This is because the discount rate unexpectedly becomes more attractive. A more attractive discount rate means that all asset classes, which price versus cash, need to offer a higher return as well. In order to raise the expected future returns of an asset, its price must fall. As an example, think about the impact on bonds of rising interest rates—as interest rates rise, the price of bonds go down. Again, since cash competes with all asset classes, the higher the yield of cash, the more attractive asset class prices have to be to entice investors to exchange their safe cash for risky assets. Of course, there may be other factors that may also influence the price, but the goal here is to isolate each factor to help you better appreciate the root causes of price changes.

There are times when the Fed may unexpectedly modify the current interest rate of cash. This may occur if there are renewed concerns about inflation or growth conditions in the future. This is what happened in 1994 and 1995 when the Fed surprised the market by raising interest rates by 3 percent over a one-year period because of fears about rising inflation. This surprise move negatively impacted all asset class returns because the rate of cash suddenly became more attractive than had been anticipated. A change in risk-free rate from 3 percent to 6 percent will have a large impact in how you view the attractiveness of current asset prices. As cash rates unexpectedly move up, you would expect forward-looking asset class returns to move up as well, to remain competitive with the higher cash rate. As a result, a negative impact to asset prices will occur.

An extreme example of this dynamic should help clarify the concept. Imagine that you own stocks and are expecting to earn the historical average excess return above cash. Let's say the average excess return above cash is 5 percent. If you expect to earn 1 percent in cash during the target time period, then that means you expect a 6 percent total return from the stocks that you own. If cash is currently yielding 1 percent and the Fed suddenly announces that it has increased the yield of cash to 10 percent, then the price of the stocks you own will likely fall considerably. Why would you own risky stocks with an expected return of 6 percent when you can now earn 10 percent just by holding risk-free cash? The price of the stocks would have to fall enough to make them worth investing in. More specifically, the price would have to fall by an amount that makes it more likely that you would earn an excess return above cash similar to what you had expected when you first purchased the stocks. Thus, it is clear that shifts in the cash rate *that are unexpected* would influence asset class prices.

How do you know if cash rates shift unexpectedly? An easy way to assess what the market is expecting is to look at the Treasury yield curve. This curve provides a rough estimate of how the market anticipates cash rates will change over time. For instance, an upward sloping curve implies that the Fed will increase interest rates over time. A downward sloping, or inverted, yield curve means that the market is anticipating that the Fed will lower interest rates in the future. The steeper the slope—either positively or negatively pointed—the faster the expected rate of change.

Importantly, if current cash rates roughly follow the path anticipated by the yield curve, then these changes in the rate of cash are not significant as it relates to asset class returns because they are *expected* shifts. Recall that your focus should be on *unexpected* changes to the rate of cash and not those that are already discounted. It is the surprises that impact asset class returns because the expected changes in the rate of cash are already factored into the current price. This is a critical distinction that you should emphasize in your understanding. This is why the surprise move by the Fed in 1994 and 1995 had such an impact. The market had not discounted rapidly rising rates and was shaken by the surprise.

It should be noted that the unexpected shifts in cash rates do not have to create a negative impact on asset class returns. It works both ways. If cash rates suddenly fall more than expected, then that generates a positive influence on all asset class prices for exactly the opposite reasons described above. Lower cash rates produce an easier hurdle for risky asset classes versus the risk-free rate. The price of asset classes rise in order to adjust to the lower hurdle. Alternatively, a lower discount rate results in a higher present value.

What happened in 2013 is another good example of shifts in expectations of future cash yields. With interest rates at 0 percent there was quite a bit of discussion about when the Fed would actually increase rates from this floor. In early 2013 there was newfound concern that the Fed may raise rates faster than what had been expected, and as a result longer-term interest rates jumped up. This event negatively impacted the returns of all asset classes simultaneously. This happened even though the Fed did not *actually* change interest rates. It was the change in *expectations* of the Fed's future actions that led to longer-term interest rates rising. The way to think about this dynamic is that the yield curve shifted up to a steeper slope because the anticipated future rate of cash changed. This outcome had a similar impact on asset class returns as when the Fed surprised the market by actually changing interest rates in 1994 and 1995.

One final critical point: Shifts in the rate of cash, both current rates as well as future expected rates, *simultaneously impact all asset class prices* and therefore asset class returns. There is only one risk-free return and that is cash. Every other asset takes some risk to own, and each offers some premium for taking that risk. If the baseline cash rate changes, then all else being equal, the price of *all* asset classes needs to reflect this shift. This impact can be positive (if cash unexpectedly falls) or negative (if it unexpectedly rises). This is precisely why the risk of unexpected shifts to current or future cash rates is not something that can be mitigated. If you take the leap of foregoing safe cash returns to invest in risky asset classes (and all of them are risky), then this is part of the primary risk you take.

## PUTTING IT ALL TOGETHER

A helpful way to visualize what I have covered thus far is presented in Figure 3.3.

Risky asset class returns are a function of the return of cash plus the excess return above cash. The return of cash is fairly stable through time.

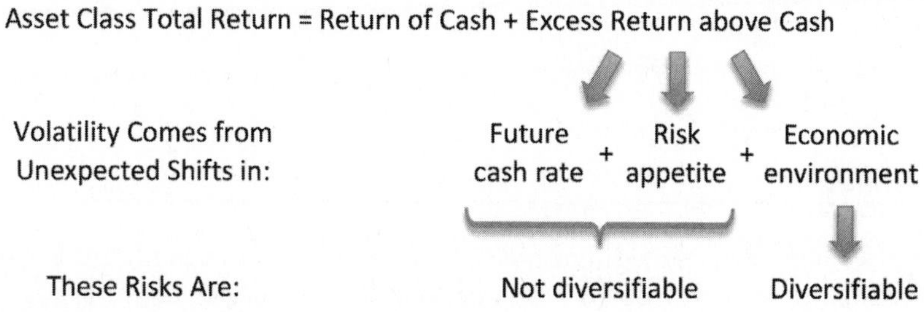

Asset Class Total Return = Return of Cash + Excess Return above Cash

| Volatility Comes from Unexpected Shifts in: | Future cash rate | + | Risk appetite | + | Economic environment |

| These Risks Are: | Not diversifiable | Diversifiable |

**FIGURE 3.3**  Asset Class Volatility Framework

Excess returns are highly volatile. The volatility can be explained by three core fundamental drivers. Unanticipated movements in future cash rates is a risk that cannot be diversified away because it simultaneously impacts all asset class returns in a similar direction. Likewise, shifts in the general market appetite to take risk cannot be neutralized since they concurrently impact all asset classes in the same manner. Fortunately these undiversifiable risks do not negatively impact returns frequently and are short-lived (as will be fully explained in later chapters). You, as an investor, are compensated for taking this risk over the long run.

Conversely, an unexpected shift in the economic environment is a risk that is diversifiable. In fact, unexpected shifts in the economic environment represents the biggest hazard to investors of asset classes. Unlike the other two risks, which don't negatively impact returns too often and don't persist for long, this source of volatility can be diversified with a good balance of asset classes. This is only because different asset classes react differently to various economic climates. Moreover, you are not compensated for taking this risk. This makes it foolhardy to not try to properly neutralize this risk in constructing your asset allocation.

*Your excess return will then depend on how the future rate of cash changes versus expectations, how general risk appetites shift, and how economic conditions actually transpire relative to what was originally expected. The goal of efficient portfolio construction is to capture the excess returns above cash offered by the first two parts and diversify away the risk of shifts in the economic environment. The whole objective of this book is to teach you how to diversify away the latter.*

Note that I have isolated each of these three risks to help better explain them. In reality, several may hit at once. Risk appetite may decline at the same time as the economy weakens (which is typical). Thus, all asset classes take a hit from declining risk appetite, but stocks get a double whammy for falling growth while Treasuries receive a positive push from the same economic climate. These influences net out to result in positives and negatives for each asset class. The severity of each outcome also provides various degrees of influence by factor. If the economy materially weakens but risk appetite only falls a little, then the resulting asset class return would be determined by the more impactful factor.

## SUMMARY

Since we have determined that two of the three key sources of risk are not diversifiable, we will focus on the one that is diversifiable. Another way to

| Growth | Inflation | | Growth | Inflation | | Growth | Inflation | | Growth | Inflation |
|:---:|:---:|---|:---:|:---:|---|:---:|:---:|---|:---:|:---:|
| ⬆ | ⬇ | | ⬇ | ⬇ | | ⬇ | ⬆ | | ⬆ | ⬆ |
| Equities | | | Treasuries | | | TIPS | | | Commodities | |

**FIGURE 3.4**  Economic Bias of Each Major Asset Class

think about asset allocation, and really the bottom line of this core chapter, is to appreciate the fact that *each asset class is merely a package of different economic structural biases.* Each asset class is impacted differently by unexpected shifts in growth and inflation. Some asset classes are positively influenced by rising growth, while others do better when growth underperforms expectations. There are asset classes that are biased to do well during rising inflationary environments and others that favor falling inflation. *By isolating each asset class into the key factors that drive its returns (and therefore are the main cause of volatility) you will be analyzing portfolio construction from the appropriate perspective, which will lead to building a truly balanced portfolio.* Figure 3.4 provides a visual of how each asset class is prepackaged with a bias toward these two key factors.

Each asset class has some long-term expected return above cash and expected risk (or volatility around that long-term expected excess return). Both the long-term excess return and the volatility around that mean are somewhat reliable over time. It is the timing and direction of the variability that is highly uncertain (largely because of changes in the economic environment) and it is that uncertainty that you should try to neutralize. The key is to appreciate the underlying fundamental drivers of each investment's pricing and how it is linked directly to changes in the economic environment. These are reliable linkages because they are fundamental to the understanding of how investments work. For instance, equities are biased to outperform when growth is rising and when inflation is falling, as illustrated in Figure 3.4. Each asset class can be encapsulated using a similar analysis of its core fundamental economic bias.

With this core appreciation, the next step will be to dive into the details of how to view various asset classes through a balanced portfolio lens. It is important to see each asset class as having predisposed biases to unexpected shifts in economic conditions. The next five chapters will use this lens to explain why major asset classes have these inherent biases and why such a cause-effect relationship can be reliable. Chapter 4 starts with stocks (or equities) since that is the most common asset class in portfolios. Treasuries, TIPS, and commodities will follow in Chapters 5 through 7, respectively. Chapter 8 will use the same perspective to look at additional asset classes that you may want to consider for your balanced portfolio.

In each of these five chapters I begin by describing the conventional perspective of each asset class. This is the way most people think about and use this asset class. The focus of each chapter, however, is on assessing each asset class through the balanced portfolio perspective. With this new lens, you will see asset classes in a different light and more fully appreciate the benefits of each within the context of a well-balanced portfolio. How each asset class fits within the bigger picture rather than the attractiveness of each on its own should be the focus.

# CHAPTER 4

# Viewing Stocks through a Balanced Portfolio Lens

**A**n investment in a stock represents an equity ownership in a public company. This is why stocks are also referred to as *equities*. If you buy Google stock, for example, you instantly become a part owner of Google. As an owner of the company, you benefit from the company's profits, which are largely reflected in the price of the stock. The current price of the company's stock reflects future expectations of the company's fortunes. When profits surprise to the upside, the stock price rises, and vice versa. Google is one company. The broad stock market consists of a basket of publicly traded companies like Google.

Most investors already understand what a stock is and what makes up the stock market. However, as you will read in this chapter, the traditional perspective of how to think about stocks within a portfolio contains many oversights.

## INTRODUCTION

When people ask how the market did today they are undoubtedly referring to the stock market, even though there are many markets to consider. The vast majority of headlines, analysis, and conversations are about how the stock market is faring. Bond, commodities, and real estate markets are just a few of many other major markets that do not seem to receive the same attention as stocks. For some reason our nation is gripped by the stock market (more so when it is going up than when it is not doing well, of course).

Consequently, equities are a staple in nearly every long-term portfolio. Those that are well balanced, as well as the imbalanced variety, are certain to contain some allocation of public companies. Thus, equities do not require a compelling argument for their inclusion in portfolios (unlike several of the other asset classes that will be covered later). Rather, the discussion needs to focus on why a heavy allocation to equities, as is commonplace in conventional portfolios, leads to portfolio imbalance.

The flaw centers on the way investors generally *view* stocks. Using a *conventional lens*, the high expected excess returns of stocks relative to other public markets attracts a high allocation in portfolios. Who wouldn't want more of the best performing asset (when viewed from this perspective)? There are several problems with this approach. First, stocks can underperform for uncomfortably long stretches of time. Moreover, the assumption that stocks offer higher returns is misleading when factoring in returns *per unit of risk*. Finally, a major drawback of an overweight to equities is the resulting portfolio's overdependence on the consistent returns of equities to produce successful results. All of these oversights will be fully explored in this chapter.

Ultimately, by discarding the conventional lens and analyzing equities using a *balanced portfolio perspective*, the appropriate role of equities will become more clear and the flaws in conventional logic far more apparent. Thus, the key emphasis in this chapter, and in the entire book, is to introduce a more thoughtful perspective that will help make it easier to build a balanced portfolio.

## THE CONVENTIONAL VIEW: WHY INVESTORS OWN A LOT OF STOCKS

I begin with the perspective used by most. Investors are attracted to stocks largely because they offer one of the highest long-term average returns of the major publicly traded asset classes. Of the assets I discuss in this book, equities have achieved the highest average excess return above cash since 1927 (see Table 4.1).

**TABLE 4.1** Annualized Asset Class Excess Returns (1927–2013)

| Asset Class | Average Excess Return | Average Volatility | Return-to-Risk Ratio |
| --- | --- | --- | --- |
| Equities | 5.6% | 19.2% | 0.29 |
| Intermediate-Term Bonds (Used in Conventional Portfolio) | 1.4% | 4.8% | 0.29 |
| Long-Term Treasuries | 1.4% | 10.0% | 0.14 |
| Long-Term TIPS | 4.6% | 10.6% | 0.43 |
| Commodities | 2.0% | 17.1% | 0.12 |

Cash returns from 1927 to 2013 averaged 3.8 percent per year. Thus, total returns can be approximated by adding 3.8 percent to the average excess returns provided above.

Equity returns stand out on this list when looking at historical returns. Most of the other popular options have produced much lower returns over time. Long-term TIPS, which come in second, have only been around since 1997. Thus, they don't have stocks' historical record and don't garner as much attention.

Conventional wisdom also recognizes that along with higher returns, stocks come with greater risk. This means that their returns fluctuate over time more than other assets. However, the assumption is that if you are willing to take the risk and have a long enough time horizon, then you should own a high allocation to stocks. This is how you achieve higher returns over time. Based on conventional logic, it is generally the time horizon and your risk tolerance that dictate the proportion equities represent in your portfolio. The conventional view holds that if you are younger, you should own more stocks; if you are retired, a smaller allocation to equities is appropriate. Many professionals simplify the math by arguing that you can take 100 and subtract your age as a general guideline to determine the equity allocation. If you are 30 years old, then 70 percent stocks (100 minus 30) is about right. If you are 70, then a 30 percent allocation is probably appropriate.

Another key factor that is traditionally used is your emotional risk tolerance. How much volatility can you handle? If your portfolio lost 20 percent in a year, would you feel compelled to sell at the low or would you be able to hold on and wait for the cycle to reverse? Can you stomach the roller coaster ride or are you more of a merry-go-round type? The rule of thumb holds that the more risk averse you feel, the fewer equities you should own.

One final traditional approach to the equity allocation decision is based on liquidity: If you might need to liquidate your equities over a shorter time frame (typically defined as five years or shorter), then a lower allocation to stocks is prudent. Again, the main logic is based on the *amount of time that you are able to hold on to your stocks*. The longer you can avoid selling, the more stocks you should own because stocks outperform over the long run.

The conventional asset allocator uses the previously described rationale to identify the right allocation to stocks in a portfolio. The net result of this common mindset and approach is a portfolio that generally contains a *high allocation to equities*. This bias is so prevalent that a 60/40 portfolio is widely considered to be balanced, even though it maintains a 60 percent allocation in one asset. *Three major oversights* in this thinking should be considered.

## Oversight #1: The Risk of Long-Term Underperformance in Stocks

Stocks are viewed as the ultimate long-term asset. Conventional wisdom holds that the longer your time horizon, the more equities you should own.

The major flaw in this logic is that stocks can perform extremely poorly for a very long period of time. In essence, *the long run may be too long for you to wait.*

Stocks only offer higher *average* returns over the long run. Averages can be very misleading. Imagine an asset class that averages 10 percent per year, but only delivers positive returns once every 100 years. It earns 0 percent every year with the exception of once a century, when it produces a positive 1,000 percent return. An attractive average return is not terribly useful in this extreme example. By investing in this asset class you will most likely earn 0 percent regardless of the average. Obviously stocks generate more reliable and consistent returns than indicated in this example, but the difference is probably less stark than you realize.

The reality is that the stock market is highly cyclical. It enjoys great runs followed by long episodes of severe underperformance. These prolonged periods are not just the three- to seven-year period that is commonly referred to as the full market cycle. They can last 15 to 20 years or longer, which by anyone's definition is a very long time. Regardless of your level of conviction about investing for the long run, a couple of decades of underperformance can truly test your patience. In reality, five years is a long time for most people and it seems as if the time horizon has been shrinking, not increasing, over the years. Indeed, it appears that we live in a world that demands immediate gratification. The trend certainly does not support greater patience over time. Every major market move is highlighted and exploited by the growing number of media outlets, which has made it quite challenging to try to maintain a long-term focus.

Table 4.2 provides a summary of the major long-term equity market cycles since 1927. This table breaks down the excess returns of equities into long-term periods from peak to trough and then back to the next peak. The main message is there exist lengthy periods of great results and drawn-out periods of near zero excess returns.

**TABLE 4.2**  Long-Term Equity Cycles (1927–2013)

| Period | Annualized Equity Excess Returns | % of Total Time |
|---|---|---|
| 1927–1929 | 41.9% | 2% |
| 1929–1948 | 0.4% | 22% |
| 1948–1966 | 13.5% | 21% |
| 1966–1982 | −3.0% | 19% |
| 1982–2000 | 12.7% | 21% |
| 2000–2013 | 1.2% | 16% |
| **Entire Period** | 5.6% | 43% above average |
| | | 57% below average |

Notice the time periods presented in the table. These are typically 15 to 20 year cycles. The up periods (1927–1929, 1948–1966, and 1982–2000) offer significant gains. However, the down cycles leave much to be desired. In most cases, the down legs have provided negative excess returns above cash, meaning that cash beat stocks for a long period of time lasting a decade or more. These bear markets account for 57 percent of the measurement period since 1927. In other words, we have lived through a secular bear market in stocks for more than *half of history*. Most people miss these obvious cycles simply because they are viewing the market too closely by focusing on 3- to 5-year cycles (which may feel like a long time to them).

The other important point to draw from Table 4.2 is the randomness of the cycles. It may appear that every 15 to 20 years the cycle turns, so you just need to wait another several years and then you can load up on equities. The randomness lies in the timing of the inflection points in the cycles. The table makes it look like the transitions occur regularly and smoothly. In reality, each of these bull and bear markets contains mini market cycles within them. Thus, you really don't know if the cycle has turned until a far later point in time.

The key lesson is that the stock market goes through very long periods during which it underperforms expectations and its average long-term returns. By concluding that you can afford to take risk and then overweighting equities, *you are taking a huge risk in the timing of your decision.* If you happen to pick the wrong half of time, then you will likely be quite disappointed with your asset allocation decision. Would you really be willing to flip a coin to determine the outcome of your portfolio? Heads you win and tails you lose. This is not the most prudent and rational approach, particularly since having a balanced portfolio (as will be shown later) would largely alleviate these risks.

Another way to analyze the long-term trends of the stock market through history is to observe rolling 10-year returns since 1927. If we assume that 10 years is a long time, then it would be informative to see the historical range of 10-year returns based on all the possible starting points since 1927. The percentage of time that the rolling 10-year returns were above and below average is also instructive. The results are presented both in chart (Figure 4.1) and table (Table 4.3) formats. Figure 4.1 illustrates that stocks have spent long stretches above and below their mean excess return of 5.6 percent. The chart uses 10-year rolling periods.

Table 4.3 segregates the results by the percentage of time spent above and below the average excess returns.

Based on this data, if you randomly picked a 10-year period that occurred sometime between 1927 and today, the odds that the returns you would earn from equities would fall below cash is about 20 percent.

**FIGURE 4.1**  10-Year Rolling Equity Excess Returns

**TABLE 4.3**  10-Year Rolling Equity Excess Returns
(1927–2013)

| Excess Returns | % of Periods | |
|---|---|---|
| 10%+ | 24% | |
| 8%–10% | 11% | |
| 5.6%–8% | 20% | Above average |
| 4%–5.6% | 10% | Below average |
| 2%–4% | 9% | |
| 0%–2% | 6% | |
| Less than 0% | 20% | |

This means that the *stock market underperformed cash for 10 years*! From a probability perspective, this implies that you have a *one in five chance* of picking a very bad *10-year period* in which to invest in equities. Nearly half of the rolling 10-year periods produced below average returns, meaning that you would have been disappointed with the results. Since 10 years is a relatively long time for most people, this is a fact that should not be quickly dismissed. Ten years of underperformance is typically enough to cause significant financial pain. It is also sufficiently prolonged as to reasonably produce shifts in investor behavior. A bad year or two may be easily forgotten, but 10 years of dreadful results can leave a lasting impression and cause second thoughts about original assumptions.

It is also unrealistic for you to assume that you possess the prescience to avoid the bad times. You might think that you will certainly identify red flags before the fact and successfully sidestep bear markets. Your actual experience, you might argue, will likely be different from that listed in Table 4.3. The problem with this perspective is that the reality suggests exactly the opposite conclusion. That is, most investors are actually predisposed to jump in, not sell, before major bear markets. In fact, the odds of investors over-weighting stocks during the next 10-year bear market is probably greater than the straight 20 percent odds would imply. This is because investors are saddled with the disadvantage of emotion. Even the most collected, rational investors are hardwired emotionally to want to do the wrong thing at the wrong time. Why does this continue to happen? The answer, in short, can be largely explained by the human motivations of fear and greed. Greed causes investors to chase returns after an upturn, while fear forces them to sell underperforming investments for worry that the poor results will continue.

The normal cycle typically repeats as follows: The stock market begins to string together impressive returns, optimism builds, and strong animal spir-its develop. Strong returns attract capital, which pushes prices even higher. Momentum ensues and eventually causes long-time bears to succumb to the pressure of sitting on the sidelines and watching friends achieve great invest-ment success with little effort. During the late stages of these long-term bull markets, manias form and fundamentals are largely ignored while talk of "this time is different" dominates. Widespread overconfidence, significant risk taking, excess leverage, or all three often signal that the end is near.

Fear begins when markets turn for the worse, often without sufficient warning. Just as was the case on the upside, recent returns are extrapolated into the future as hope of a market rebound fades. Fundamentals once again become important and risk tolerance reverts to the opposite extreme. Risk takers and highly leveraged investors are punished as too many rush for too few exits. Prices suffer and a long-term bear market has begun. The excesses are slowly worked off until the market becomes attractive once again, just before the inception of the next bull market (which has tended to coincide with widespread pessimism about future prospects).

This may sound like an oversimplification. However, since these long-term periods tend to last as long as 15 to 20 years, there is enough time between bull and bear markets for investors to forget their mistakes and fall into the same traps over and over again. In reality, these long-term periods include various shorter-term bull and bear markets within them, which makes them even more difficult to distinguish.

A recent example of these cycles will perhaps resonate with you. The last set of 10-year rolling periods during which equities earned a negative excess return occurred in the 1998 to 2000 start period (therefore ending from 2008 to 2010). You may recall the level of general optimism during the dot-com Internet boom. In fact, it was a time marked by substantial exu-berance over the forward-looking prospects of the economy and the stock market. Many investors loaded up on stocks that promised to grow to the sky. That period may have marked one of the peaks in U.S. infatuation with the stock market.

## Oversight #2: Equities Are Just Prepackaged to Offer Higher Returns

The conventional view's core argument is that stocks offer higher expected returns over the long run. A major flaw with this assumption is that this is only true because stocks are prepackaged to offer attractive returns. When I say prepackaged, I mean to describe the structure in which this asset class is normally available to investors. If you bought a broad U.S. stock market index fund (such as the S&P 500 Index) in 1927 and held on until today, you would have earned attractive average excess returns. Notice, however, that other asset classes have achieved a similar long-term *return-to-risk ratio* as equities.

For instance, the other component of the traditional 60/40 mix— intermediate-term bonds (also known as core bonds)—has achieved a lower excess return than stocks (1.4 versus 5.9 percent), but they have also experienced lower volatility (4.8 versus 19.2 percent). The key is that the ratio of return to risk was about the same as that of the stock market (approximately 0.3 each). This means that you could have levered core bonds since 1927 to earn the same return with the same risk as stocks. The leverage could be achieved by investing in futures of the core bond index, the Barclays Aggregate, to package the asset differently. The asset is prepackaged to provide lower returns with lower risk, but you can easily change that. You don't have to take this asset class off the shelf since you have the ability to customize it to better fit your needs. Most investors neither know they can do this nor would take advantage of it because it sounds risky and unconventional. With recent advancements and growth of investment products, there are prepackaged exchange traded funds or mutual funds that you can purchase just like a stock or bond fund that provide such characteristics. Thus, it is easier than ever to take advantage of this inefficiency.

Regardless of your aversion to lever other asset classes, *the bottom line is that higher returns should not be the main reason you buy equities.* You can get the same return from bonds or other asset classes by restructuring them. Likewise if you are looking for lower risk and return than that offered by equities, you can simply add cash to the portfolio to bring down the volatility and returns. This is another way of customizing the asset class. Again, I am not espousing such a strategy, but it is an option you should be aware of.

## Oversight #3: The Conventional Approach Results in Imbalanced Portfolios

The third major reason to conclude that the conventional perspective of equities is highly flawed is because a simple, high-level review of the portfolios that result from such an approach tells us they are *grossly imbalanced*. An important question to ask is how do portfolios that own a high allocation to stocks generally behave? In other words, if you followed the conventional mind-set of adding stocks to a portfolio merely because of their high expected returns, then what might your portfolio end up looking like?

One simple way to observe the resulting portfolio characteristics is by comparing the correlation of the portfolio to the stock market. *Correlation* is just a statistical method of measuring how two streams of returns are co-related. Correlation data can be used to compare the dependence of traditional portfolios to the success of equities. A high correlation means that the two generally move in sync. A negative correlation signals that the two perform the opposite of one another. They don't have to go up and down to the same degree so long as they move in the same direction. Thus, the correlation can be as high as +100 percent (or 1.0) or as low as −100 percent (or −1.0). A correlation of 0 indicates no correlation. Any number higher than 80 percent suggests a very high correlation between the two return streams you are comparing.

The thinking is that if the total portfolio is highly correlated *to the stock market*, then it can't be considered well balanced because we already know that the stock market can easily experience prolonged periods of underperformance. Table 4.4 lists the correlation of various conventional portfolio mixes *to the stock market*. These portfolio allocations represent typical outputs using conventional inputs. My objective is for you to appreciate the extraordinarily high correlation that all of the conventional portfolios have to equities. Note that the data used goes back to 1927, so this is not an aberration.

What the data shows is that even a portfolio commonly viewed as conservative using conventional methods is highly correlated to the stock market. In other words, you may think that your portfolio is conservative but its results are almost entirely conditioned on how well the stock market performs. The more aggressive mixes are even worse. Consider that a so-called

**TABLE 4.4** Conventional Portfolio Correlations to Equities (1927–2013)

| Portfolio | Asset Allocation | | Correlation with Equities |
| --- | --- | --- | --- |
| | Equities | Fixed Income | |
| Aggressive | 90% | 10% | 100% |
| Moderately Aggressive | 75% | 25% | 100% |
| Moderate | 60% | 40% | 99% |
| Moderately Conservative | 45% | 55% | 96% |
| Conservative | 30% | 70% | 88% |

moderate allocation of 60/40, which is widely considered to be a traditional portfolio allocation, is 99 percent correlated to the stock market. *Clearly, this is not well balanced!* Believe it or not, most investment professionals are completely unaware of these simple-to-calculate statistics. Indeed, most would be absolutely shocked at these figures and would probably not believe them to be true (you can check for yourself using a simple formula in Excel).

If you were to ask a business school professor what he thought the correlation would be between a 60/40 equity/fixed income portfolio and a 100 percent equity portfolio he may apply the following logic (which he probably learned in business school and likely teaches his students now). When you take two asset classes that have a low correlation to one another—such as stocks and bonds—the correlation of the combined portfolio should be reduced due to the benefits of diversification. Thus, if you own 60 percent stocks and 40 percent bonds, then the correlation between that mix and one with all stocks should be less than 60 percent. The logic suggests that this must be true because you only own 60 percent of the asset class that you are comparing to a portfolio that consists of 100 percent of the same asset. Because the other 40 percent is invested in something you know has low correlation to the 60 percent holding, then the combined portfolio should benefit from this diversification to result in a mix that has a correlation less than 60 percent. This thought sequence may sound intuitive, but it is completely erroneous.

How can this be? In order to see how obvious this result is you must ensure that you are *looking through the correct lens*. The traditional approach would leave you confused, as it does most investors. If instead you observe these portfolios from a balanced portfolio standpoint, the results will become evident.

## THE BALANCED PORTFOLIO VIEW: HOW TO THINK ABOUT EQUITIES

Equities are very volatile and can go through decades of underperformance, as you just read. Therefore, it makes much less sense to focus on the returns than it does to try to understand what *drives* the returns. If you emphasize the high expected returns and build a portfolio with the expectation that you will earn those returns, then you will be putting yourself in the unenviable position of having too high a probability of underachieving your expectations. Moreover, if the success of your portfolio requires equities to perform well, then you are effectively putting all of your eggs in the equity basket. Recall that most portfolio combinations using the conventional perspective lead to portfolios that have a high correlation to equities, which signifies an overreliance on this asset class. *There has to be a better approach.*

Fortunately, there is. In order to see asset classes through the lens of a balanced portfolio, you need to consider each asset class in two ways. First (as explained in the last chapter) the key driver of asset class returns, including equities, is unexpected shifts in the economic climate. The economic drivers to emphasize include unexpected changes in growth and inflation. Second, the volatility of each asset class matters. This is because the more volatile the asset the greater the impact to the total portfolio.

In this chapter, equities will be examined through the lens that looks at them in terms of their economic bias and volatility. By understanding what influences the returns of equities within this context, you will establish a solid foundation on which to make a well-informed asset allocation decision. You will then be armed with the insight needed to build a well-balanced mix of asset classes and to better understand the role of equities within the total portfolio.

## Economic Bias: Rising Growth Bias of Stocks

Positive growth is a huge plus for equities because it directly impacts the top-line revenues of most companies. This is due to the stronger economic activity that has led to increased spending. More spending results in higher company revenues since someone's spending is someone else's income and that process generally runs through companies. Higher revenues, all else being equal, produce greater profits for corporations. Better than expected profits generate upward pressure on stock prices since ultimately it is company's profits that make a company worth something. When the economy grows faster than discounted, this logical sequence typically leads to higher equity prices because the old price had not reflected the improved conditions.

As a result, equity prices are impacted by unexpected shifts in economic growth. When growth comes in better than conditions that had already been discounted in the stock price, then a positive influence results. The opposite is also true: Negative surprises generally lead to price declines.

## Economic Bias: Falling Inflation Benefit to Equities

There are two parts of the profit equation: revenues and profit margins. Rising growth positively influences revenues, while falling inflation can improve profit margins. Inflation is a measure of the increase in the cost of goods and services. These same items are inputs into the cost of doing business for corporations. Moreover, falling inflation exerts downward pressure on interest rates, which also benefits companies as the cost of borrowing money declines. As company costs decline (both from lower borrowing and input costs), profit margins increase, all else being equal. Thus, if growth transpires as expected and inflation falls more than expected, then revenues may come in as priced but the margins may improve. The net result is positive because profits have increased more than discounted. Note that if growth is rising and inflation is falling simultaneously, then such an economic outcome marks a double positive for stocks and generally results in the best overall environment for this asset class. Such an economic outcome largely explained the unprecedented equity returns during the 1980s and 1990s bull market. Consequently, unexpected decreases in inflation positively impact stock prices and vice versa.

### Combining the Two Economic Biases of Equities

Together, the rational cause-effect relationship between unexpected shifts in growth and inflation reliably impacts stock prices and results in price fluctuations over time. Moreover, so-called good environments characterized by rising growth or falling inflation relative to expectations generally exhibit stronger equity returns than so-called bad periods during which the opposite sets of conditions exist. Not only do the conceptual linkages make sense, long-term historical data also supports this cause-effect relationship. The historical data backing this outcome are summarized in Table 4.5.

Notice how much better equities have historically performed during good economic climates versus bad times. You may also recognize that the average excess return since 1927 of 5.6 percent is just about midway between the positive growth environment returns (10.7 percent) and the negative growth climate returns (1.3 percent). The same observation holds for falling inflation periods (9.5 percent) and rising inflationary environments (1.9 percent). The reason the average is almost exactly in the middle of the two ends of the spectrum is because of the frequency of each economic environment. As I've mentioned before, each economic climate occurs roughly

**TABLE 4.5** Annualized Equity Excess Returns by Economic Environment (1927–2013)

| Annualized Excess Return for All Periods (Good and Bad) | Good Environment (Avg. Excess Return) | Bad Environment (Avg. Excess Return) |
| --- | --- | --- |
| 5.6% | Rising growth (10.7%) Falling inflation (9.5%) | Rising inflation (1.9%) Falling growth (1.3%) |

*Source*: Bloomberg and Bridgewater. Methodology used to determine whether growth and inflation are rising or falling: current growth or inflation rate compared to average of the trailing 12-month period. If the current rate (of growth/inflation) is higher, then that is considered a rising growth/inflation period and vice versa. The logic is based on the observation that most people expect the future to closely resemble the recent trend line.

**FIGURE 4.2**   10-Year Rolling Equity Excess Returns versus Growth and Inflation

half the time because what really matters is how the future transpires relative to what had been expected to occur. In fact, about half of the months
since 1927 can be characterized as rising growth and about half as falling
growth. Rising inflation and falling inflation each also cover about half of
the measured environments.

Figure 4.2 provides the historical rolling 10-year excess returns of equities to help you observe the results over long time horizons. Periods of outperformance understandably occur during environments characterized by
either rising growth or falling inflation (or both). Likewise, long-term underperforming years occurred during falling growth or rising inflationary economic climates.

## The Importance of Volatility

The economic bias of equities is a critical input into assessing how equities fit
within a truly balanced portfolio. The second important input into the asset
allocation decision-making process is to factor in the volatility of equities.
Why does the volatility of an asset class make a difference in how it fits
within the balanced portfolio framework?

Remember that the objective is to build a portfolio using various asset
classes to capture the excess returns offered by them with as little variability
around that mean as possible. Therefore, in order to determine the allocation
of each to own you need to think about *how much* each asset class is likely
to move around its mean. Those asset classes that are highly volatile will
fluctuate around their average more than those that are less volatile. The
reason that assessing volatility is a key step in the process is because it is this
measure that identifies the magnitude of the fluctuations around the average
excess return. The more an asset class moves around its mean, the greater
the impact to the total portfolio. Economic bias tells us *when* the asset class
is biased to outperform or underperform its average return. Volatility tells us

*how much* it is predisposed to fluctuate around its mean. *Both characteristics are important inputs into the balanced portfolio decision-making process, since both have a direct impact on the return pattern of the total portfolio.*

Consider an extreme example to help understand the significance of volatility in the balanced portfolio framework. Imagine two asset classes: One is super volatile and the other has very low price volatility. Further, assume that the economic bias of both is identical. Consider the difference in impact to your total portfolio if you included one asset class versus the other. With the super volatile asset class your total portfolio would perform very well during economic environments during which the asset class is biased to do well and exceptionally poorly during the opposite climates. On the other hand, the low-volatility asset class has much less impact on the total portfolio even though it shares the exact same economic bias as the first asset class. Why is this? Since low volatility means that the returns do not fluctuate materially from year to year, then a return during a good year will not be much better than a return in a bad year. Conversely, a highly volatile asset will experience huge swings in its returns. Years characterized by positive economic environments will produce great returns, and negative environments will result in very poor returns. Putting numbers to it, the high-volatility asset may return +30 percent or −30 percent while the low-volatility version may return +3 percent or −3 percent. Obviously the wider swings in returns will cause greater fluctuations in the returns of the total portfolio (assuming the same allocation to each).

Of course, volatility will change over time. There are periods during which equities will experience greater volatility and other times when the volatility will be lower. The goal here is not to predict the exact volatility over your investment period. Rather, try to view volatility at a broad level. Perhaps you can characterize equities as containing high volatility relative to other asset classes such as bonds, which may have low or medium volatility (longer-maturity bonds have more volatility than shorter-maturity bonds). *Do not attempt precision.* It is nearly impossible to predict the exact volatility of the future based on the past. However, a range of volatility expectations or a broad categorization of future volatility is likely to yield a more successful approach.

At this point, the key insight you should appreciate as we go through each asset class is that the volatility of each is an important factor when considering how it fits within the balanced portfolio. Along with the economic bias of the asset class, these two inputs are the key criteria that will be used to construct a truly balanced asset allocation.

In terms of equities, you know that stocks are likely to outperform their average excess return when growth is rising, when inflation is falling, or when both conditions are present. You can also determine with some reliability roughly how much above or below the mean stocks are probably going to oscillate on average. This is clearly not an exact science, but you can reasonably anticipate that stocks will experience greater volatility than bonds, as an example, both because of actual experience and because conceptually it makes sense for this to be the case. Furthermore, common sense and history suggest that the bigger the shock from shifts in the economic climate, the bigger the moves around the average. For instance, if growth significantly outperforms expectations, then the upside for a pro-growth asset class will likely be material (just as the downside would be drastic for a falling growth biased asset class). You saw this in 2009 as expectations for growth were very weak following the financial crisis. Equities delivered very strong returns as economic growth, while not strong, far exceeded overly pessimistic expectations. Conversely, if growth comes in just slightly stronger than discounted, then the upswing above the average may be more muted.

Recall that one of the major flaws in the conventional approach to asset allocation is the noticeable imbalance in the resulting portfolios from such a process. With this understanding of the importance of volatility, you are now better positioned to appreciate *why* the conventional mind-set has led to such poorly balanced portfolios. We have already discussed the oversight in conventional thinking of not considering the economic bias of each asset class. The second missing element in the conventional analysis is the volatility of the asset classes in terms of how that factor influences the total portfolio.

With this new lens you can see why 60/40 is so weakly balanced. If you take two assets and one has high volatility and the other has low risk, then the more volatile of the two will obviously impact the total results more. Think of the 60/40 portfolio within this context. The *60* is four times as volatile as the *40* and will therefore drive the total portfolio returns. When stocks perform well, the 60/40 mix does well and vice versa. The returns of the low-volatility bonds effectively don't make much of a difference to the portfolio's overall results because they don't move around enough. By overallocating to the more volatile asset class, you actually hurt the balance in the portfolio even more. As I will describe further in the chapters about Treasuries and TIPS, this is one reason owning longer-duration, more volatile bonds actually improves the balance in the portfolio (even though individually they are considered more risky by conventional measures).

In a nutshell, the simplest way to view the equity asset class within the newly introduced balanced portfolio framework is as depicted in Figure 4.3.

When I look at an equity asset class, I visualize these two boxes. In fact, the boxes are more important than the *equity* label, since the boxes represent the biases of the asset class. A different asset class with the same biases should be viewed the same as equities, since the key drivers of returns are the crucial input into building a balanced portfolio (as will be shown later).

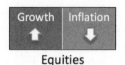

Equities

**FIGURE 4.3** The
Economic Bias of
Equities

Equities are predisposed, for perfectly rational reasons, to perform better than average when growth is rising and when inflation is falling. When both occur, that is the best environment for stocks. When the opposite climate dominates, that predictably results in the worst outcomes. There are other variations too. Sometimes growth, inflation, or both can come in as expected and therefore not materially influence the results. Other times, these factors may shift meaningfully from trend and significantly influence returns. In these cases, the factor that dominates more from expectations will generally have the greater influence on the price. For example, if growth is in line and inflation falls, then the inflation factor will dominate for that period. In the case of equities, since it is a falling inflation asset, such an economic outcome would be favorable. The data supports this outcome, but, more importantly, because of the logic described above, this cause-effect relationship simply makes sense.

Ultimately, *you don't need to guess the economic outcomes.* You merely need to have confidence in the cause-effect relationships between whatever the economic result and the general impact to equities. *If* growth unexpectedly accelerates, *then* equities are biased to outperform their average returns. *If* inflation falls, *then* equities are biased to outperform. It is the *relationship that should be the focus rather than the outcome.* Adding to this, the volatility of equities tells us roughly *how much* the price can generally be expected to fluctuate around its average long-term returns.

Thus, together, we have two reliable factors that do not change much over time. We know *when* equities tend to perform well and we know *how much* better than average they are predisposed to perform during these environments. *These two key insights are far more reliable characteristics of equities than their absolute returns during any forward-looking period.* If the foundations on which you are basing the all-important asset allocation decision are unstable, then the resulting portfolio is likely to also be unstable. If the key input in the process is a high expected return of equities, then the core input is far more likely to disappoint than if the main reason for using equities in a portfolio is because of its more reliable cause-effect relationship to various economic outcomes and its general volatility over time.

When you view equities using this perspective, the portfolio construction process naturally leads you down a very different path. However, if you view equities using conventional logic, then the focus will be on returns. Since equity returns are inherently unreliable because they can produce unacceptably low returns for decades at a time, why would you base the critical asset allocation decision on this factor? Rather, it seems more prudent to depend on the cause-effect relationship between growth and inflation conditions and equity returns since that connection is logical and *far more reliable over time*. Following this methodology, how then should equities be considered within a total portfolio? What is the *role* of equities within a total portfolio context using the balanced portfolio framework? To these vital questions I now turn.

## The Role of Equities in a Truly Balanced Portfolio

Based on its bias to rising growth and falling inflation, equities fulfill an important part of a well-balanced portfolio. Since growth and inflation are the primary drivers of asset class returns, a portfolio of asset classes should allocate among asset classes in a way that tries to neutralize these primary drivers. After covering the major asset classes in the next several chapters, I will explain in detail how to accomplish this ultimate objective. For now, I will focus on how you should think about equities and how this particular asset class fits within the bigger picture.

Since you know that unexpected shifts in growth and inflation are largely responsible for changes in individual asset class pricing, a required characteristic of a truly balanced portfolio is that it does not share this attribute. That is, the underlying asset classes may be impacted by economic shifts, but a cleverly constructed mix of them should result in much greater stability at the total portfolio level. The stability comes from a *total portfolio that has no inherent bias to growth and inflation*. If the portfolio is not predisposed to perform better or worse during rising growth or falling growth, or rising inflation or falling inflation, then that represents true balance.

Equities play a role in reaching that ultimate objective. Since equities do well during periods of rising growth and falling inflation, then it naturally follows that this asset class checks off those boxes. Thus, by including equities in a portfolio, if the economy is surprisingly strong or if inflation unexpectedly drops, then the portfolio will have a component (equities) that will be biased to deliver strong results. This outperformance will likely offset underperformance in other parts of the portfolio, which are biased to do well during opposite economic environments.

Conventional portfolios clearly own too high a proportion of equities. However, my goal is not to talk you out of owning any equities. The argument should not be taken too far. The objective is to keep good balance and that requires a deep understanding of the key drivers of asset class returns. Even if you are a very conservative investor and feel that the volatility of the stock market is too much to bear, you should probably still own some equities. If you take it to the other extreme and avoid the entire asset class, then you would be leaving your portfolio exposed to the environments in which equities outperform. The logic works both ways. This may sound a little counterintuitive since stocks are far riskier than bonds. The problem is that bonds, like stocks, can go through long bear markets as well. Bonds have their own economic bias and if the environment plays out in an adverse direction, then bonds can perform quite poorly for a prolonged interval. This is what happened during the 1970s and early 1980s as interest rates surged from 5 percent to 15 percent when inflation far exceeded expectations. In that scenario stocks would not have helped as they too underperformed, but the inflation hedges would have added significant value. If interest rates rise again in the future, it may be because economic growth outperformed discounted levels. In that case, equities may actually fare well and provide some offset to bond market weakness. We saw this dynamic play out in 2013 as equities performed strongly while bonds lost money.

## SUMMARY

Most investors start with the assumption that they should own as high a proportion of equities as they can handle because stocks offer the highest expected return of the major asset classes. Then bonds are added to fill the remainder and lower the overall volatility of the portfolio. My main aim in this chapter was to emphasize evaluating the equity allocation decision from a different perspective. You should think about it in balanced terms. Treat the equity decision the same as you would the other asset classes. Ask in what economic environments is it biased to outperform and how does it fit within a balanced portfolio framework.

*Using the conventional lens* to view equities, you would conclude that a high allocation to this asset is warranted. Equities have historically produced high expected returns relative to most other liquid asset classes. Conventional wisdom holds that if the objective is to achieve strong returns, then you must own a lot of stocks. This argument sounds intuitive and logical, but *only if viewed from a conventional perspective.*

The reason you now know that the conventional view is flawed is because of major oversights in some of its core assumptions. Stocks can underperform for far longer than most investors' patience can bear. Additionally, the assumption that stocks offer higher returns can easily be debunked by adding leverage to other asset classes to match the expected return of stocks. Finally, you understand that a portfolio created using this approach results in significant imbalance: If the output of the process is poor, then there must be something wrong with the input. To fully appreciate the flaws with the input, you need to remove the conventional lens and view asset classes—equities in this case—through a different lens.

I refer to the lens that is being introduced in this book as the *balanced portfolio lens* because our objective is to build a balanced portfolio. You learned in previous chapters that unexpected shifts in economic conditions (growth and inflation) are largely responsible for variations in asset class returns. Most importantly, this is the factor that can cause the most harm but also the factor that is diversifiable. Thus, by looking at each asset class through a lens that involves an analysis of its economic bias, then we are better positioned to construct a well-balanced portfolio. Notice that expected returns are not part of the process. The goal is merely to identify the economic bias of each asset class and put them together so that the total portfolio is neutral to shifts in growth and inflation.

Within this context, equities are rising growth and falling inflation assets. For good reasons, these biases are reliable indicators that can be used to build a balanced portfolio. In the next four chapters, a similar analysis of Treasuries, TIPS, commodities, and several other asset classes will be developed.

# CHAPTER 5

# The High Value of Low-Yielding Treasuries within the Balanced Portfolio Framework

**T**reasury bonds are government guaranteed instruments that promise to pay a fixed interest rate over time. The principal value of the bond has nearly zero risk of loss because the issuer, the U.S. government, effectively has the ability to print money to repay the bondholder. As a result, Treasuries are often considered to be risk-free. However, this is only true if you buy a bond and hold it to maturity. The price of Treasuries fluctuates every day because these bonds are publicly traded. The price moves as the future economic environment unfolds and as expectations of the future shift. Thus, you can lose money if the bond is sold prior to maturity. When I discuss Treasuries in this chapter and in this book, I am referring to bonds that are generally *not* held to maturity, as my emphasis is on trying to achieve stable returns through time. Thus, the volatility in the price of the bonds becomes an important consideration.

## INTRODUCTION

In the last chapter we covered one of the most popular and widely owned asset classes, equities. In this chapter, we turn perhaps to the other end of the spectrum. Many investors believe that Treasuries, because of their low yields, are one of the least attractive asset classes. Today, Treasuries may be the one asset to which you are most averse. You might question why anyone in their right mind would invest in an asset class that offers a very low yield with limited upside and significant downside risk. It would be one thing if Treasuries were yielding double digits as they were in the 1980s, but yields near historic lows seem to make this an obviously poor asset class. This mind-set, while ostensibly reasonable, is extremely flawed.

I will begin the discussion about Treasuries with a review of this asset class as it is commonly viewed from a conventional perspective. Similarly to the approach taken with equities, most investors simply look at the expected return of Treasuries, which they base on their current yield, to assess their attractiveness. A low yield suggests poor future returns and therefore a bad investment. As a result, few investors choose to include this asset class in their portfolios. The major flaws in this thought process and conclusion will be detailed in the first part of this chapter.

The discussion will then turn to how Treasuries should be assessed when analyzed through a balanced portfolio lens. Not only will this new insight help you to better understand the important role of Treasuries in a balanced portfolio, but you will also more clearly appreciate the flaws in conventional thinking when viewing Treasuries using this different viewpoint.

## THE CONVENTIONAL PERSPECTIVE

As was described in the last chapter, the conventional approach to assessing the attractiveness of asset classes, including Treasuries, is to consider the upside. The main question that is asked is how much Treasuries can return over a reasonable time frame. Most investors look at the current yield as an indicator of the future return potential of Treasuries since the principal value is guaranteed. If interest rates are low relative to historical levels, then the assumption is that there is more downside risk than upside potential in Treasuries. This is because if rates are low, then they are more likely to rise than fall. Rising rates cause a loss in principal in Treasuries, while falling rates are a positive. This simplistic approach effectively covers the preponderance of the analysis done on this important asset class.

The current view of Treasuries *from this perspective* seems to make sense. In late 2007, the 10-year Treasury yield fell and stayed below 4 percent for the first time since the 1950s. Most investors concluded that interest rates were too low to warrant buying Treasuries. Many are absolutely convinced that the yield is far too unattractive to provide a decent expected return. As a result, since 2007 investors have reduced their exposure to Treasuries by replacing them with higher yielding, lower quality alternatives. In addition, investors have been shortening their bond portfolio's duration to protect against what they view to be an inevitable rise in interest rates.

Despite this conventional view, long-term Treasuries produced excess returns above cash of 44.1 percent from October 2007 through December 2013. This return far exceeded expectations and was stronger than the returns of the stock market during the same time frame. The S&P 500 Index beat cash by 36.1 percent during this time (nearly all of the gain coming in the final year—2013—of the measurement period). Many contend that the outsized returns of Treasuries have been an aberration that no one could have confidently predicted.

The truth is that underweighting Treasuries during the past six years has exposed the highly flawed belief that the only thing that really matters is the interest rate. *The real mistake is not in the results, but in the perspective used.* The most important message is for you to understand *why* Treasuries performed far better than many had expected and *why* the predictable reaction to low interest rates was misguided. After all, the results could have easily turned out differently. The objective is to provide you the needed insight to help minimize the likelihood of making a similar mistake in the future.

In the first section of this chapter I will walk you through the main arguments used in the conventional perspective and identify major oversights in each key point. The main argument for underweighting Treasury exposure follows a familiar logical sequence, which is laid out in Figure 5.1.

This conventional thought process contains several major flaws at each step of the argument. The first point that current Treasury yields are low is certainly true; however, the rest of the logic quickly falls apart. The flaws can be summarized into three groups:

1. Interest rates have to rise *more than expected* in order to negatively impact Treasury *excess* returns.
2. Long-term Treasuries can produce *strong returns* over shorter time frames despite a low starting yield.

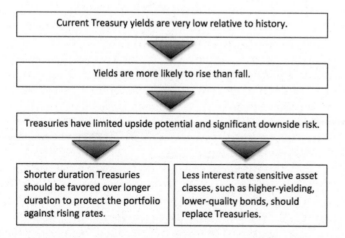

**FIGURE 5.1** Conventional Thought Process for Underweighting Treasury Exposure

3. Cutting Treasury duration or replacing Treasuries with higher yielding, lower quality bonds makes portfolios *less balanced and more risky*.

I will address each of these major flaws separately.

### Major Flaw #1: Interest Rates Have to Rise *More* than People Expect for Treasuries to Underperform Cash

Earlier in the book I emphasized the importance of breaking down returns into their core components. The return of cash plus the excess return above cash make up the total return of an asset class. Since the return of cash is risk-free, you should focus on the excess return above cash when analyzing asset class returns. You can get the cash rate with no risk, so if you are going to take risk you need to understand how much you can expect to be compensated.

When you decide to exchange cash for a long-term Treasury bond, you are effectively making a bet that you will be compensated a little more than what you would earn if you just held cash over time. Since both cash and Treasuries are considered risk-free in terms of principal value, you would only take the price risk associated with Treasuries if you were compensated with excess returns above cash. Since Treasuries are merely a longer-duration version of risk-free cash—because they, too, do not contain credit risk—the excess returns Treasuries offer are understandably low relative to other, riskier asset classes.

The actual excess return above cash that you will receive with your Treasury investment, like all other asset classes, depends on how events transpire relative to market expectations. The future discount is relatively straightforward to discern for Treasuries because it is reflected in the slope of the yield curve. Specifically, the yield curve tells us the market's expectation for the future path of cash rates. An upward sloping curve demonstrates the discounted increase in cash rates over time. Cash rates and short-term interest rates are nearly identical and are set by the Federal Reserve. The steeper the slope, the faster short-term interest rates are expected to rise.

Therefore, when you think about whether Treasuries are attractively priced relative to cash the key question to ask is whether you expect interest rates to rise faster than what is currently priced in. If you do, then you should underweight Treasuries (relative to an efficient, neutral mix); and if you don't, then you ought to hold more. For example, if cash is yielding 0 percent and long-term Treasuries are offering a 4 percent yield, then that implies that interest rates are expected to rise significantly over time. If they do rise, but less than priced in, then you would be better off buying Treasuries than holding cash. In this case Treasuries would earn excess returns above cash because cash rates rose less than expected.

From this perspective it should be apparent that contrary to the popular view, *the current yield by itself does not matter.* You need to look at the entire yield curve to identify what future conditions it is discounting. A 4 percent long-term Treasury yield means something very different when cash is yielding 0 percent versus when it is yielding 6 percent. At 0 percent, the yield curve is extremely steep and at 6 percent it is inverted (signifying the anticipation of falling short-term interest rates). In both cases, the excess return above cash is dependent on the future path of interest rates versus the discounted levels. In fact, since 1927 *the correlation of future excess Treasury returns and the starting yield is just 10 percent or 0.1* (meaning there is effectively very little correlation between the two). The excess return depends on how the future plays out relative to what was already priced in (and you know that the odds of it going one way or another are about fifty-fifty).

To illustrate this point, let's review the yield and returns of Treasuries during the past six years. The 10-year Treasury fell below 4 percent in December 2007, at which time nearly every bond investor concluded that interest rates were near historic lows and destined to rise. Shortly thereafter at the onset of the financial crisis, short-term interest rates fell to almost 0 percent. With the framework described above, the appropriate way to have analyzed interest rates was to consider the steepness of the yield curve to gain a more complete perspective of what the low rates meant. Since everyone expected rates to rise, this market view was already reflected in the yield curve with low rates at the short end (the end closest to the present) and much higher relative rates at the long end (the end farther out).

A well-informed investor would have asked what has caused short-term rates to fall. Historically, interest rates have gone down to zero only in times of great distress and when there is need for massive monetary stimulation. The last time interest rates were near zero in the United States was during the Great Depression, and they stayed there for 15 years, from 1933 to 1948. In Japan, interest rates approached zero in 1995 and have remained there ever since (19 years and counting). Monetary policy dictates lowering short-term interest rates to stimulate growth. When interest rates are lowered to zero, that suggests that the economic environment is so fragile that zero rates are warranted. In today's environment, zero rates are in fact insufficient to stimulate growth because of the overly indebted balance sheets of many developed economies (the United States included). Thus the question to ask is *how long* short-term interest rates may stay near zero given the economic environment, as opposed to just automatically concluding that they must rise *just because they are low.* The timing is crucial because it ultimately drives long-duration bond excess returns to a greater degree than the starting yield.

The reason Treasuries performed so strongly was because everyone expected rates to rise rapidly, and instead rates fell. Why did they fall? Economic growth underperformed levels discounted in the market, which were far too optimistic given underlying economic conditions. This is a major oversight of the vast majority of investors.

In reality it is not the low yield of Treasuries that has been unusual *but the near zero yield of cash*, which rarely occurs. *Since all asset classes price relative to cash, low yields impact everything.* They are just more easily observable in low Treasury yields. This is a crucial insight: *low cash yields lower the total returns of all asset classes* since they are all priced relative to cash. The excess returns should be your focus, and they remain unchanged as a result of low-yielding cash. If you observe every asset class relative to cash as described in an earlier chapter, then this thought process should make sense. This point is most obvious when considering Treasuries because of the close similarity between this asset class and cash.

Another argument against holding Treasuries in a portfolio is that the yield is said to be artificially low because the Fed is printing money and buying these bonds. The thinking goes that this is not normal and is in effect artificially depressing rates far below where they would be were it not for the government's manipulation. And, once the Fed stops doing this, rates are surely going to rise. Thus, in today's unique environment, the argument continues, it is not just how the future transpires relative to expectations but the role government plays in the process—it is not a free market, but one that is being controlled by a noneconomic participant. Many experts have proposed this line of thinking.

However, the flaw in this perspective is that it fails to fully appreciate *the reasons* for the Fed's involvement. Think of our discussion in the first chapter. The deepest economic collapse since the Great Depression forced the Fed to first lower interest rates to zero and then engage in quantitative easing (or printing money) to push longer-term interest rates lower and inject money into the economy. The last time this was done to this degree was during the Great Depression, when similar economic conditions existed. In other words, interest rates are low *because the economy is extremely depressed*, which is the type of environment in which Treasuries are biased to do well (and they have).

In fact, it is debatable whether interest rates would be higher or lower if the Fed were to stop buying Treasuries. The first few times Treasury purchases ceased shortly after 2009, *interest rates actually fell* even lower *because the lack of printing of currency caused the economy to weaken*, which caused rates to fall further. *The forces of the economic environment outweighed the reduced buying by the Fed to force rates even lower.* Conversely, each time the Fed started to buy bonds, rates actually rose because the economy strengthened. Thus, the answer to the question of whether rates are artificially low is unclear. Had the Fed never bought a single Treasury bond interest rates might be significantly *lower* than current levels because of the probability of an economic collapse. Perhaps interest rates are artificially *high*! Consider, for instance, that several European countries have interest rates lower than those in the United States even though the ECB, as of this writing, has printed far less than the Fed.

## Major Flaw #2: Long-Term Treasuries *Can* Deliver Sizable Gains over Shorter Periods

Please note that in this section when I refer to owning long-term Treasuries, I am suggesting maintaining a constant duration to these bonds rather than buying a bond and holding it to maturity. This is an important distinction. If you buy a 10-year Treasury bond, for example, and you hold it until it matures, then the return you will earn is known at the time of your purchase. It will simply be the yield to maturity of the bond. This is the return that most investors think about when they consider investing in Treasury bonds. This logic may sound intuitive because when you analyze the potential return of a bond it seems to make sense to look at the yield it offers plus a return of your principal. From this perspective, a low yielding Treasury bond would understandably look quite unappealing.

However, if instead you buy that same 10-year bond today and then after a year sell it and buy another 10-year bond and continue the process indefinitely, then you will maintain a constant long-maturity Treasury bond. The return stream of this portfolio may be different from that in the first example when the bond is held to maturity, depending on the economic environment.

When considering Treasuries, most investors are concerned that the potential upside is limited when the yield is low. Many are also concerned that there is significant risk of loss because rising interest rates means that Treasuries will lose money. These commonly held views are simply not true when considering the *excess returns above cash*. We already know the return of cash is low, but this reality lowers the returns of *all* asset classes, not just Treasuries. The focus should be on excess returns above cash, as I've reiterated multiple times.

The excess return of Treasuries, like other asset classes, is based on how the future transpires versus what was discounted. If interest rates are priced to rise rapidly and they actually fall, then significant returns can be expected. This is because of the huge mismatch between what happened and what was anticipated to occur. You can see that when nearly everyone expects a certain outcome, the pricing in of that eventuality actually creates an opportunity for significant outperformance because of the extreme view. On the other hand, if few expect rates to rise and they do rise because of the shifting economic conditions, then that would lead to underperformance in Treasuries. Treasury outperformance versus cash is possible, then, even with low starting yields.

There is one condition, however: To achieve high returns investors must own longer-duration bonds. *Duration is key*. It is duration that can produce the high returns and it is duration that helps build balance. Investors have been reducing duration because they are afraid of losing money. Instead they should be increasing duration, *not because they expected interest rates to fall, but to improve the balance in the portfolio*. If rates happened to rise more than expected, then other segments of the portfolio could have benefited (such as equities, if rates rose because the economy was strong). If rates fell (as they did), then the Treasuries would have appreciated enough to offset the losses in the other asset classes. This critical point will be fully explored later in this chapter and in the subsequent discussion about the makeup of the balanced portfolio at the end of the book. The key argument I am trying to make at this point of the discussion is that you can achieve very good excess returns even if the starting yield is low—if you maintain long duration.

Once again, recent experience provides a helpful example of the dynamic described above. The 30-year Treasury yield on June 30, 2011, was 4.4 percent and it closed at 2.9 percent just three months later. The reason it fell so much was because the economy materially weakened unexpectedly during that short time horizon because the Fed stopped buying Treasuries. Since the duration is so long, the excess return during that three-month period was 30.9 percent! The S&P 500 dropped 14.1 percent during that three-month span and investors who didn't own long Treasuries were fully exposed and likely lost significant capital.

What about the consensus view among experts that going forward it is highly unlikely that interest rates will fall again? The problem with this argument is the simple fact that the consensus view has been an extremely poor indicator of future returns time and again. Consider that the *three best years in the history* of the Treasury market all occurred at a time when Treasuries were *most out of favor* (+32 percent excess returns in 1982 after an 18-year run of rising interest rates, +39 percent in 2008, and +35 percent in 2011 when interest rates were widely considered to be too low). Not only did Treasuries outperform consensus expectations, but they emphatically delivered record returns!

What about the argument that bond yields do not sufficiently compensate investors against inflation? The *current yield* may be less than *expected* inflation, but that does not necessarily mean that the *total return* (yield plus principal gains) will be less than *actual* inflation. In terms of total return, the example above clearly demonstrates that with enough duration, the total return can far exceed inflation. Furthermore, we do not yet know what inflation is going to be over time. It may be much higher or it may be much lower (or even negative as it was for a moment in 2008). The key consideration is whether the future plays out as expected. Far too often, investors are guilty of placing too much confidence in their ability to accurately predict the future despite having a subpar track record (selective memory in this area tends to obscure reality).

## Major Flaw #3: Cutting Treasury Exposure *Reduces* Balance and Makes Portfolios *More* Risky

Many investors have been cutting their exposure to Treasuries as a response to their concerns about limited upside and big downside risks in this asset class. The act of reducing Treasury exposure can take two main forms, both of which have a similar impact on the total portfolio (as you will see shortly).

First, you might cut the allocation to Treasuries to add other asset classes. Some investors have tried to replace Treasuries with bonds of lower credit quality to increase yield and decrease exposure to what they view as inevitably rising interest rates. The problem with this approach is that a bond with a lower credit quality has a different economic bias than Treasuries. This makes sense because Treasuries have virtually no credit risk, while bonds of other issuers do have varying degrees of risk of default. During weak economic periods the general risk of default rises and therefore adversely impacts lower quality bonds. On the other hand, Treasuries thrive in such an environment because of the flight to quality. In this way, Treasuries are unique securities and there are very few, if any, true substitutes (within the United States at least; of course you can always buy high quality sovereign bonds overseas).

A second way to reduce exposure to Treasuries is to shorten the duration of your Treasury holdings. The thinking is that the shorter the duration, the less interest-rate sensitive the bonds. And since interest rates are expected to rise, reducing duration seems like a reasonable reaction to this problem. It is true that shortening the duration of the Treasury holdings reduces volatility, but more importantly, it also *negatively impacts the effectiveness of these holdings*. What if rates actually fall instead of rise, or if they don't rise as much as everyone expects? What economic environments would those outcomes likely involve, and what would be the consequences to your portfolio? These are crucial questions that ought to be part of the thought process. Table 5.1 summarizes the changes investors have made in response to concerns about low interest rates and their corresponding impacts on the portfolio.

We can test the conceptual linkages described in Table 5.1 by comparing the actual returns of the various substitutes for Treasuries during the period

**TABLE 5.1**  Fear of Rising Rates Has Led Investors to · · ·

| Action | Impact | Because |
|---|---|---|
| Cut Treasury allocation | Underperform during falling growth | Other bonds don't do as well during falling growth |
| Reduce Treasury duration | Underperform during falling growth | Shorter duration Treasuries don't go up as much during falling growth |

from October 2007 (when interest rates first fell to theoretically low levels) to December 2013 (when this book was written). By analyzing how each conventional solution to low interest rates behaved during various environments, we can gain insight into the diversification attributes of each asset class. When you look at the data, try to focus on how each market segment performed when the stock market was going up or down: How did Treasuries do when equities were performing well and how did they do when equities experienced declines? How did shorter-term bonds and lower quality fixed income perform during similar environments? The correlation between asset classes is a critical part of building a balanced portfolio, so the intent here is to demonstrate performance using recent examples of the types of relationships that you might expect.

The results are presented in Table 5.2. The table divides the time frame since 2007 into bull and bear market phases of the stock market, which mostly correspond to strong and weak economic growth cycles, respectively (since inflation has been relatively stable during this period). In addition to long-term Treasuries, the returns of three other asset classes are compared to equity returns during each cycle. Intermediate bonds and cash represent the strategy of reducing bond market duration to protect against rising interest rates. High-yield bonds offer a higher yield and theoretically better downside protection against rising interest rates.

None of the popular substitutes for Treasuries offered similar upside *during periods that equities suffered losses*. The critical lesson to draw from the analysis in Table 5.2 is an appreciation of *why* the return patterns of the recent past materialized. The economy underperformed expectations and therefore long-term Treasuries, which are biased to outperform in such periods, soared in value. It certainly could have gone the other way. In fact, there were periods during which Treasuries did poorly during this great run. Of course, equity gains during those times more than offset the underperformance in Treasuries.

Clearly, of all the bond substitutes—intermediate-term diversified bonds, cash (both of which are proxies for shorter-duration bonds), and high-yield fixed income—Treasuries proved to be the *best diversifier*. This analysis has nothing to do with the fact that Treasuries outperformed most of the rest (high-yield bonds ended with better absolute performance, although the pattern of returns generally matched those of equities). Indeed, the opposite result would have yielded the same conclusion. The returns shown in Table 5.2 should be expected because of the environmental bias of this crucial asset class. Intermediate diversified bonds, although they are of high quality, do not have sufficient volatility to materially help the portfolio during economic weakness. Cash and low-duration fixed income strategies don't move enough to make a difference. High-yield bonds, which are more credit-sensitive than interest rate-sensitive, predictably tend to correlate with the ups and downs of the stock market. All three commonly used bond alternatives offer inferior diversification benefits when compared to long-term Treasuries.

The three major oversights that I just covered help demonstrate the flaws in conventional thinking as it relates to the Treasury asset class. In the rest of this chapter I reintroduce Treasuries using a balanced portfolio perspective.

**TABLE 5.2**  The Diversification Benefits of Treasuries: Excess Returns during Equity Bull and Bear Markets since 2007

| Equity Market Highs and Lows | Period | Equities | Long-Term Treasuries | Shorter Duration Intermediate Bonds | Cash | Higher Yield High-Yield Bonds |
|---|---|---|---|---|---|---|
| Peak to Trough | 10/07–3/09 | −58.2% | 30.4% | 7.2% | 2.9% | −29.5% |
| Trough to Peak | 3/09–4/10 | 84.2% | −12.9% | 9.5% | 0.2% | 72.4% |
| Peak to Trough | 4/10–7/10 | −15.6% | 13.5% | 3.0% | 0.0% | −2.1% |
| Trough to Peak | 7/10–4/11 | 35.5% | −4.9% | 3.0% | 0.1% | 16.1% |
| Peak to Trough | 4/11–10/11 | −18.6% | 36.7% | 5.4% | 0.0% | −7.5% |
| Trough to Peak | 10/11–4/12 | 30.5% | −8.6% | 1.0% | 0.0% | 12.6% |
| Peak to Trough | 4/12–6/12 | −9.6% | 17.5% | 2.2% | 0.0% | −0.7% |
| Trough to Peak | 6/12–12/13 | 49.7% | −19.9% | −0.5% | 0.1% | 18.9% |
| Total Period | 10/07–12/13 | 36.1% | 44.1% | 34.8% | 3.5% | 69.8% |

*Source:* Bloomberg.

All returns cumulative.

Indexes used are as follows: equities (S&P 500), long treasuries (Citigroup US 30 Year Treasury), intermediate bonds (Barclays Aggregate Bond), cash (3 month Treasury repo rate), and high yield (US High Yield Master II).

Specific time periods used are as follows: 10/9/07–3/9/09, 3/9/09–4/23/10, 4/23/10–7/2/10, 7/2/10–4/29/11, 4/29/11–10/3/11, 10/3/11–4/2/12, 4/2/12–6/1/12, 6/1/12–12/31/13.

These represent peak to trough and trough to peak periods for the S&P 500 Index since October 2007.

As you will read, the focus will not be on the future expected return of Treasuries as is the conventional approach.

## CONSIDERING TREASURIES THROUGH A BALANCED PORTFOLIO PERSPECTIVE

Treasuries, despite their low yield, still play an important role in well-balanced portfolios. In order to more fully appreciate this conclusion, I will cover the economic bias of Treasuries in terms of growth and inflation and the volatility of long-term Treasuries. You have already seen how these two factors represent the key inputs in the asset allocation process of a balanced portfolio, so a continuation of a similar thought process will now be applied to Treasuries.

### Economic Bias: Treasuries Favor Falling Growth

Weak growth benefits Treasuries because of the increasing likelihood of falling interest rates. This occurs because a weakening economic environment produces a reaction by the central bank to consider lowering interest rates to encourage borrowing to spur economic growth. When growth unexpectedly declines, it results in a move by the Fed that had not been anticipated by the market since the falling growth itself had not been expected. As a consequence, interest rates decline because cash rates suddenly are discounted to rise less than previously anticipated.

Declining interest rates are great for Treasuries because the bonds you own have a fixed interest rate. If prevailing rates are lower than those discounted at the time of your purchase, then the higher coupon of your bond relative to market rates makes your bond a more attractive investment. Consequently, the price rises to reflect the new reality of lower interest rates as this gradually becomes apparent to the market.

Moreover, Treasuries tend to do well during weakening growth periods because of a *flight to quality* during adverse economic environments. When bad things happen to the economy, it seems reasonable that investors would react by becoming more cautious and risk averse. Treasuries, which have no credit risk, all of a sudden become more attractive investments because the focus shifts from maximizing returns to protecting capital. The high-quality bias of Treasuries attracts frightened investors who are seeking a safe place for their money.

Within this context you might better appreciate how low interest rates can go even lower. All it takes is for economic growth to underperform what is already discounted. Since growth underperforms expectations roughly half the time from a historical standpoint, it makes sense that the odds of low rates dropping are similar to the odds of them rising (even with low starting yields).

## Economic Bias: Falling Inflation Benefit to Treasuries

Lower inflation also benefits bond prices. As I expressed in the opening chapter, the Fed attempts to keep inflation at bay by raising interest rates to deter borrowing when inflation is too high and lowering rates to stimulate debt growth when inflation is too low. Each incremental change in inflation produces an expectation of its future path. How that expectation relates to what has already been discounted in the original price is then reflected in the current price. If inflation falls more than expected, then that leads to a greater likelihood of the Fed lowering short-term interest rates. This new discovery then feeds into the increased probability of lower future long-term interest rates, which benefits Treasury prices.

**Important Distinction: Deflation versus Falling Inflation** One quick note on deflation needs to be pointed out. Inflation has been the natural state of the economy during nearly all of U.S. history. Inflation means that prices are rising. Falling inflation implies that prices are rising less than they were before: That is, the rate of price increases has declined, although prices are still rising. This scenario is called disinflation. An important distinction needs to be made between disinflation and deflation, the latter of which means a period in which prices are actually falling.

Deflation is not good for an economy, even though you might argue that you would prefer to pay less for what you buy. The reason deflation is such a negative outcome is because of the vicious cycle to which it normally leads. In the first chapter I described the economic machine as a system that vitally depends on increased spending. The more spending there is, the better the economy, since spending improves incomes and provides for a virtuous, self-reinforcing cycle. When there is deflation, people tend to reduce their spending. This is particularly true when deflation becomes entrenched for an extended period of time. Imagine if you anticipated that prices would be lower next month than present levels. Wouldn't you most likely wait to make that big ticket purchase at the lower price? A short-term drop in overall prices of goods and services is fine because spending would likely continue, if not pick up, as consumers take advantage of sale prices. However, the longer deflationary conditions exist, the greater the negative impact on spending patterns as people start to realize that they would benefit from postponing their purchases. The problem with this reaction is when the majority simultaneously cut spending it results in falling incomes, which then leads to reduced spending. This negative spiral is difficult to break and can lead an economy into a major prolonged depression. The Japanese economy since the early 1990s provides a prime example of this dynamic, as does the U.S. Great Depression in the early 1930s.

The severe negative consequences of deflation—in contrast to the benefits of falling inflation—are precisely why central banks are so focused on avoiding this economic outcome. When inflation rates fall too low, there is great incentive for central banks to lower interest rates to stimulate more borrowing in order to improve growth and increase the inflation rate. Central banks, generally speaking, prefer for inflation rates not to hover too close to zero for long. Keep in mind that deflation is historically quite rare, mainly because of the central bank's ability and willingness to avoid it at any cost. Further, the recent Japanese and European deflationary periods offer central banks vivid reminders of the severe social, political, and economic costs of such dire circumstances.

This background about deflation relates to this section of the book because this particular economic environment should be examined on its own. It does not fit cleanly into the rising-falling growth and rising-falling inflation construct described earlier. Like the economic shock that comes from deflation, the impact of this environment on asset class returns can also be drastic. Stock prices collapse an average of 90 percent and in many instances it leads to widespread bankruptcies. Commodities and inflation-linked bonds, both of which are pro inflation investments, generally lose significant value as well. In fact, few asset classes hold their value as a mad rush into cash often dominates during such periods. Treasury bonds may provide a safe haven since their prices are most directly impacted by shifts in interest rates. Deflation is normally met by a drastic cut in rates in an effort to promote borrowing and spending.

Therefore, Treasuries carry with them some deflation protection in addition to the falling inflation bias. Deflation does not occur frequently, so don't overvalue this characteristic. That said, if it does occur, you would be very glad that you own some long-term Treasuries. Think of it as insurance: You rarely need it, but it is prudent to keep it just in case. Given where we are in the long-term debt cycle, holding some deflation protection may not be such a bad idea in the present economic climate.

### Putting It Together: Falling Growth and Falling Inflation (and Deflation) Economic Bias

As described above, lower interest rates benefit bond prices. More precisely, it is the future path of cash rates that influences bond prices. This is because the bond yield at various maturities from short-term to long-term merely

**TABLE 5.3**  Annualized Long-Term Treasuries Excess Returns by Economic Environment (1927–2013)

| Average Excess Return for All Periods (Good and Bad) | Good Environment (Avg. Excess Return) | Bad Environment (Avg. Excess Return) |
|---|---|---|
| 1.4% | Falling growth (5.5%) Falling inflation (2.6%) | Rising inflation (0.2%) Rising growth (−3.0%) |

reflects the discounted changes in cash rates. Since the Fed controls cash rates and the Fed responds to changes in the economic environment (in terms of growth and inflation) by adjusting cash rates, then these economic shifts together impact discounted cash rates. Changes in cash rates then impact longer-term interest rates, which directly affect Treasury bond prices.

Table 5.3 provides historical data that supports these cause-effect linkages. The rare deflationary periods that we've experienced have been bundled with falling inflation economic climates in this table.

As you might expect, at 1.4 percent the historical average excess return above cash is not very high. Treasuries have the same credit risk as cash, so investors in long-term Treasuries only receive compensation for the interest rate risk that is taken. As is the case with equities, the difference in returns by economic environment is meaningful. During falling growth periods the excess return of Treasuries has averaged 5.5 percent per year. This is a very strong average return that is *nearly identical to the 5.6 percent equity average excess return* (for all periods). Considering that about half the time growth is falling relative to expectations, it is easy to see the benefits of owning Treasuries as part of a balanced portfolio.

Of course, the opposite environment of rising growth has historically been very bad for Treasuries, with an average excess return of −3.0 percent. Predictably, Treasuries benefit from falling inflation and underperform during periods of rising inflation, as demonstrated in Table 5.3.

Figure 5.2 provides similar data for longer-term rolling 10-year periods. Notice that the good times occurred during predictable economic climates, as did the bad environments.

## The Benefits of Higher-Volatility Treasuries

One very important and somewhat counterintuitive point about the returns in Table 5.3 needs to be reinforced. The only reason the returns diverge materially between the good and bad periods is because we are using long-duration Treasuries. Shorter-duration Treasuries would share exactly the same environmental bias as longer-term Treasuries. In fact, the excess

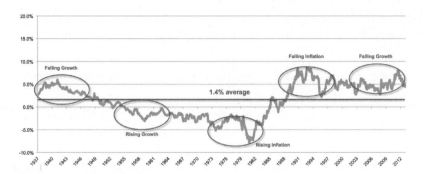

**FIGURE 5.2**   10-Year Rolling Long-Term Treasuries Excess Returns versus Growth and Inflation

returns above cash are nearly identical. However, the returns during good environments and bad environments would not be too different. Good periods would outperform the average excess return by a little bit and bad environments would produce slight underperformance. This is simply because longer-duration bonds have more volatility than short-term bonds. More volatility means that the return pattern will fluctuate more, which leads to the wider divergence in returns during good and bad economic climates.

*From a conventional perspective,* when you have two asset classes that produce the same returns you would always select the one that has less risk or lower volatility. Why get the same return for more risk? However, from a *balanced portfolio viewpoint,* you do not make asset allocation decisions based on the same criteria. Instead the emphasis is on identifying the economic bias of each asset class and determining its volatility. As is apparent from Table 5.3, the reason more volatility is preferred over less volatility (and therefore long-duration instead of short-duration Treasuries) is because of the better returns *when you need them.* This is the whole idea behind building balance. *You focus less on each individual asset class and more on how it fits within the bigger picture.* Each asset class is part of a team and serves a bigger purpose.

## THE ROLE OF TREASURIES IN THE BALANCED PORTFOLIO

Treasuries do well when growth comes in below expectations, when inflation falls below consensus views, or when both conditions are present, as shown in Figure 5.3.

Economic growth has historically underperformed about half the time. This observation has been true since 1927 and is very likely to persist looking forward. This is a reasonable outcome because what really matters is

Treasuries

**FIGURE 5.3** The
Economic Bias of
Treasuries

how future economic conditions play out versus what had already been discounted. The consensus view about future growth is factored into today's
price of Treasuries (as well as equities, commodities, TIPS, and all other
asset classes).

It makes sense that the consensus, or average, view is wrong about half
the time for two main reasons. First, the middle point of a data set means
that half the outcomes fall below and half above that point. Second, the
consensus view generally represents an extrapolation of the recent past into
the near future. Most people expect the next 6 to 12 months to resemble the
last 6 to 12 months. Few try to anticipate inflection points, and even fewer
foresee major shifts before the fact.

The same can be said about inflation. Roughly half the time what transpires is above what had been discounted and the other half below. Importantly, this *range of outcomes exists whether interest rates are high or low.*
Everyone can easily observe the level of current interest rates and therefore
factors this into expectations of future growth and inflation.

This background is repeated here because it is fundamental to describing
the important role of Treasuries in the balanced portfolio. The same background is also crucial for establishing the importance of each asset class
within the context of a truly balanced asset allocation.

Importantly, since 2007 short-term Treasuries have not enjoyed success
similar to long-term Treasuries. This is because shorter duration reduces
volatility both ways. When rates rise more than discounted, then long duration hurts more, but when rates don't rise as fast as expected, then long
duration helps more. One core idea behind the concept of maintaining a
well-balanced portfolio is that you do not have to correctly guess which way
it is going to go. If rates move against you, then other parts of the portfolio
are biased to outperform during that environment. If rates move favorably
for Treasuries, then that is likely because of an adverse economic environment that would simultaneously cause other parts of the balanced portfolio
to underperform. Therefore, if you don't maintain sufficient duration, then
you leave the portfolio exposed to environments during which Treasuries are
biased to outperform. If the economy suddenly weakens and you don't have

sufficient duration in your Treasuries, then this part of the portfolio would not go up enough to offset underperformance elsewhere.

Each asset class in the balanced portfolio fills a specific role because it serves to cover certain economic environments. If one of the asset classes were removed from the efficient starting point, then the portfolio would naturally be exposed to the economic environment that had been previously covered by that asset class.

The two economic environments that Treasuries cover are weak growth and falling inflation (or deflation). Weak growth is the more important of the two, since most portfolios are already underweight weak growth assets (either because of a lower quality bias in bonds, smaller total allocation to Treasuries, or a shorter duration). In other words, if long-term Treasuries are reduced from the efficient mix, then there is effectively a big bet that the economy will not underperform expectations. Remember that economic growth is falling about half the time, since it is relative to market discounted conditions. If you underweight Treasuries and the economy does weaken, then overall portfolio underperformance is likely to result because of the imbalance in the portfolio due to the underweight to Treasuries.

Rather than focusing on how Treasuries may perform if interest rates rise (as is nearly universally the concern), you should view the role of this important asset class within the framework of a balanced portfolio efficient mix. Viewed through this lens, you would be less worried about the performance during rising interest rate environments, since other segments in the balanced portfolio are biased to do well during that period (namely, commodities or TIPS if rates rise due to rising inflation, or commodities and equities if rates rise due to rising growth; you'll see this as we cover additional asset classes). Another question that will become apparent when thinking in balanced portfolio terms is what would happen to the portfolio if interest rates *fall* and Treasuries are missing? Even if rates are low, they can certainly go lower (as you've seen not just recently but throughout the history of financial markets).

## SUMMARY

Of all the potential economic environments that you would likely want to cover in your portfolio, it is the *falling growth* scenario that is perhaps the most significant. The worst equity bear markets in history occurred during the weakest economic environments, and more accurately, during the periods in which most investors had expected continued good times but were suddenly blindsided by unexpected downturns (i.e., 2008–2009, 2000–2002, 1973–1974, 1929–1932, etc.).

With this understanding, the recent moves by investors to cut exposure to Treasuries in favor of lower quality, higher yielding bonds and to drastically reduce duration can be reexamined. It may be more apparent now why these actions have actually increased the risk in the portfolio by making the allocation less diversified. Nearly everyone is afraid of rising interest rates. Yes, there is risk of loss in Treasuries if interest rates rise (as they did in 2013), but there is also risk of loss in the rest of the portfolio if interest rates *fall* (usually because of a weakening economic environment). This became apparent in 2008 and 2011. The most important message to remember is that *it is far better to hedge the interest rate risk by adding asset classes that are biased to do well during environments in which rates rise than to significantly reduce Treasury exposure.*

Putting it all together, it should be understandable why a core allocation to long-term Treasuries should have a permanent place in your balanced portfolio. Furthermore, the low yield should not deter you from owning this asset class because of the critical role it plays within the foundation of a well-balanced mix of asset classes.

# Why TIPS Are Critical to Maintaining Balance (Despite Their Low Yield)

In the previous two chapters I recommended that you view equities and Treasuries through a balanced portfolio framework as opposed to seeing them through the conventional lens and discussed how to do that. You may have noticed that equities and Treasuries tend to complement each other well when considered within the context of a balanced portfolio. Equities outperform when economic growth is increasing, and Treasuries do well in the opposite environment of decreasing growth. The reason you can't end there and construct a balanced portfolio using just these two asset classes is because there are *two* key economic inputs into asset class price fluctuations. Stocks and Treasuries successfully cover you for different growth outcomes, but what about unexpected shifts in inflation? Both equities and Treasuries are biased to underperform during rising inflation (and outperform during falling inflation). In order to adequately build a truly balanced portfolio, you need to include additional asset classes in your tool kit that are biased to outperform during rising inflationary climates. In this chapter I discuss the benefits of incorporating TIPS into a balanced portfolio. TIPS are the first of two major asset classes offering inflation protection that will be analyzed (commodities will be covered in the next chapter).

Most investors do not fully appreciate the benefits of TIPS. In fact, this asset class is entirely missing in most conventional portfolios. In this chapter I first clarify what TIPS are and how they work. Similarly to Treasuries, many investors are opposed to adding TIPS as part of their portfolio simply because the yield is low relative to historical levels. The flaws in this conventional perspective will be addressed next. I then shift to viewing TIPS through a balanced portfolio lens, which will involve an analysis of the environmental bias and volatility of TIPS. Finally, I explain the crucial role TIPS play within the context of a balanced portfolio and why this unique asset class is so difficult to replace.

## WHAT ARE TIPS AND HOW DO THEY WORK?

TIPS, or Treasury Inflation-Protected Securities, are bonds issued by the U.S. government. Accordingly, they carry the same credit risk as Treasury bonds, which were addressed in Chapter 5. That is to say that TIPS, like Treasuries, are widely considered to be a risk-free asset, since the U.S. government holds the world's reserve currency and has the capability to print U.S. dollars to repay its obligations. If you owed me money and had the flexibility to print it out of thin air, I would not be too worried about being paid back. This is particularly true given the long-term negative consequences of defaulting on your debt.

TIPS generally pay a coupon that is less than that paid by Treasuries. This is because TIPS returns are inflation-adjusted (measured by using the CPI, or the consumer price index). For example, if you buy a TIPS bond that provides a 2 percent yield to maturity, your total return will be 2 percent plus actual inflation if you hold the bond to maturity. If inflation turns out to be 3 percent, then you get 5 percent (2 percent plus 3 percent). The main idea behind a TIPS bond is to provide investors the inflation protection that they do not get with Treasuries. Other than the inflation component, TIPS and Treasuries are the same. Of course, that inflation factor makes a world of difference (as you may have guessed).

Another way to compare Treasuries to TIPS is by calculating the break-even inflation rate. For instance, if a 10-year Treasury offers a yield of 4 percent and a comparable maturity TIPS bond has a yield of 1 percent, then that implies that the market is discounting inflation to be 3 percent over the maturity time frame. This must be true because the two bonds are identical otherwise (same maturity and credit quality). The only difference between the two is that one provides a yield without inflation protection and the other offers a lower yield with inflation protection. As an investor, you have an opportunity to choose between the two securities. Therefore, if you feel that inflation will be greater than the break-even rate—3 percent in my example—then you would opt for the TIPS bond. If you were concerned that inflation would come in less than 3 percent, then you'd buy the Treasury because it would provide a higher total return if you are correct.

You might sensibly consider TIPS to be one of the safest investments you can make: They are bonds and therefore your principal is safely returned to you at a predetermined maturity date. Your investment is guaranteed by the U.S. government and is backed by its ability and willingness to print money to pay you back. For lending your money, you are paid a fixed interest rate that is also guaranteed. Additionally, and perhaps most importantly, your investment is protected against the long-term negative consequences of inflation. Other bond investments do not share this benefit. Treasuries, for instance, are just as safe in terms of principal and interest payments but because they are not linked to inflation you are taking the risk that the money paid back to you will be worth less due to inflation. Thus TIPS are arguably *safer* than Treasuries, since an investment in this asset class does not contain inflation risk as does an investment in Treasuries.

For example, if you lend me $100 today and I promise to pay you back in 10 years, then the expected rate of inflation is a big factor in the amount of interest you will charge me for that loan. If you anticipate inflation to be low, then less interest is required. However, if you suspect that inflation rates will spike, then you will demand a higher rate of interest in order to be compensated for the diminished purchasing power of your money. With TIPS, this concern is generally eliminated.

## THE CONVENTIONAL VIEW THAT THE YIELD OF TIPS IS TOO LOW AND WHY IT'S FLAWED

The same argument that is widely used against Treasuries generally applies to TIPS. Most investors look at the low yield of TIPS and conclude that the upside return potential is limited while the downside risk is too much to warrant an allocation to this asset class. The rationale is that a low yield is unsustainable and will inevitably rise back to historical norms, and that rising yields are a negative influence on the price of TIPS and therefore TIPS must be a bad investment. The majority of investors view this unique asset class in this light. As a result, TIPS are heavily under owned in conventional portfolios. In fact, the standard 60/40 allocation completely excludes TIPS. Absolutely zero allocation!

It seems that TIPS are not widely followed securities and are misunderstood by many investors relative to Treasuries and other nominal (as opposed to inflation-linked) bonds. This is partly understandable as TIPS are relatively new securities. In the United States they were first created in 1997, while other parts of the world initiated similar instruments a few decades earlier. The confusion is probably due partly to this asset class's relative young life and partly because of its distinctive structure. It simply does not function like most other bonds because it is hedged against inflation (one of the greatest enemies of a bond holder).

The manner in which TIPS deliver returns is a little different from many other asset classes. As is the case with Treasuries (and other asset classes), the excess returns of TIPS above cash depend on how future economic conditions transpire relative to discounted rates. The market's expectation of future shifts in cash rates over time is reflected in the TIPS yield curve. The difference here relative to the Treasury yield curve is that the TIPS yield curve is *net of inflation*. This is called the real yield curve and is used because TIPS returns are inflation-adjusted. Thus, changes in actual inflation are paid through TIPS so the price needs not vary to reflect shifts in conditions (as is the case with Treasuries). Therefore, the excess returns of TIPS above cash depend on how real rates of cash (that is, cash yields net of inflation) change over time relative to how they were expected to shift with the passage of time. The only difference between future returns for TIPS versus Treasuries is that TIPS use the real yield curve and Treasuries use the normal, or nominal, yield curve.

For instance, a very steep real yield curve indicates the anticipation by the market that real yields will rapidly rise over time. An easy way to think about the real yield is to take the nominal yield and subtract inflation. Unlike nominal yields, real yields can be negative if inflation is higher than nominal rates. If nominal one-month rates are 1 percent and inflation is 3 percent, then the real yield is −2 percent (1 percent minus 3 percent). If the yield for 10-year TIPS is 3 percent with 3 percent expected inflation, then the real yield at 10 years is 0 percent (3 percent minus 3 percent). These represent two points on the real yield curve: one at one month and the other at 10 years. Following this process through various maturities sets the real yield curve from short- to long-term maturities. As cash rates change through time and as the rate of inflation shifts, the actual real yields unfold year by year. If the real yield curve is upward sloping and steep, then that implies that real yields are anticipated to rise quickly over time. If they rise less than priced in, then TIPS outperform the real yield of cash.

From this analysis, you should recognize that TIPS could produce attractive excess returns above cash regardless of the starting yield. *It is the low yield of real cash that is unusual and not the low yield of TIPS.* The focus should be on excess returns above cash, so a low or zero cash yield simply lowers the hurdle. This is a major oversight in conventional thinking.

Another way to think about the potential performance of TIPS during rising interest rate environments is as follows: If interest rates rise due to increasing inflation, then there are two potentially offsetting effects on TIPS pricing. Rising cash rates to fight inflation are a negative if the increase is greater than that discounted by the yield curve. However, rising inflation is a positive for TIPS. Depending on how much either goes up, the net effect on TIPS could be positive or negative. In contrast, Treasuries generally do poorly no matter what the reason for interest rates rising (assuming they rise faster than discounted). TIPS at least have some upside potential if interest rates rise due to increasing inflation.

## TIPS VIEWED THROUGH A BALANCED PERSPECTIVE

The two key insights about each asset class that I focused on when discussing equities and Treasuries will be repeated with TIPS. The economic environments in which TIPS are biased to outperform will be explored and the logical connections analyzed. Since limited actual history is available for TIPS, the reasonableness of the cause-effect relationships is even more significant than it is with other asset classes. Also, it will be critical to consider the importance of including higher-volatility TIPS rather than lower-volatility bonds in a balanced portfolio. Ultimately, my objective is to help you analyze this asset class within the context of how it fits within a well-balanced asset allocation mix.

### Economic Bias: Rising Inflation

TIPS are fixed income securities that are biased to outperform during periods of rising inflation. The rising inflation benefit is more obvious with TIPS than with just about any other asset class. Returns to TIPS owners are adjusted by the actual rate of inflation. Therefore, the higher the rate of inflation, the greater the amount received. In many ways TIPS are debatably the *purest inflation hedge* available to investors. There is a direct pass-through from rising inflation to TIPS investors.

Note that TIPS, in this sense, have the opposite environmental bias to inflation than Treasuries, which do better during falling inflationary periods. This makes sense since TIPS returns are inflation-adjusted while those from Treasuries are not. With Treasuries you are betting that inflation won't be higher than discounted, because if it is, then the fixed interest rate that the Treasury pays you would be too low. With a TIPS bond you don't have to worry about the inflation rate because you will automatically receive it.

The inflation component of TIPS is the key attribute that makes this asset class particularly attractive. There are few inflation hedges available to investors and none of the other options offers as clean a hedge as TIPS, particularly over the long term. We have not experienced high inflation since the 1970s and early 1980s, so you may be wondering why you need inflation protection. Keep in mind that inflation does not have to be high for inflation hedges to outperform. Recall that with all asset classes, the pricing is impacted by how the future transpires relative to what was discounted. If inflation expectations are low, then all it takes is a little more inflation for TIPS to be positively impacted. This is especially true when no one is expecting high inflation (perhaps because it has not occurred for several decades) and such an outcome transpires. Most asset classes would perform very poorly in this scenario. Going back to the first chapter, this potential outcome is certainly possible in the current economic environment because what happens will be largely dependent on how much money the Fed eventually prints. If the amount of printing is large enough such that total spending (including credit) increases materially, then high inflation is certainly a possibility. In short, it would be a mistake to assume that the relative stability of contained inflation over the past few decades is likely to continue indefinitely, particularly given present unusual and uncertain economic circumstances.

### Economic Bias: Falling Growth

Falling growth periods are also positive for TIPS because of the prospect of falling interest rates in response to weakening economic conditions. The fixed interest rate component of TIPS results in a positive influence on the price, as downward pressure on competing interest rates materializes. Note that if inflation declines more than discounted during these periods TIPS would be negatively impacted. Thus, it is the net effect of *nominal* (or normal) interest rates and inflation shifts that ultimately move TIPS prices. TIPS move on changes in *real* interest rates (which are nominal rates minus inflation). By taking the nominal yield curve and subtracting expected inflation at each maturity date, you get the real yield curve. How real cash rates change through time versus discounted levels is what ultimately influences TIPS prices and performance. Unexpected shifts in economic growth have a direct impact on real interest rates and therefore TIPS prices are heavily influenced by this factor.

### Putting It Together: Rising Inflation and Falling Growth

TIPS are biased to outperform their average excess return above cash during rising inflation and falling growth economic climates. Table 6.1 summarizes the data that supports the conceptual conclusions just covered.

As can be expected, TIPS far outperformed their average returns during rising inflationary periods. Falling growth climates also produced very strong returns. Unsurprisingly, the opposite environments—rising growth and falling inflation—delivered subpar results, with falling inflation actually producing negative excess returns.

How can the returns be negative? Returns below the return of cash do not suggest that deflation existed during these time frames. In fact, newly issued TIPS bonds are deflation-protected, meaning that if inflation turns

**TABLE 6.1**  Annualized Long-Term TIPS Excess Returns by Economic Environment (1927–2013)

| Average Excess Return for All Periods (Good and Bad) | Good Environment (Avg. Excess Return) | Bad Environment (Avg. Excess Return) |
| --- | --- | --- |
| 4.6% | Rising inflation (10.7%)<br>Falling growth (7.9%) | Rising growth (1.1%)<br>Falling inflation (−1.1%) |

out to be negative, then zero inflation will be used to calculate the return of TIPS. However, excess returns may still be negative because the returns are based on what happens versus what was expected to occur. If the market is discounting high inflation rates and inflation fell, then the excess returns above cash could very easily be negative. This is often true even if there was positive inflation and could even be true if there was high inflation. Again, it is all about how the future transpires relative to discounted conditions.

Another understandable conclusion from Table 6.1 is that at 4.6 percent, the average excess return above cash for TIPS may seem high. Because TIPS history only goes back to 1997, actual data prior to that period does not exist. Due to the relatively small data set and the desire to use longer historical returns for all the asset classes to cover a wider range of historical economic environments, I have used simulated TIPS data for periods prior to 1997. Bridgewater Associates, one of the originators of TIPS (it assisted the U.S. government in creating TIPS in the mid-1990s), prepared the simulation. Bridgewater used its deep understanding of the mechanics behind TIPS pricing and applied its insight to actual historical economic developments to create a simulated TIPS return stream going back to 1927. Conceptually, the numbers make sense. During rising inflationary and falling growth climates TIPS outperformed. Conversely, TIPS underperformed during the opposite set of economic outcomes. Moreover, the simulated results very closely align with actual returns since 1997, further adding credibility to the proprietary methodology used to create the return series. Note also that since 1997 TIPS excess returns have been even stronger than the longer-term data presented here (7.4 versus 4.6 percent).

Simulated data is undoubtedly imperfect. For this reason, you should emphasize the relationship between various economic outcomes and return patterns rather than the absolute returns produced by the simulation. The former is far more reliable looking forward. It is the logical sequence of why investing in TIPS within the context of a well-balanced portfolio that should be the prevailing insight. The numbers help support the concepts, but you should not depend overly on the data, particularly since most of what is represented did not actually happen. What we can be confident about is

**FIGURE 6.1**   10-Year Rolling Long-Term TIPS Excess Returns versus Growth and Inflation

that TIPS are biased to outperform during rising inflation and falling growth economic environments and few, if any, other asset classes share that beneficial bias.

The same data can also be observed over longer time frames. Figure 6.1 illustrates rolling 10-year TIPS excess returns. Periods of outperformance and underperformance seem to logically correspond to the economic bias I have described.

## TIPS Volatility

For exactly the same reasons that I suggested the use of long-term Treasuries rather than shorter-term bonds, longer-duration TIPS are appropriate within the context of a balanced portfolio. It is probably even more critical to include longer-term TIPS than long-term Treasuries in a balanced portfolio because of the unique economic bias of TIPS. Rising inflation and falling growth is exactly the opposite economic bias of equities. Since most conventional portfolios own a high allocation to equities, TIPS turn out to be the perfect diversifier and should be included in nearly every portfolio. Moreover, a more volatile version of TIPS is prudent in order to provide sufficient exposure to the underexposed economic biases covered by TIPS.

As with Treasuries, you should not be overly concerned about rising interest rates negatively impacting the returns of the long-duration TIPS in your portfolio. The economic climate that tends to be the worst for TIPS is the best for equities. Thus if TIPS perform poorly it is most likely because of unexpected shifts in the economic climate that would concurrently produce outperformance in the most commonly held asset in portfolios: equities. We saw this play out in 2013 as TIPS suffered big losses as growth outperformed expectations and inflation fell. Of course, equities performed brilliantly during the same environment, as you should expect. Ultimately, the reason to own longer-duration TIPS is to properly hedge against environments of falling growth, rising inflation, or both so that you will have sufficient upside to cover for weakness elsewhere in the portfolio.

## THE CRUCIAL ROLE OF TIPS IN THE BALANCED PORTFOLIO

TIPS have a prepackaged bias to rising inflation and falling growth as depicted in Figure 6.2.

Every component of the balanced portfolio serves a critical role. TIPS, however, are possibly the most influential of the asset classes. As I have discussed throughout this book your objective in portfolio construction should be to ensure that you have efficiently covered all four key economic environments (rising growth, falling inflation; falling growth, rising inflation; rising growth, rising inflation; and falling growth, falling inflation) with the asset classes you have selected. As it turns out, some of the boxes are *easier to fill than others*. There are many asset classes that are biased to do well during rising growth environments. Falling inflation is also easy to cover since both stocks and bonds, which are widely used, benefit from this outcome. There are a handful of asset classes that are predisposed to outperform during falling growth periods, but after that the list starts to shrink. As previously mentioned, even fewer benefit from rising inflation. In fact, the list of good candidates for this environment is quite limited. Therefore, due to the scarcity of viable replacements to cover the rising inflation *and* falling growth outcomes, *TIPS serve as an excellent diversifier for most portfolios.*

Since the growth-inflation boxes for TIPS are exactly the opposite from those used for equities, you might conclude that a balanced portfolio can be constructed by using just these two asset classes. After all, between the two all four potential economic outcomes would be covered. Indeed, this is a valid argument, and a portfolio that only consists of these two assets would probably be more balanced than conventional portfolios.

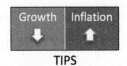

TIPS

**FIGURE 6.2**   The Economic Bias of TIPS

However, one unique nuance about the *timing* of TIPS returns should be mentioned. Since TIPS returns are adjusted for actual inflation, it is generally shifts in *actual* inflation that impact TIPS returns rather than shifts in *expected* inflation (or how future inflation transpires relative to expectations). This distinction is significant in terms of the exact *timing* of the underperformance and outperformance of TIPS. Because of the fact that TIPS are bonds that account for the current inflation rate, over the *short-term* their price is not impacted by shifts in future expectations of inflation changes. However, over *longer time periods* the changes in inflation do make a difference in the returns of TIPS, because investors receive returns reflecting the inflation that actually transpires. This characteristic is only important because of the potential *timing mismatch* between TIPS returns and those of the other asset classes. Since the returns of the other asset classes mentioned—equities, Treasuries, and commodities—are impacted by changes in inflation *expectations* and how inflation transpires relative to what had been expected, then the key impact to the returns of these asset classes is how these variables shift over time. Consequently, TIPS may not move if inflation expectations suddenly increase, as would the other asset classes. Of course, over time TIPS do react to these changes, but the shift in returns experiences a lag relative to the other asset classes.

Think of it this way: TIPS prices over the short run are based on changes in growth while shifts in inflation flow through TIPS over a longer time frame. In contrast, the other three asset classes experience changes in the current price from shifts in growth as well as inflation over the short run (as well as the long run). The upshot is if inflation expectations suddenly jump, then the lag in TIPS returns reacting to this new environment may not immediately be reflected in the price. This means that the balanced portfolio may underperform for a short time until TIPS returns catch up to the change in conditions. They need to catch up because the other three asset classes would have already reacted to the shift in inflation expectations while TIPS experienced a delayed reaction. Over time, this distinction is smoothed out so it is not that important over the long run. I only mention it so that you are aware of this unique dynamic as it relates to TIPS. One way to mitigate this factor is to own commodities (which will be covered in detail in the next chapter) as an inflation hedge because this asset class does tend to react immediately to shifts in inflation expectations. For this reason, there is a benefit to further diversify a balanced portfolio by adding more assets within the framework presented.

## SUMMARY

In summary, TIPS are an excellent diversifier that cannot easily be replaced. Their role within the context of the balanced portfolio is crucial because they cover the two economic scenarios that are most often underweighted: falling growth and rising inflation. Moreover, the low starting yield should not dissuade you from adding them to your portfolio because attractive excess returns above cash are still achievable looking forward.

# CHAPTER 7

# Owning Commodities in a Balanced Portfolio

**A**ssets that hedge against the risks of *rising* inflation are hard to come by. The traditional asset classes of stocks and bonds are both biased to outperform during periods of *falling* inflation. Consequently, traditional portfolios—which are mostly invested in stocks and bonds—are highly exposed to environments in which inflation is *rising*. These types of portfolios tend to perform extremely poorly during climates dominated by rising inflation, as should be expected given the predictable return patterns of these asset classes in terms of their economic bias.

In the last chapter I discussed how the inflation protection TIPS offer is a benefit to portfolios. TIPS provide direct inflation protection because returns to TIPS holders are inflation-adjusted. Commodities represent another asset class for your portfolio that covers the rising-inflation environment category. In this chapter I will first explain how commodities investments work, since the investment structure is different from the asset classes previously discussed. Next, commodities will be viewed through the conventional lens and the flaws in this thinking will be exposed. Finally, I will walk you through how to analyze commodities through a balanced portfolio perspective to help you appreciate how this asset class fits within a total balanced portfolio framework.

## WHAT ARE COMMODITIES INVESTMENTS?

There are various commodities in which you can invest. A short list of the main commodities includes oil, gas, industrial metals (copper, aluminum, etc.), precious metals (gold, silver, etc.), agricultural commodities (soybeans, corn, sugar, etc.), and livestock (cattle, hogs, etc.). Commodities are very different investments from mainstream stocks and bonds. Unlike equities and fixed income securities, commodities do not generate income or pay dividends or interest. The return you receive is based solely on the price change of the underlying commodity (or, more precisely, the futures price as will be discussed later in this chapter). If the price rises over time you earn a positive return, and vice versa.

The other big difference between this asset class and the others we have covered thus far is that commodities are *real* assets. Stocks, bonds, TIPS and most other asset classes, in contrast, are *financial* assets. A real asset is something that is tangible and that you can touch; a financial asset is merely a contract that reflects a claim in an underlying asset. The reason I make a distinction between real and financial assets is because this attribute is actually one of the main reasons why commodities tend to be better inflation hedges. The supply of commodities cannot easily be increased with financial engineering. It takes time for the supply to change as production of each commodity is adjusted based on underlying demand and the cost of production. A relatively fixed supply generally results in price changes stemming from shifts in demand for the commodities. Changes in demand come from the economic cycles that you are trying to diversify against.

Due to the tangible nature of commodities, investing in this market segment is unlike investing in the other asset classes that I have covered. Holding a stock or a bond is easy because buying and selling is as simple as a click of a button. No physical asset needs to be stored because stocks and bonds are financial assets that only require a computer entry or certificate of ownership. The stock or bond appears on your monthly statement and can be easily tracked. Buying a commodity is quite different since you cannot effortlessly store a commodity such as oil or cattle.

There are generally two ways to invest in commodities without having to deal with the administrative burden and cost of holding the physical asset. First, you can buy the stocks of the corporations that invest in commodities such as metals miners or oil producers. The logic is that as the price of the commodities rise, the profits of these companies also improve and therefore lead to higher stock prices. Since stocks are liquid investments, you can gain exposure to commodity prices with little effort and none of the cumbersome restrictions that come with holding physical commodities. The challenge with this approach is that the stock price may not be highly correlated with the underlying commodity price. The companies may be mismanaged or they may hedge out the price risk of the commodity, thereby giving up the upside price movement. Another way to say this is that by investing in commodity stocks, you are taking on additional stock market risk on top of the risk of commodity price changes. Therefore, you may have periods during which the commodity price goes up but the stock price falls, and vice versa. Recall that the key to building a balanced portfolio is to ensure that the various economic environments are adequately covered. Thus, it is imperative that your commodity allocation tracks the price of the underlying commodities as closely as possible. For these reasons commodity stocks may not be an ideal fit for the balanced portfolio.

Entering into a futures contract with another party for the price of the commodity is probably a cleaner approach to investing in commodities, and is the strategy used in this book. This process in effect converts this real asset into a financial asset, just like the rest of the asset classes. This conversion provides increased liquidity and tighter correlation with the underlying commodity price. The way these agreements work is that you invest in a contract with another party in which you promise to pay a fixed price at a future date for a specific commodity. This price, called the *futures price*, may be higher or lower than the current price of that commodity, termed the *spot price*. For example, if the spot price of oil is $100 per barrel today, the price you might agree to pay for a barrel of oil (in say, three months) may be $102. With this agreement, you have the obligation to pay $102 for a barrel of oil in three months and the counterparty is required to physically deliver the barrel of oil to you. Since investors in commodities rarely want to actually receive the barrel of oil (and the other party normally doesn't want to deliver it to you), nearly all commodities futures contracts are settled before the predetermined delivery date. The settlement terms are simply the difference between the then-current price and the futures price that had been established at the inception of the contract. In the example above, if the price of oil is $105, then the winning party who purchased the commodity future earns $3 ($105 current price minus $102 agreed-upon futures price) and the losing side that sold it pays $3. It is a zero sum game because the gains of one party are equal to the losses of the other.

In practice, entering these futures contracts is far simpler than it may seem at first. You do not actually have to go find someone who will take the other side and hire an attorney to draft the documents. These contracts are actively traded in highly liquid, regulated exchanges that are not too different from the stock and bond markets. Long-term investors, short-term speculators, and those who are looking to hedge themselves against adverse commodity price movements trade in these markets. The hedgers are typically commodity producers who often prefer to know today the price they are going to sell the commodity for in the future. These market participants can take both sides of the trade and together create sufficient buyers and sellers of commodity futures contracts to establish a fluid tradable market.

The main goal with commodities investing is to gain *exposure* to a diversified basket of the price of these items in order to achieve the target of hedging against inflation risk. A balanced basket can easily be purchased via a commodities index fund that has a specific, predetermined weight to a large number of commodities in order to provide sufficient diversification to investors. This also takes the guesswork out of picking the right commodities to own.

## THE CONVENTIONAL VIEW OF COMMODITIES

Most conventional portfolios include a very small proportion, if any, of commodities investments. To better understand why this is the case, it will be helpful to look at the attributes of commodities *through a conventional lens.* The conventional approach to assessing the attractiveness of most asset classes is to review their historical returns to determine whether they offer upside potential. This expected return might also be compared to expected risk to assess the return-to-risk ratio. A question that is often asked is whether the investment provides a compelling return for the risk taken. Asset classes that offer higher returns per unit of risk are deemed to be the most attractive, and those with low expected returns and high risk are considered to be unattractive. The conventional logic follows that if the goal of a port-folio is to have high returns with low risk, then a collection of asset classes that share the same attributes would efficiently accomplish this objective.

*When viewed through this lens,* the commodities asset class does not look very appealing. It has historically produced low excess returns rela-tive to its high volatility. Table 7.1 summarizes the average historical excess returns and standard deviation (or risk) of each of the four key asset classes I have covered.

*From a conventional standpoint,* commodities jump out on this list. This asset class is one of the riskiest investments because of its high standard deviation, but its average excess return is one of the lowest. The risk is similar to that of equities, but the long-term return is like that of bonds. Low return and high risk: why would anyone want to own this asset class? Consequently, the conventional allocation to commodities tends to be very low.

Such an outcome seems to make sense when approaching the asset allo-cation decision *within the conventional framework.* Most investors look at each asset class *as a stand-alone investment* and try to identify those market

**TABLE 7.1**  Returns and Risk of the Major Asset Classes (1927–2013)

| Asset Class | Average Excess Return | Average Volatility |
|---|---|---|
| Equities | 5.6% | 19% |
| Long-Term Treasuries | 1.4% | 10% |
| Long-Term TIPS | 4.6% | 11% |
| Commodities | 2.0% | 17% |

segments that offer compelling prospective returns with lower risk (which are often based on historical returns). This approach can be contrasted to a balanced portfolio context in which each asset class is examined in terms of its *contribution to the total mix rather than its own merits*. Thus, some asset classes may be unattractive on their own but warrant inclusion in the portfolio because of the benefits they provide when looking at the bigger picture. In other words, the true diversification benefits of owning commodities are only obvious when looking through a balanced portfolio framework, which depends on reliable cause-effect linkages as opposed to through the traditional lens, which tends to overemphasize historical data (returns, risk, and correlation).

A second drawback to commodities *from a conventional perspective* is that this particular asset class, unlike many others, contains some structural impediments. First of all, the fact that commodities do not generate income or pay a dividend or interest makes it difficult to calculate their fair value. How would you know what an asset is really worth if it doesn't earn or pay anything? A commodity's value and return is based entirely on what others will pay for it in the future. As a result, this asset class is often missing from the menu for investment portfolios focused on investing in undervalued or cheap asset classes because investors simply cannot determine whether it is a good buy at the current price.

The second structural concern for commodities investments is the potential discrepancy between the price of commodities futures and current (or spot) prices. That is, the price of the actual commodity may rise but the futures price may not follow suit. Thus, by investing in commodities futures you are taking the risk that even if the underlying commodity appreciated in value you may not benefit from the gain.

These two major arguments against commodities stem from using a conventional lens and are overstated. Each of these reasons to avoid commodities contains major flaws that I will explain next.

## Major Flaw #1: Low Returns and High Volatility—Why Would I Ever Invest in Commodities?

The bottom-line reason to own commodities is because they are biased to outperform *when you really need them to*. This holds true even though the *average returns* over time may be unattractive. A perfect analogy is insurance, which tends to share similar characteristics. Insurance protects you in the event of a disaster (be it a fire, an accident, death, or whatever you are insuring against). If the event you are insuring against doesn't occur, you lose a little by owning insurance, since you have to a pay a premium to stay insured. You can think of commodities in the same way. Even if the total excess return above cash is very low over the long run, you still benefit from owning it because it pays off during periods in which your other assets may be doing poorly (particularly during rising inflation economic climates). The higher the inflation relative to expectations, the more it earns. When considered from this perspective, a low average excess return over time actually makes it even more attractive than insurance. Insurance has a negative return almost all the time and probably a net negative expected return to you over the long run even if it does pay off every now and then (which is precisely why insurance companies exist and are highly profitable). Think of it as insurance that you do not have to pay for. The same rationale applies to TIPS, Treasuries, and every other asset class. Each is there to protect you in a different economic environment. Even stocks are there to protect you against periods of rising growth and falling inflation. You may not feel you need protection against these encouraging periods, but owning stocks protects your portfolio from potential underperformance of the rest of the assets. They all work together and have a specific role. This important concept will be more fully fleshed out later in this chapter when I discuss the role of commodities in a balanced portfolio.

## Major Flaw #2: Two Structural Issues—They Pay No Income and Futures Prices Can Diverge from Spot Prices

Commodities produce no income. Your return is based solely on the difference between the price you pay to buy and the price when you sell. Most other asset classes, such as equities, Treasuries, and TIPS, offer interest or dividends in between buying and selling, providing an additional source of returns. Even stocks and bonds that pay no dividends or interest accrue some value while they are being held. Companies earn profits, and if they choose not to pay a dividend they simply reinvest the cash into their businesses. This theoretically adds some value that benefits shareholders. A zero coupon bond that does not pay interest compensates investors with a gradually increasing bond price until it reaches its full par value at maturity.

That commodities produce no income should not dissuade you from including commodities in your balanced portfolio. Due to the pronounced benefits of this asset class's unique characteristics, it is still worthy of a place in a balanced portfolio, regardless of the aforementioned issue. The bottom line is that value is less important than its economic bias. And since there is a scarcity of good inflation hedges, commodities can add value when included in portfolios. The response to this objection will become even more evident when we go through how commodities fit within the context of a balanced portfolio later on.

Another concern involves the unique structure of commodities futures. The apprehension stems from the fact that the spot price of the commodity can rise, but you may still lose money depending on the shape and slope of the futures curve. In reality, you are not investing in the current price of a commodity. Since you are buying a commodity futures contract, you are effectively making a bet on the future price and how that future price may change. Consider the following example: oil today is $100 per barrel and the futures contract three months from today is $102. If you buy the three-month futures contract and during that period oil rises from $100 to $102, then you do not gain anything. This is because you bought a contract for $102 (even though today's price was only $100). Therefore, even though you were right that oil went up $2, you were not able to profit from this foresight since you effectively had to overpay for the investment. The opposite, as argued, is also true. If the futures price is lower than the current price, then that makes investing in commodities a more attractive endeavor. *This is the thinking among many market participants.*

Although this logic may seem intuitive, *it misses a big component of how you should think about investing in commodities futures.* Remember that the return you earn from any investment, not just commodities, is based on how the *future transpires relative to what had been expected* and already factored into the purchase price. I discussed this notion in the section that noted that Treasuries may produce attractive excess returns even though the starting yield is low. The reason for this, as I explained, is that the concern that interest rates may rise (because they are low) is probably already priced into the yield curve. Said differently, longer-term Treasuries offer a higher yield than shorter-term bonds and cash because of the expectation that interest rates are going to rise. This is reflected in an upward sloping yield curve that may be very steep. Your excess return above cash will depend on whether interest rates rise more or less versus what is already discounted. Thus, if everyone expects rates to rise and they actually rise less than the level priced in (but they nonetheless rise), you earn an excess return from holding long-term Treasuries because the increase was less than expected.

A commodities futures curve and the return you ultimately achieve both *follow a parallel rationale.* If the futures price is higher than the spot price (the current price) that signifies that the *market is anticipating that the price will rise* between now and the end of the futures contract. If the price rises more than that amount, then you earn a profit. If the price underperforms expectations, then you underperform cash. This is exactly the same dynamic as for Treasuries and stocks, real estate, and any other asset class. It all depends on how the future transpires relative to discounted conditions.

Another simple example involves inverted curves. If the futures curve is inverted that means that the futures price is lower than the spot price. This reflects a market expectation that the price in the future will fall. This may be the case if there is excess supply of the commodity, anticipated economic weakness, or for many other potential reasons. Regardless, if the price falls less than expected you will earn a positive return. For instance, if today's oil price is $100 and the 3-month futures price is $98, even if oil prices fall to $99 you still earn $1.

This is the same thought process that is used to analyze an inverted yield curve for bonds. There are times when a 5-year Treasury may offer a yield that is less than that of a 3-month Treasury. You might reasonably ask why investors would want to tie up their money for five years and be compensated with a lower yield than they can get by locking in their cash for only three months. Going back to the core principles applied above, an inverted yield curve—just like an inverted commodities futures curve—indicates a market expectation that interest rates are going to decline over time. This often occurs because of an expectation of an economic downturn that would cause the Fed to lower interest rates. (You may have heard of the familiar connection between inverted yield curves and recessions: Every time that there's been an inverted yield curve, an economic recession has occurred.) If interest rates actually fall more than is priced in, you would be better off locking in a lower rate for a longer period because you would earn more interest in total (even though your starting interest rate may be lower). In other words, the interest rate for a 3-month Treasury is temporary and when your bond matures you would reinvest your principle in a lower-yielding Treasury. After adding up all the reinvestments over a five-year period, you would have been better off locking in the lower five-year rate in the beginning. Conversely, if rates fall less than is priced in you would outperform with the shorter-term bond. It simply comes down to how the future plays out as compared to what was priced to occur. As a result, the concern that the spot price may be different from the futures price becomes a nonissue.

## CONSIDERING COMMODITIES THROUGH A BALANCED PORTFOLIO PERSPECTIVE

Rather than looking at commodities in terms of how they may perform on their own, you should consider how they fit within the context of the total portfolio. What attributes do they possess that may add value to the total portfolio? To think from this perspective requires you to evaluate commodities with an eye toward the two key factors that influence the total portfolio's returns: its economic bias and its volatility.

## Economic Bias: Rising Inflation

Commodities are biased to outperform their average returns during periods dominated by rising inflation. This bias is reasonable and reliable. In fact, commodities are actually part of the inflation calculation. Rising prices in commodities such as energy, metals, and food directly and indirectly lead to broader increases in inflation measurements. The direct impacts on inflation measurements come from the fact that the methodology used to calculate the CPI incorporates changes in the prices of commodities. Meanwhile, indirect effects of rising commodity prices find their way into inflation of other items in the CPI basket because of the fact that these commodities are inputs into the prices of these items. For instance, higher gas prices lead to higher prices for traveling or shipping items because of the increased costs to those companies providing these services. At least a portion of the higher input expenses are typically passed on to consumers via higher prices, which results in higher overall prices for goods and services.

The fact that commodities represent a portion of the input cost of goods and services is another reason there is an inflation link in their returns. As general increased demand for goods and services pushes overall inflation rates higher, the higher demand for the goods and services leads to greater demand for the inputs (the commodities). The higher demand in turn exerts upward pressure on commodity prices. If the demand was greater than expected, then the price generally rises, because the demand originally expected was compared to the original supply to determine the price. This discounted future price is then reflected in the futures curve. Again, your profit depends on whether the future price comes in higher or lower than that price. This outcome will be based on how the future transpires relative to expectations, just as is the case with the other asset classes.

## Economic Bias: Rising Growth

Commodities are not only pro-inflation assets, but also are biased to outperform during rising growth environments. As the economy outperforms to the upside, greater commodity demand naturally follows. If I earn more money than I had anticipated, then I am likely to spend a portion of that higher income. Part of that spending will either be directly on commodities (perhaps higher quality food, oil or precious metals) or on other goods and services that will require more commodities to produce. Because economic growth is greater than expected, it is reasonable that the original supply of commodities is insufficient to meet the higher, unexpected demand. This mismatch generally results in upward price pressures. It comes down to expectations versus actual results. Imagine if there was great optimism about the future prospects of the economy: We are living in a boom period and this prosperity is expected to continue. This view would likely result in higher futures prices for commodities, as well as an uptick in the production of commodities. If you are a commodities producer and feel that the economy is trending positively and commodities prices are rising, you will have the incentive to produce more commodities to meet the anticipated growing demand. Such lofty expectations are often not met since the margin of safety has shrunk. Even if the economy performs well, it would have to do better than expected in order to positively impact commodities prices (or stock prices, or the price of any pro-growth asset class). In the case of commodities, changes in both supply and demand lead to price changes and both are directly impacted by expectations of future economic conditions.

### Putting It Together: Rising Inflation and Rising Growth

The historical average excess return of a diversified basket of commodities since 1927 is 2 percent per year and the average volatility has been a very high 17 percent, which is slightly less than the volatility of equities. Most importantly, however, during rising inflation periods (favorable times for commodities) the average excess return has been 8.4 percent per year. This represents the second-best asset class return (behind long-term TIPS at 10.7 percent) of the four major asset classes. Since rising inflation periods occur about *half the time* (relative to expectations), the benefits of owning this asset class should be apparent. The same analysis holds for the other economic environment in which commodities are biased to outperform: rising growth. Commodities have averaged a 7 percent excess return above cash when there is rising growth, which ranks second to equities. The average return of commodities during different economic environments is presented in Table 7.2.

Using rolling 10-year returns, as displayed in Figure 7.1, commodities have outperformed and underperformed as you would expect, given their economic bias.

**TABLE 7.2** Annualized Commodities Excess Returns by Economic Environment (1927–2013)

| Average Excess Return for All Periods (Good and Bad) | Good Environment (Avg. Excess Return) | Bad Environment (Avg. Excess Return) |
|---|---|---|
| 2.0% | Rising inflation (8.4%) Rising growth (7.0%) | Falling growth (−2.3%) Falling inflation (−4.0%) |

**FIGURE 7.1** 10-Year Rolling Commodities Excess Returns versus Growth and Inflation

## The Advantage of the High Volatility of Commodities

Seen from a conventional viewpoint, the high volatility of commodities appears to be a negative attribute. However, when considering how commodities fit within the framework of a balanced portfolio, something remarkable occurs. You will discover that commodities are actually more valuable to the balanced portfolio *because* they are highly volatile. If they were not volatile, they would provide *less* of a benefit. This may sound like an exaggeration, but the following example provides support for this highly counterintuitive statement.

To prove this point, I will take an extreme example. Imagine if there were another asset class that offered exactly the same return as commodities but with *zero* risk or volatility. In other words, this asset class, which I will call *no-risk commodities,* has returned the same long-term percentage return as regular commodities (2 percent excess returns since 1927) but was able to achieve these results through a perfectly smooth return path. Commodities averaged a 2 percent return per year but had years when they were up by 60 percent and periods during which they were down by 50 percent. On the other hand, the hypothetical no-risk commodities earned 2 percent excess returns by earning 0.17 percent per month every month (which is 2 percent divided by 12) without exception. On its own this looks like a very attractive asset class and would score off the charts using traditional risk-return metrics. You are guaranteed to beat cash by 2 percent every year. You would think that this asset class is far superior to normal commodities.

As it turns out, *the opposite is true.* To demonstrate this I will compare the long-term average historical return of a balanced portfolio with regular commodities with the same balanced portfolio with our hypothetical no-risk commodities. For the balanced portfolio I have used the allocation that is presented in the final chapters of this book. At this point the makeup of

**TABLE 7.3** The Balanced Portfolio and Commodity Volatility (1927–2013)

|  | Average Excess Return |
| --- | --- |
| With Regular **High-Risk** Commodities | 4.3% |
| With Hypothetical **No-Risk** Commodities | 4.0% |

this portfolio is not important. This comparison is presented here to demonstrate the significance of the volatility characteristic of commodities. You just need to know that the percentage of commodities in the two portfolios we are comparing is identical and the only difference is the substitution of the commodities return stream. One portfolio uses regular commodities and the other substitutes no-risk commodities. The goal is to completely isolate the impact of volatility on total portfolio returns.

The balanced portfolio's results are actually *worse* with no-risk commodities than with regular commodities. In this case, *higher volatility is better than lower volatility*! The comparison is highlighted in Table 7.3.

Does this result make sense from a conceptual standpoint when looking through the balanced portfolio lens? Of course it does. Regardless of the results, my objective is to ensure that you now understand why this result is actually more sensible. As I've covered previously, it is the concepts that stand the test of time as the environment will undoubtedly change in the future and new investment strategies and structures will be introduced. You can take these concepts and apply them to various economic environments and asset classes. The reason this outcome makes sense is because the strong returns arrive *when you need them* to balance underperformance in other parts of the portfolio. By producing a more stable return stream and by minimizing the losses during the really bad times, the improved overall balance that comes from owning commodities outweighs their individual unappealing return-risk characteristics. In this sense, commodities are the true team player!

## THE ROLE OF COMMODITIES IN A BALANCED PORTFOLIO

Commodities are biased to perform better during rising inflation and rising growth economic climates, as depicted in Figure 7.2.

Putting the inflation and growth bias together, the role of commodities in a balanced portfolio is to offer upside during these periods to help offset weakness in other asset classes not biased to outperform during these climates. The inflation hedge is crucial because of the lack of great options

**Commodities**

**FIGURE 7.2**
Economic Bias of
Commodities

in this area. This is another reason why you might consider including commodities even though investing in this asset class is not as structurally clean as the others.

## SUMMARY

If you approached investing the conventional way by analyzing each asset class on its own and putting together a handful that looked independently attractive, then you would immediately dismiss commodities (as most do). With a line of thinking that emphasizes the balanced portfolio you are better able to assess the attractiveness of each asset class based on its role within the context of a truly balanced portfolio. The change in perspective and approach leads to a completely different outlook, asset allocation, and ultimately, improved long-term results.

*This is a very important point because it diffuses many of the arguments you may hear about commodities or other asset classes that may appear unappealing as a stand-alone investment. That the various economic environments are adequately covered is more important to the bottom line than the relative attractiveness of the portfolio's individual parts.*

# CHAPTER 8

# Even More Balance

## Introduction to Other Asset Classes

In order to emphasize core concepts, I have intentionally oversimplified the discussion thus far to cover only four basic asset classes. The fact that the economic biases of these four asset classes are relatively straightforward to analyze has also helped clarify the main ideas. In the end, understanding the cause-effect relationship between shifts in the economic environment and asset class returns is the most critical lesson to draw from this discussion. The specific asset classes used, their historical and prospective returns, and whether a particular moment is a good time for the strategy are far less important factors. This is because it is the concepts that survive through time and can be relied upon looking ahead.

### HOW TO DECONSTRUCT OTHER ASSET CLASSES USING THE BALANCED FRAMEWORK

Using the cause-effect relationships that have been introduced in previous chapters, we now turn to a similar analysis of other asset classes. The first step when considering other asset classes, as you might suspect, is to determine their bias to shifts in economic growth and inflation. As a reminder and guide in this initial process, Table 8.1 provides a summary of the economic biases of each of the four asset classes covered up to now. More importantly, the reasoning behind each bias is included. You need to possess a strong grasp *of the rationale* in order to effectively apply the same logic to new asset classes.

After identifying the economic bias of each asset class you need to determine the general volatility of the asset (low, medium, or high). This information will enable you to regulate its overall weighting in the total portfolio. Table 8.2 summarizes the volatility of the four major asset classes covered

**TABLE 8.1**   The Economic Bias of Four Major Asset Classes

| Asset Class | Growth | Rationale | Inflation | Rationale |
|---|---|---|---|---|
| Equities | Rising | Higher company revenues | Falling | Lower input costs, cheaper financing |
| Long-Term Treasuries | Falling | Falling interest rates to stimulate economy | Falling | Falling interest rates to increase inflation |
| Long-Term TIPS | Falling | Falling interest rates to stimulate economy | Rising | Pays inflation rate |
| Commodities | Rising | Rising demand for commodities | Rising | Higher commodity prices part of inflation measure |

**TABLE 8.2**   The Volatility of Four Major Asset Classes

| Asset Class | Volatility | Average Volatility since 1927 |
|---|---|---|
| Equities | High | 19% |
| Long-Term Treasuries | Medium | 10% |
| Long-Term TIPS | Medium | 11% |
| Commodities | High | 17% |

thus far. To simplify this process I have categorized each asset class as having low, medium, or high volatility to make it easier to compare them with each other.

Note that there are no low-volatility asset classes listed. Treasuries and TIPS are normally low-volatility assets, but they have been transformed into medium-volatility assets by using bonds with longer duration. You can certainly use specific numbers for volatility; however, it is not necessary to be precise since this exercise is not an exact science. The goal is to use the right approach and a ballpark weight based on the asset's approximate relative volatility.

## ADDITIONAL ASSET CLASSES

Once you have mapped the economic bias and volatility of each market segment the goal is to ensure that each of the four economic climates is represented in your portfolio such that the impact to the total portfolio from each environment is roughly equal. In the next few chapters I will walk you through how to do this. At this point, you should focus on identifying the environmental bias and overall volatility of each asset class as I go through them in the following sections. Obviously I will not cover every asset class, but the idea is to provide you with a sample of popular market segments to help you apply the logic to whatever area you wish to include in your portfolio.

## Global Stocks and Bonds

All the assumptions and data used for the balanced portfolio to this point reflect a 100 percent domestic portfolio. Equities used the S&P 500 Index as a proxy. Obviously Treasuries and TIPS are both U.S.-based. Commodities are global assets, although most are denominated in U.S. dollars. Thus, the balanced portfolio could be much more diversified by simply expanding outside of U.S. markets.

Incorporating global equities (those from countries outside of the United States) and fixed income securities into the mix could improve the overall return-to-risk ratio over time. This is because instead of being dependent on the U.S. economic environment alone, you are able to spread the risk across multiple economies across the globe. U.S. stocks may be performing poorly, but stocks in Japan may be doing fine because Japan's economic growth may be stronger. Going global applies to fixed income assets as well, including non-U.S. inflation-linked bonds, which were actually created long before TIPS were introduced in the United States in 1997. Exposure to multiple countries and economies simply spreads the risk without giving away much upside.

Global diversification is one of the easiest diversification enhancements that can be made to the balanced portfolio structure that I have presented because global equities and fixed income securities generally share the same economic characteristics as I have described for the U.S. asset classes. Global stocks are biased to outperform during rising growth and falling inflation environments just like U.S. stocks. The difference is that a global equity portfolio consists of exposures to several countries, each of which is biased toward its own economic conditions (although global economic conditions may ultimately impact cross-border companies due to international ties).

The one difference between a global portfolio and one that is domestically based is the potential volatility. Non-U.S. equities may be more volatile relative to U.S. equities due to increased risks from currency fluctuations, politics, and so on. Emerging markets equities are usually more volatile than U.S. stocks because the aforementioned risks are generally perceived to be even higher in these regions (even though the balance sheets of many of these countries are currently superior to those in the developed world, including that of the U.S.). The bottom line is that their economic bias is similar to that of U.S. stocks, but their slightly higher volatility should be noted when determining how to weight asset classes.

## Equity Subsets

Stocks, being a popular asset class, come in a variety of sizes and flavors. I just discussed expanding equities to include non-U.S. regions. You also have the option of selecting a subset of this broad market. For instance, equities can be subdivided into growth or value, and into large or small capitalization. Although these segments do experience diverging returns over time and different levels of volatility, their general economic bias to growth and inflation are similar to the equities that I have already described. This connection is reasonable since broad groups of public companies, whether they are large or small, generate profits similarly. Likewise, growth companies and cheap value companies by and large earn money similarly when profits are considered within the context of broad economic themes.

You may break down equities further into categories that are more directly linked to either growth or inflation factors. For example, you may be able to find a basket of stocks that are more hedged against rising inflation than the average public corporation. Perhaps companies that can consistently raise their dividends may provide superior inflation protection than the broad stock market can. Moreover, there may be certain industries that are better able to pass through cost increases to their customers and that therefore are less sensitive to inflation. Likewise, some types of companies seem to withstand weak economic environments better than others.

All of these distinctions within the stock market may be valid, but they may only make a difference at the margins. If you do find an equity subsegment that you are confident can withstand (and better yet, appreciate during) inflation and weak economic periods in the future, then you are free to plug it into your portfolio. You just need to make sure you account for it correctly when determining its economic bias and volatility.

Also, recognize that the analysis goes both ways. If you decide to only hold stocks that are biased to perform better during weak economic periods, during rising inflationary times, or both, then you leave yourself exposed to the opposite environment: If the economy is very strong, then your stocks may not keep up with the market. More importantly, the gains may be insufficient to make up for the underperformance elsewhere in your balanced portfolio. Again, the key is to ensure that you have balanced it appropriately and that comes from categorizing it correctly at the beginning.

Since we are still talking about stocks, the volatility of these subsets will be roughly similar to that of the overall stock market. However, the slightly higher risk of smaller companies should be noted. This segment includes riskier business ventures because the companies are often less mature than larger capitalization stocks (i.e., small businesses trying to become large companies). Growth and value stocks, on the other hand, have not experienced markedly divergent volatilities through time, particularly as compared to bonds, TIPS, commodities, and other asset classes. Some research may suggest different levels of volatility, but many of those findings are highly dependent on the time period observed and results may vary depending on the starting and ending points used in the analysis.

## Corporate Bonds

Another variety of bonds, outside of Treasuries (or sovereign debt of other countries), includes corporate bonds. As their name indicates, these bonds are issued by corporations rather than by governments and therefore are not backed by the full faith and credit of the government. Due to the greater risk of default, or credit risk, these bonds typically offer a higher yield than Treasuries. This asset class also contains a wide range of credit ratings. There are companies that are rated AAA, meaning that their debt is considered very safe. Consequently, these bonds have a lower yield to reflect their relative safety. Companies rated BB and below are viewed as high yield, or junk, bonds because of the higher yield they offer and the greater risk of default.

The excess yield above Treasuries that corporate bonds offer is termed the credit spread, which is the difference between the yield of corporate bonds and that of Treasuries (the risk-free rate). In general, the greater the odds of default, the higher the credit spread. The credit spread is effectively the excess return that investors receive for taking risk (minus the expected default rate of these bonds). This is the same concept that I've covered throughout this book when comparing the expected returns of each asset class to the returns offered by risk-free cash. Treasuries are used here instead of cash in order to match the duration of the bonds and simplify the math.

The critical observation to appreciate is the material difference between Treasuries and corporate bonds in terms of their economic bias. Treasuries, as you know, are biased to outperform during *falling* growth (and falling inflationary) periods. Corporate bonds benefit from *rising* growth as opposed to falling growth. Like Treasuries they are biased to do better during falling inflationary outcomes; however, unlike Treasuries, they can get absolutely crushed if inflation falls too much and nears deflationary levels. You will notice that even though corporate bonds are structured like Treasuries, they actually share the same economic biases as equities. Although *they are technically bonds, they act more like stocks.*

The way to understand and figure out these biases on your own is to appreciate the factors that ultimately lead to improved conditions for the

asset class. Corporate bonds generally yield more than Treasuries, but do so because the risk of default is higher. Thus, it is reasonable that these bonds will perform better as the odds of default decline. Based on this core understanding of what drives the returns of the asset class, you can take the next step in the logical sequence. Stronger economic growth makes it more likely that the company will not default because its profits are biased to improve (just as is the case when thinking about the economic bias of stocks). Moreover, falling inflation is a plus because it lowers input and borrowing costs, further improving profit margins. This is exactly the same rationale for the economic bias of equities. You should then understand why deflation is so bad for corporate bonds. In a deflationary environment the economy has collapsed and corporate earnings have likely plummeted. Treasuries fare well during this environment because they do not have credit risk, while the credit of corporations (or at least the perceived creditworthiness) takes a catastrophic hit. Finally, corporate bonds also benefit from falling inflation because of the increased prospects for falling interest rates. The fixed coupon of corporate bonds, like Treasuries, becomes more attractive with falling rates.

The volatility of corporate bonds lies somewhere between that of stocks and similar-duration Treasuries. This should make sense: Corporate bonds can be considered a hybrid investment because they share characteristics of both equities and Treasuries. Like equities, corporate bonds are issued by public companies. When public companies do well, both the stocks and bonds of that issuer benefit, and vice versa. Similarly to Treasuries, corporate bonds are debt instruments, and the upside (if held to maturity) is limited to a return of the original principal plus the coupon. Consequently, the volatility of corporate bonds can be approximately categorized as medium, or somewhere along the spectrum between low-risk intermediate dated bonds and high-risk stocks. Of course, high yield bonds typically come with even higher volatility, as they tend to be even more sensitive to economic shifts.

## Emerging Market Bonds

Similarly to corporate bonds, debt issued by emerging markets offers a higher yield than U.S. Treasuries. This *spread* can vary significantly by emerging country because of variations in credit, political, social, currency, and other risks that exist among countries. One way to think about emerging market bonds is they lie somewhere between Treasuries and U.S. corporate bonds. Similarly to Treasuries, these are sovereign fixed-income securities backed by the emerging economy's government. Like corporate bonds, these securities are not as safe as Treasuries and therefore offer a yield spread above Treasuries.

In order to determine the appropriate economic bias some understanding of these economies and how they generally differ from developed nations is required. Many of these developing countries are able to expand their economies by taking advantage of demand that comes from outside their borders. By definition, these are economies that are in an early phase of their maturation periods and that are working toward becoming fully developed, self-dependent countries. Thus, much of their growth comes from selling abroad rather than to domestic consumers. Goods, services, and commodities are produced in emerging markets and exported to richer nations. Therefore, the growth and inflation dynamics that support these factors tend to benefit emerging markets, which consequently creates upward pressure on emerging market bond prices.

Emerging market bonds are biased to do better during periods characterized by rising growth and rising inflation. Stronger growth is a positive outcome because that normally leads to more purchases of the goods, services, and commodities that these countries are trying to sell. Improved overall profits make it more likely that the government will make good on its promise to repay its debt (the bonds in which you have invested).

Rising inflation is also a benefit because the items that are being sold—the goods, services, and commodities—cost more. The higher revenues that come from selling these items results in greater profits, which ultimately improves the probability of the country paying off its debts.

Due to their beneficial economic bias (which is similar to commodities), emerging market bonds can be an interesting asset class to include in your balanced portfolio. The inflationary component may be particularly useful given the lack of available inflation hedges.

The volatility of this asset class tends to fall in line with that of corporate bonds. This is because these two areas generally share similar characteristics due to the existence of credit risk. Note that emerging market bonds, depending on the specific structure used, may contain currency risk as well. Oftentimes, the volatility that comes from changes in the currency may be even greater than the volatility of the underlying bond in local currency terms. When analyzing the volatility to use for this asset class in your balanced portfolio framework, make sure to first understand the extent of the currency factor impact in your investment and adjust your volatility estimates accordingly.

## Municipal Bonds

Municipal bonds are debt obligations issued by states and local government entities. Investors who pay taxes generally purchase these securities because municipal bonds are usually tax-free investments. That is, the interest rate paid on these bonds is typically exempt from federal and state taxes (under certain conditions).

This unique asset class tends to share characteristics with Treasuries, although lower rated bonds can act more like corporate bonds. Higher quality municipal bonds—those with strong credit ratings—are similar to Treasuries. These bonds are considered relatively safe because they are backed by entities that have historically exhibited fairly low default rates. In fact, municipal bonds normally offer even lower yields than Treasuries because of their tax advantage (note that Treasuries are federally taxable). High quality municipal bonds are widely considered a more tax-efficient version of the risk free asset and therefore have the propensity to outperform during falling growth and falling inflation environments (like Treasuries). Their volatility is also similar to that of Treasuries (both of which largely depend on the duration of the bond).

Lower quality municipal bonds, however, can act more like corporate bonds. They tend to offer a higher yield because of the increased credit risk. Consequently, lower quality municipal bonds are biased to outperform during rising growth and falling inflation climates like corporate bonds. Moreover, like corporate bonds, these lower quality issues also tend to be a little more volatile than higher quality municipal bonds.

## Commercial Real Estate

Commercial real estate comes in two main forms: public and private. Real estate investment trusts (REITs) are publicly traded companies that are in the business of managing real estate. The vast majority of their profits, which come from operating commercial real estate, must be passed on to their shareholders. This asset class provides investors with the opportunity to invest in commercial real estate while maintaining liquidity. The drawback is similar to that of commodity stocks. You not only gain exposure to the underlying investments (real estate in this case) but also to the management of the company. Thus, your returns are impacted both by general shifts in real estate prices as well as broad changes in stock prices. Private real estate, on the other hand, involves a direct investment in commercial buildings such as offices, industrial buildings, retail space, and apartments. This approach involves a more direct link to commercial real estate prices but does not offer the liquidity advantage of public REITs.

The environmental bias of commercial real estate in terms of economic growth should be fairly intuitive. Rising growth is a positive outcome because it results in increased rents as stronger economic growth supports incomes and corporate profits. Higher incomes make household tenants in apartments more likely to absorb higher rents. Improved corporate profits enable businesses to afford more expensive leases for office, industrial, and retail commercial space. Moreover, better overall economic conditions lead to greater demand for commercial real estate properties, which produces upward pressure on prices.

The inflationary bias of real estate is a bit more difficult to discern. Most people believe that real estate is an inflation hedge because it is a real asset. You can touch the land and the building, and as overall prices rise real estate is worth more. This is particularly true because of the relatively limited supply of commercial real estate and the long lead time required to develop new properties. These observations are accurate and support the conclusion that real estate commonly reacts positively to inflationary conditions. However, there is a competing force that makes real estate outperform during falling inflationary climates. Real estate is commonly acquired using some leverage, as most real estate transactions are not 100 percent cash purchases. Falling inflation generally leads to lower interest rates, which effectively makes real estate more affordable. Conversely, rising inflation often corresponds with higher interest rates, creating a headwind for real estate affordability. All else being equal, it costs more to buy real estate as the rate of interest climbs. Higher financing costs also negatively impact your net profit in real estate, as one of the biggest expenses is the cost of interest on your mortgage. In addition, real estate's bias toward shifts in inflation is largely dependent on the terms of the deal made between the owner and the tenants. The rent paid may be fixed or variable. The leases may be short-term or long-term. In other words, there are many variables that impact the sensitivity of commercial real estate to shifts in inflation, so the net results are mixed. That is, real estate is neither a rising inflation nor falling inflation asset, as these countervailing forces may roughly offset each other over time.

The volatility of commercial real estate can be tricky to ascertain. The volatility of REITs, which is similar to that of equities, is easier to calculate because REITs are public companies. Private real estate does not price daily because it is an illiquid asset. Even if you appraised the properties each day, the value is unlikely to shift materially over shorter time frames. Therefore, the volatility can only be estimated. Given this limitation, a medium level of volatility seems appropriate. It should be less than that of public REITs, which trade daily and involve equity as well as real estate risk. Like a bond that pays a steady stream of income, private real estate does experience less volatility than many other asset classes. Even though the income from private real estate may be relatively stable over time, the price of the real estate does change. Combining these factors, categorizing it as a medium-volatility asset class seems to be reasonable. Of course, if your real estate is highly levered or has below average liquidity, then the volatility may be higher.

## Private Equity

Private equity is very similar to public equity (the category that I have spent a considerable amount of time covering). The only difference is that it is privately held as opposed to publicly traded. Both are investments in the equity of companies. Private equity is not marked to market or priced daily as are public stocks. Some investors categorize private equity as an *alternative investment*, suggesting that it is a completely different type of asset class. The reality is that public and private equity are quite similar in terms of their behavior, even though you may not see it day to day (because the price of private equity does not reflect changes in conditions on a shorter-term basis).

This asset class is quite simple to categorize: It is a rising growth, falling inflation asset, just like public equities. This is a long-term assessment since the price is typically only updated a few times a year. Notwithstanding the illiquid nature of private equity, the underlying fundamentals of the companies represented are impacted by shifting growth and inflation conditions, just as are public companies.

Similarly to private commercial real estate strategies, private equity does not offer daily pricing. In fact, this asset class is typically even less liquid than real estate. That said, the underlying volatility of private equity is essentially the same as that of public equities, if not greater. From a pure measurement standpoint, since private equity does not price often, the volatility of the returns may appear low. However, this is more of a measurement shortfall; the true risk is at least as great as it is for public companies. Many experts compare the risk of private equity to that of small capitalization public stocks, which tend to experience higher volatility than larger companies. I share this caveat to point out that you shouldn't take the low calculated volatility figure and plug it into your balanced portfolio process.

## Hedge Funds

Hedge funds represent a wide array of investment strategies. The term hedge fund merely refers to the structure of these funds, just as mutual funds or exchange traded funds refer to different investment structures. The actual investments that can be found inside hedge funds vary greatly. That said, the vast majority of hedge funds tend to be overweight equity risk. This is basically because hedge funds, generally speaking, invest in stocks and bonds. They also typically employ some leverage and most are able to short various markets. Certainly there are exceptions, but hedge funds as a broad group tend to have a similar environmental bias as equities (just like 60/40 portfolios). The equity risk is much higher than that of bonds and therefore it tends to drive overall results.

Consequently, the *general* economic bias of this broad asset class is rising growth and falling inflation. Since this is an area in which extreme diversity exists, it can be difficult to reach general conclusions. Thus, you should analyze each strategy separately to determine its particular bias. Perhaps you can observe how a particular hedge fund has reacted in the past to shifts in economic growth and inflation (which may be difficult since many of these funds have not been around very long). You may also dig deeper to understand its primary holdings.

Since there are so many different types of hedge funds, there is no way to generalize the volatility of this asset class. Part of your analysis when considering hedge funds is to identify the expected volatility in addition to the economic bias as described above.

## SUMMARY

Table 8.3 provides a summary of the economic biases of all the asset classes discussed, including the rationale for the economic sensitivity of each.

**TABLE 8.3** The Economic Bias of Major Asset Classes (Expanded List)

| Asset Class | Growth | Rationale | Inflation | Rationale |
|---|---|---|---|---|
| Global Equities/ Private Equity | Rising | Higher company revenues | Falling | Lower input costs, cheaper financing |
| Long-Term Global Sovereign Bonds/ High Quality Municipal Bonds | Falling | Falling interest rates to stimulate economy | Falling | Falling interest rates to increase inflation |
| Long-Term Global Inflation-Linked Bonds | Falling | Falling interest rates to stimulate economy | Rising | Pays inflation rate |
| Commodities | Rising | Rising demand for commodities | Rising | Higher commodity prices part of inflation measure |
| Corporate Bonds | Rising | Higher company revenues | Falling | Lower input costs, cheaper financing |
| Emerging Market Bonds | Rising | Higher country revenues | Rising | Higher revenues due to higher price of items exported |
| Real Estate | Rising | Higher rents, greater demand | Mixed | Pos.: Real asset; Neg.: Higher interest rates |
| Hedge Funds | Rising/ Mixed | Overweight equity risk | Falling/ Mixed | Overweight equity risk |

**TABLE 8.4**   The Volatility of Major Asset Classes (Expanded List)

| Asset Class | Volatility |
| --- | --- |
| Global Equities/Private Equity | High |
| Long-Term Global Sovereign Bonds/High Quality Municipal Bonds | Medium |
| Long-Term Global Inflation-Linked Bonds | Medium |
| Commodities | High |
| Corporate Bonds | Medium/High |
| Emerging Market Bonds | Medium/High |
| Real Estate | Medium/High |
| Hedge Funds | Mixed |

Table 8.4 summarizes the volatility of each asset class. Note that exact volatility figures were not provided in the table because the volatility of these market segments can vary depending on the particulars of each. In general, you could use about 14–20 percent volatility for those areas characterized as having high volatility, 8–12 percent for medium-risk areas, and 4–6 percent for low-volatility market segments.

The lesson I hope you take away from this chapter is to learn the concepts so you can apply them to various investment options available to you. Certainly new investment structures will emerge in the future just as TIPS came into existence not too long ago. If you are able to understand *why* each of these asset classes is biased as I have described, then you will be in a much better position to assess any asset class within a balanced portfolio framework.

Now that you understand these two factors (economic bias and estimated volatility), you are well positioned to move on to the final step of building a balanced portfolio. In the next couple of chapters, I will walk you through the process of constructing your balanced portfolio and implementing many of the concepts introduced to this point.

CHAPTER **9**

# How to Build a Balanced Portfolio

## Conceptual Framework

This chapter is about how to achieve a balanced portfolio. For reasons I will explain here, the best portfolio is the most balanced portfolio. What I am going to show you was discovered by Ray Dalio and his team at Bridgewater.

It is easy to make money when economic growth is rising and the stock market is soaring. You really don't need to read a book to enjoy success during those environments. However, the key to successful long-term investing is whether you are able to survive economic troughs. How does your portfolio perform during the difficult times? How vulnerable is it to adverse economic climates, and are the potential dips in asset value so significant as to result in catastrophic losses? The framework behind construction of a balanced portfolio is to account for all contingencies so that you have a good chance of surviving the inevitable bad times and participating in strong economic environments.

More specifically, the idea behind a balanced portfolio is to achieve *steady returns* over the long run and to *minimize the risk of major drawdowns* and *prolonged periods of underperformance*. In order to achieve these objectives, you need to first identify where returns come from and why they are volatile. Earlier in the book I identified the key drivers of asset class returns. I established that returns fluctuate due to *unexpected changes* that inevitably occur in the following three areas:

1. Economic environment (in terms of growth and inflation)
2. General risk appetite
3. Future cash rate

Further, I explained that unexpected shifts in the economic environment occur frequently and can last a very long time. These surprises are responsible for producing significant underperformance in asset class returns both as it relates to *severity* (peak to trough drawdowns) and *longevity* (the length of an extended period of poor returns). Recall that these two negative outcomes are the two major downside risks that we are trying to minimize in constructing a balanced portfolio. We want good returns, but want to avoid big losses and long-term underperformance. Since unexpected shifts in the economic environment are largely responsible for these two outcomes that we seek to avoid, it makes a lot of sense to think of building a portfolio from this perspective. Fortunately, and perhaps most importantly, the existence of unanticipated shifts in the economic climate is a risk that can be diversified with a proper asset allocation.

The other two risks negatively impact asset class returns *infrequently* and for *short time frames*. Since exposure to these risks is inherent in earning excess returns above cash, they are not something you can diversify away (without giving up the excess returns taking these risks provides). You have to live with the potential downside that may result from these forces when you invest your risk-free cash into risky asset classes in order to earn the excess returns—or risk premiums—they offer.

Based on these fundamental understandings, it is sensible that the portfolio construction process should be rooted in the philosophy of trying to *neutralize the risk of unexpected shifts in the economic environment*. This is the biggest risk to investors in asset classes and it can be diversified with a thoughtful asset allocation. The purpose of this chapter is to establish the *conceptual framework* for building a balanced asset allocation. The main objective is to efficiently capture the excess returns (or risk premiums) above cash offered by the various asset classes by appreciating the cause-effect linkages between changes in the environment and their returns.

Ray Dalio developed the understanding of asset class drivers and the portfolio structuring framework that I have been describing, in particular the idea of risk-adjusting assets and the identification of growth and inflation as the primary environmental drivers of asset class returns. He always believed that it is important to "know where neutral is," by which he means to know what portfolio you would hold if you had no opinions about where the markets were going. Once you know where neutral is—that is, what a balanced portfolio is—you should tactically deviate from it only if you are smart enough to bet against other market participants with respect to the direction of the market. This *neutral* asset allocation mix is also called one's strategic asset allocation mix. It is based on the knowledge of how markets are likely to move in relation to each other. For example, if you don't know the direction of the markets, but you do know that when one market goes up another goes down, then you know something important about how to achieve a balanced portfolio.

These concepts form the basis of Bridgewater's All Weather approach to asset allocation, which Ray Dalio developed to be the permanent asset allocation mix for the inheritance money for his children and grandchildren, and that led Bridgewater to launch its All Weather strategy in 1996 and manage it for some of the largest institutional pools of capital in the world. It was other managers drawing from the All Weather principles in various ways that gave the rise to the recent *risk parity* movement. The framework for building a balanced portfolio I describe in this chapter draws from my understanding of All Weather, but is not meant to reflect exactly how Bridgewater actually manages its strategy.

## INTRODUCTION: TWO SIMPLE QUESTIONS

There are essentially two key questions that you should ask yourself when deciding how to build a balanced portfolio:

1. Which asset classes should I own?
2. How much should I invest in each?

Putting together a portfolio is truly that simple. There is no need to overly complicate the process, as is far too common in the investment community. Anyone can do this well, but the thought process for each of these steps should be based on a solid logical foundation. Furthermore, you need to get both parts right. If you don't own the right asset classes, then you can't get balanced, because you are likely to do really well during the economic environments that you are heavily exposed to and poorly during other economic climates. If you don't weight the asset classes properly, then the positive returns of the winners may not be large enough to offset the negatives of the losers during certain economic periods.

## QUESTION ONE: WHICH ASSET CLASSES?

Because we are trying to build a portfolio that in aggregate is not biased to outperform or underperform in any growth or inflation environment, the first step is to identify asset classes in terms of their individual economic sensitivities. When you look at asset classes, you need to consider them by their economic biases so that you have the right information to put together a portfolio of these assets that is neutral to the economic environment. Think of each asset class as being prepackaged to provide exposure to various economic climates. *Try to see asset classes in this light.*

Going back to the fundamental understanding of what drives asset class returns and the goal of neutralizing these factors, the strategy should be to identify asset classes that are biased to outperform during different economic environments. Some do well during rising growth periods and some do well during falling growth periods; some favor rising inflation and others falling inflation. Such an approach provides the opportunity for the portfolio to own something that is biased to perform well regardless of which economic climate dominates in the future. If the economy suddenly and unexpectedly weakens (as it is predisposed to do), then such an outcome would probably result in losses in pro-growth assets. However, by owning investments that have a falling growth bias and which outperform their average excess return in such an environment, then at least one segment of the portfolio would potentially offer a positive offset to the negative returns. The same logic holds for the other economic climates.

The crucial insight to appreciate is that the *same environment that causes one asset class to underperform its mean simultaneously helps another outperform* its average. Even though shifts in the environment may be difficult to anticipate, it is the understanding of what causes the excess return to fluctuate around its mean that is the instructive part of the analysis. You do not have to know *when* an asset class's excess return is going to perform well or poorly, you just need to understand what would *cause* it to do well or badly. *The cause-effect relationships are much more reliable over time than trying to forecast the right outcome each round.* You should have much greater confidence in this relationship than you should in your ability to accurately predict the timing and direction of the changes. Historically, this core principle appears logical based on experience and data. Your experience has probably taught you that the future is highly uncertain; curious and unexpected events seem to happen all the time. The data supports the fact that the next economic shift relative to discounted levels is anyone's guess. The odds are near fifty-fifty that growth and inflation will outperform or underperform expectations in the future.

How, then, should you determine which asset classes to select for your portfolio? Since growth and inflation are the two factors that truly drive asset class returns around their average long-run excess returns (as previously established), you should pick asset classes by simply ensuring that *all the possible environments are covered* by your selected asset classes. If you only pick asset classes that are biased to outperform during rising growth and falling inflation, for example, then you won't be able to build a balanced portfolio *no matter how many of these asset classes you include*. The goal should be to protect your portfolio against various economic scenarios by hedging the portfolio. The hedging is accomplished not by any sophisticated structure or strategy. Instead, you can hedge by owning various asset classes biased to outperform during the four economic environments (rising growth, falling growth, rising inflation, and falling inflation).

In previous chapters I emphasized four asset classes, but I also introduced several more. For this exercise I will begin with the four major asset classes I started with in order to simplify the discussion and because their economic biases balance out well. The goal here is to use market segments that are easy to understand, offer a long history, and are commonly used. A more diversified portfolio using additional asset classes encompassing global markets would certainly benefit investors. However, *the focus at this point is on simplicity in order to more effectively emphasize the key points being presented.* Obviously, you should concentrate on the concepts and the logic of the thought process rather than on any specifics about the particular asset classes or their histories.

The concepts that I will present can easily be used on whichever asset classes you choose to include in your analysis. For this exercise, let's begin with using the following four asset classes to build a balanced portfolio because of their varying economic biases (summarized in parentheses):

1. Equities (rising growth, falling inflation)
2. Long-term Treasury bonds (falling growth, falling inflation)
3. Long-term TIPS (falling growth, rising inflation)
4. Commodities (rising growth, rising inflation)

Figure 9.1 also provides a visual comparison of the economic biases of each of these asset classes.

Stocks and commodities tend to outperform when growth is rising; long-term Treasuries and TIPS do well when growth is falling; TIPS and commodities produce strong results when inflation is rising; and stocks and Treasuries do well when inflation is falling. Two of these four asset classes are biased to outperform in each of the four economic environments (rising/ falling growth and inflation), as displayed in Table 9.1. This table shows the average return of each asset class since 1927, the type of environment in which it beat its average, and the climate in which it is favored to underperform its average (identified as *good* and *bad* environments, respectively). You have seen these numbers separated out before, but here they are presented side by side.

Equities

Treasuries

TIPS

Commodities

**FIGURE 9.1**   The Economic Bias of Four Major Asset Classes

**TABLE 9.1** Annualized Asset Class Excess Returns by Economic Environment (1927–2013)

| Asset Class | Average Excess Return for All Periods (Good and Bad) | Good Environment (Average Excess Return) | Bad Environment (Average Excess Return) |
|---|---|---|---|
| Equities | 5.6% | Rising growth (10.7%) Falling inflation (9.5%) | Rising inflation (1.9%) Falling growth (1.3%) |
| Long-Term Treasuries | 1.4% | Falling growth (5.5%) Falling inflation (2.6%) | Rising inflation (0.2%) Rising growth (−3.0%) |
| Long-Term TIPS | 4.6% | Rising inflation (10.7%) Falling growth (7.9%) | Rising growth (1.1%) Falling inflation (−1.1%) |
| Commodities | 2.0% | Rising inflation (8.4%) Rising growth (7.0%) | Falling growth (−2.3%) Falling inflation (−4.0%) |

Return of cash averaged 3.8 percent per year from 1927 to 2013. Thus, total returns can be approximated by adding 3.8 percent to the average excess returns provided above.

Notice the wide divergences in average returns during good and bad environments for each asset class. Since these economic climates represent about half of the total time period since 1927, the differences are meaningful.

Table 9.1 provides long-term *averages*. How about returns over longer cycles? Comparing the major long-term shifts in the economic environment over time to the impact on various asset class returns provides great insight into the bias of each asset class. Table 9.2 lists each major historical economic shift since 1927 and the best and worst asset class excess returns during that period. The data further corroborates the fact that changes in the economic climate largely explain fluctuations in asset class returns over longer time frames as well.

**TABLE 9.2** Asset Class Returns during Major Economic Shifts (1927–2013)

| Period | Economic Climate Growth | Inflation | Asset Class Annualized Excess Returns Best | Worst |
|---|---|---|---|---|
| 1927–1929 | Rising | Falling | Equities +41.9% | TIPS −11.8% |
| 1929–1939 | Falling | Deflation | Treasuries +4.9% | Commodities −7.0% |
| 1939–1949 | Volatile | Rising | TIPS +15.6% | Treasuries +2.5% |
| 1949–1965 | Rising | Stable | Equities +13.4% | Treasuries −1.6% |
| 1965–1982 | Volatile | Rising | Commodities +5.8% | Treasuries −5.0% |
| 1982–2000 | Rising | Falling | Equities +12.7% | TIPS +1.5% |
| 2000–2013 | Falling | Stable | TIPS +9.6% | Equities/Commodities +1.2% |

Notice the change in the leaders and laggards during the various economic environments. The shifting economic climate predictably and reliably causes various asset classes to perform vastly different from their long-run averages during these extended periods. In each instance the actual economic outcome resulted in an asset class return that was consistent with what you would have expected given each class's underlying economic bias. Moreover, the cycles have been prolonged and have lasted for a decade or longer. Since one of our major goals in building a balanced portfolio is to minimize the risk of experiencing an extended period of underperformance, we should recognize how the economic environment is responsible for such an outcome.

I will make one final point before proceeding to the subject of how to think about weighting these four asset classes in your balanced portfolio. You may have noticed that *cash was not included as one of the market segments* offered above. Recall that we are trying to construct a balanced portfolio that is designed to capture the excess returns above cash over time while minimizing the variability around the average return.

There are environments during which cash is the best performing investment, outgaining all other market segments (often by not going down, while the rest temporarily lose money). Because of the completely divergent economic environmental bias of each of the four asset classes discussed here, it is quite rare that all four would simultaneously lose money. Regardless of whether the economy is strong or weak, or inflation is rising or falling, something is bound to perform well. Even during the extreme case of deflation, Treasury bonds will potentially outreturn cash.

The main reason cash is excluded is because over time it does worse than the other asset classes. This is because these asset classes offer positive excess returns above cash. You don't know what the economic environment will be in the future and how it will change course over time, but you do know that you can build a portfolio that by and large is immunized against these shifts.

Furthermore, the periods in which cash outperforms the other asset classes rarely occur, are short-lived, and are very difficult to anticipate in advance. Few, if any, have a successful long-term record of consistently accurately predicting when to hold cash over other asset classes. As a result, a constant allocation to cash merely lowers expected returns over time without providing much benefit. For this reason, it has been excluded as a viable asset class in the well-balanced portfolio.

## QUESTION TWO: HOW DO I WEIGHT THE ASSET CLASSES?

Now that you have selected asset classes that cover all the potential economic outcomes, the next step is to determine how much you should allocate to each. Let's start by looking at this from the highest level. The goal is to gain *exposure* to the shifts in the economic climate, since these shifts are largely responsible for the fluctuations of excess returns offered by asset classes. When one of these unpredictable shifts occurs, you want to make sure that your portfolio has sufficient exposure to that environment so that you benefit from its occurrence. Again, the goal is not to predict which environment will dominate next, but to position yourself so that you are by and large indifferent to what occurs. By exposure I am referring to the idea that the excess returns you capture from that environment are large enough to roughly offset underperformance in the rest of the portfolio, which is invested in market segments that were not favorably influenced by the economic environment that transpired.

In reality, they don't exactly offset each other so that the net result is zero. If that were the case, there would be no point in investing at all. Instead, the positives and negatives that I am talking about are related to *average excess returns*, which are all positive (rather than zero). In other words, a negative environment produces a *below-average excess return* and a positive climate generates an *above-average excess return*. For instance, if the average excess return for equities is 5.6 percent per year, then a slightly bad environment may lead to an excess return of 3.6 percent and a slightly good period 7.6 percent. Of course, a really bad economic climate would likely result in a negative excess return, but the baseline to which results should be compared is the average rather than zero. The same holds for each asset class, which has a positive average excess return.

You are trying to capture the excess returns offered by various asset classes over time while minimizing the volatility due to fluctuations of those excess returns. By neutralizing the impact of shifts in the economic environment, which is what mostly causes the fluctuation around average excess returns, you are able to roughly accrue the excess returns while minimizing volatility. Thus, the *positives and negatives net out at some positive excess return above cash over time.* Thus, when I refer to focusing on maintaining exposure to various economic climates such that the positives offset the negatives, it is to earn *a positive excess return*, rather than a zero excess return.

When thinking in terms of exposures, the analysis involves both the economic exposure as well as the *return impact of the occurrence of each environment*. It is not enough to say that you've covered all the environments and therefore have sufficient exposure to various economic outcomes. The returns during those various outcomes need to be considered as well. For instance, if you own bonds to protect against falling growth, but only own a 5 percent allocation, then when growth is falling this portfolio segment will not rise enough to offset negative excess returns elsewhere. You covered the exposure by owning the bonds, but you did not have sufficient coverage because you failed to own enough of the bonds (only 5 percent of your portfolio outperformed). *It takes both parts to make it work effectively and to produce a well-balanced asset allocation.*

You can achieve sufficient exposure by allocating more to a particular asset class. If stocks were prepackaged to offer you exposure to rising growth and falling inflation climates, then a higher allocation to stocks would naturally provide your portfolio with greater exposure to these environments. However, there is one other factor besides the weighting to the asset class that must be considered in this process.

## The Impact of Volatility

A critical step in the conceptual process of allocating the assets is to factor in the *volatility* of the asset class. *This is because the volatility also impacts the exposure provided by the asset class.* Those asset classes that are highly volatile will fluctuate around their average more than those that are less volatile. The reason the volatility is the key step in the process is because it is this measure that specifically quantifies the fluctuations around the average excess return.

Your focus here should not be on precision but on the conceptual logic that follows. You do not need to calculate the exact volatility of an asset class and you do not need to worry about whether the volatility is higher or lower than normal. Keep the analysis very simple to ensure that you are grasping the concepts of why volatility is a key input in the determination of how to efficiently weight asset classes.

*Ultimately, exposure comes from two factors: how much you own and the volatility of what you own.* Consider an extreme example. The economic exposure of a 1-year Treasury bond and a 30-year Treasury bond is exactly the same. Both are biased to outperform during falling inflation and falling growth environments. For argument's sake, let's say the average excess return above cash for each is also similar. The key difference between these two is that the short-term bond will be reliably less volatile than the longer-dated security because of the significantly shorter duration of the former. What the higher volatility means is that the price of the long-term bond is going to fluctuate much more around its average return than that of the short-term bond. If you were to allocate 30 percent of your portfolio to 1-year bonds, then during falling inflation, falling growth climates, or both, the 1-year bond will likely outperform its average excess return. However (and this is the critical insight to appreciate), the 1-year bond's return during the favorable environment *will not be much better than its return during other periods because it is not very volatile.* Therefore, the real exposure (in terms of returns you will earn with this allocation) will not move very much. You have effectively covered two of the three parts of the key inputs. You gained exposure to the right environment, which provided a boost to your portfolio. You also allocated a healthy amount to the asset class, so you benefit from that move. However, since the segment in which you invested was not very volatile, the positive return was not very high and likely insufficient to properly balance your portfolio.

Conversely, the 30-year bonds are extremely volatile. The same allocation of 30 percent to this segment would provide much greater exposure to falling inflation and falling growth environments than a similar allocation to the short-term bonds. This is because during a positive environment for this asset class, the more volatile bonds are likely to produce a very high return for the same allocation. You will notice that another way to consider this is that a lower allocation to the longer-maturity bonds could be maintained to gain the same exposure as that provided by the less volatile bonds (which carries the additional benefit of leaving more money to invest elsewhere). Recall that the only difference between these two bond portfolios is that the volatility of one is much higher than that of the other. This logic may sound counterintuitive, but within this context higher volatility is superior to lower volatility.

Using this understanding, the conceptual logic of determining the appropriate weight to each asset class is to factor in both volatility and economic bias in the process. This is precisely the reason that long-term Treasuries and TIPS are being used for construction of a balanced portfolio rather than shorter-term bonds. Since the goal is to balance the risk of the asset classes, we want greater volatility from the typically low-volatility asset classes such as Treasuries and TIPS. The reason is simple: If the volatility of the bond segment is too low, then you would have to allocate a significant proportion of the portfolio to this asset to make up for its low volatility. This higher allocation would negatively impact your total expected return because bonds are a lower returning asset class. Thus, longer-duration bonds provide greater diversification benefits than do shorter-term (lower volatility) equivalent bonds because of how they fit within the balanced portfolio framework. Too little volatility in bonds prevents them from rising enough to protect the portfolio during environments in which the other, more volatile, asset classes underperform. Likewise, when bonds underperform there is enough volatility in the remaining asset classes to offset them, since the volatilities have been matched. The key is that the same environment that causes the bonds to underperform is likely to produce upside elsewhere.

## Putting It Together

Now that we have selected a handful of asset classes that have different economic biases for our balanced portfolio, how should we think conceptually

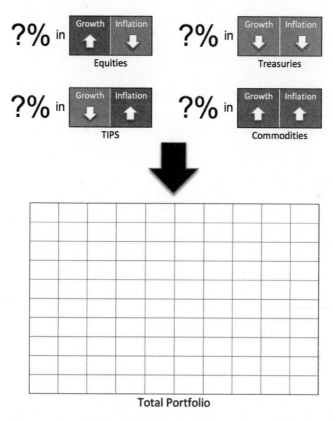

**FIGURE 9.2** Weighting the Asset Classes

about constructing our asset allocation? We need to determine how much of each asset class needs to go into our total portfolio, as depicted in Figure 9.2.

In Figure 9.2, the total portfolio is divided into 100 boxes. Each box represents a 1 percent position, or one unit. If we put one unit of equities into the portfolio, then 1 percent of the portfolio would consist of equities. Since we are thinking in terms of economic environmental biases, a portfolio of one unit of equities would have a slight bias toward rising growth and falling inflation (since 99 out of 100 boxes in the portfolio would have no bias). The total portfolio obviously takes on the economic biases of its parts. If we make the portfolio 100 percent equities, then it would be clearly biased to do well when growth is rising and when inflation is falling.

One way to visualize the impact of volatility using the asset class boxes is to adjust the number of arrows according to the asset's volatility. More volatile asset classes will have more arrows and less volatile classes will have

**FIGURE 9.3**  Factoring in Volatility: Equities

fewer arrows. *More arrows will indicate greater exposure to that particular economic environment.*

To keep it simple, we can say that highly volatile assets can be marked with three arrows, medium-volatility with two, and low-volatility assets with just one arrow. Low volatility might have a standard deviation in the range of 4–6 percent, medium 8–12 percent, and high 14–20 percent. Notice that medium has about twice the volatility of low and high is about three times the volatility of low. The idea is to indicate the magnitude of the economic bias. The direction of the arrows doesn't change since the bias doesn't change, but the greater the volatility, the more significant the sensitivity to that particular environment. Consider the diagram in Figure 9.3, which tries to convey this important conceptual link.

When the high volatility of equities is factored into the equation, the arrows for rising growth increase from one to three, as do the arrows for falling inflation. The direction of the arrows is not modified, but the greater number of arrows illustrates the magnitude of the environmental bias. If equities were medium volatility, there would only be two arrows in the rising-growth box and two in the falling-inflation box; if they were low volatility, there would just be one arrow in each box.

The difference is crucial from an exposure standpoint. Two units of a low-volatility asset class provide roughly the same exposure as one unit of a medium-volatility asset class, assuming both have the same environmental bias. Why is this? What really causes returns to fluctuate is the economic exposure. The more volatile an asset, the greater the variation between good and bad environments. Two units invested in low-volatility Treasuries provide roughly the same exposure to falling growth and falling inflation as one unit invested in medium-volatility Treasuries (assuming the volatility of the latter is twice that of the former). *It is just like owning double the allocation from an economic exposure standpoint.*

The same volatility adjustment can be made to the other asset classes, as shown in Figure 9.4.

The natural conclusion from the preceding thought sequence is that *you either need to own more of the lower-volatility asset classes and less of the higher-volatility asset classes* or somehow equalize the volatility of them all. This is an inevitable truth because otherwise the portfolio will simply not be economically balanced. And as I have emphasized, economic balance is

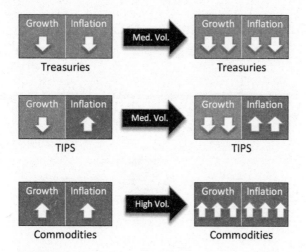

**FIGURE 9.4** Factoring in Volatility: Treasuries, TIPS, and Commodities

crucial because it is the unpredictable shifting environment that by and large impacts asset class returns.

Although I am not espousing such a strategy in this book, you should know that you could roughly equalize the volatility of the asset classes by incorporating leverage. That is, you could take lower-volatility asset classes and use leverage to increase their volatilities to match the higher-volatility segments. To keep it simple, however, the emphasis in this book will be on extending duration in the more stable fixed income assets rather than incorporating leverage. Increasing the maturity of the bonds to longer-dated securities materially escalates their volatility. Either approach works; *the key is to emphasize the core concepts behind building a balanced portfolio.*

The bottom line is that this entire process is all about *covering the various economic environments with equal exposure* because these are what fundamentally and reliably drive asset class returns. Therefore, it is the volatility of each asset class that should be used to determine the appropriate weighting.

After adjusting each asset class that we are considering putting into our portfolio by its volatility, we are left with a picture that looks more like the one shown in Figure 9.5.

This figure more accurately illustrates the decision that needs to be made because it views each asset class with a complete summary of its total economic exposure. Importantly, this full depiction incorporates the asset class's volatility as well as its fundamental economic bias.

The final step in the process is to come up with a combination of asset classes so that the total portfolio's exposure to the various economic

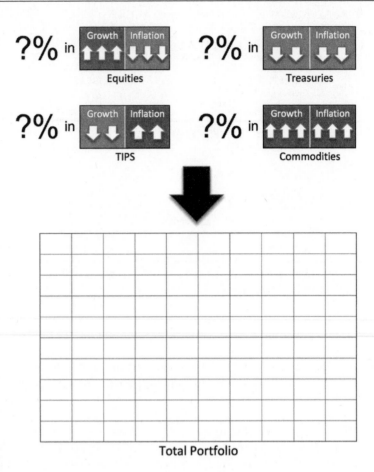

**FIGURE 9.5** Weighting the Asset Classes: Factoring in Volatility

environments is neutral. Neutral in this case means that when you add up all the economic biases of the component asset classes you end up with totals that are roughly balanced. There should be about the same exposure to rising growth as there is to falling growth and the same for rising inflation as falling inflation.

If there were one (hypothetical) asset class that was not biased to out-perform in rising/falling growth or rising/falling inflation environments, then you could simply construct a portfolio entirely made up of that single asset class to achieve this objective (assuming it also offers an attractive expected excess rate of return). However, since such an asset is not readily available, we have to construct a portfolio that consists of a mix of asset classes, each of which has different biases.

The trick is to decide how much of each asset class to insert into the portfolio so that it adds up to a neutral total portfolio that is not biased to outperform during any economic climate. This would represent a *truly balanced portfolio* with an *efficient, neutral allocation*. If you do not have strong feelings about a certain economic outcome, then a portfolio that is balanced and neutral would be an appropriate allocation. It can also serve as an efficient starting point if you do decide to tilt your allocation in favor of one outcome versus another.

From a conceptual standpoint, identifying a balanced mix is relatively straightforward using the illustrations provided. Simply *add up the arrows in each environment*. One unit (or 1 percent allocation) of equities means that you have three arrows in rising growth and three in falling inflation. By adding one unit of long-term Treasuries, you would then include two arrows in falling growth and two in falling inflation. A portfolio made up of 1 percent equities and 1 percent long-term Treasuries would then have three arrows in rising growth, two in falling growth, and five in falling inflation. This is not a well-balanced portfolio because it will likely do a little better during rising growth than falling growth (since it consists of three arrows in rising and two in falling growth). From an inflation standpoint, it is even less balanced. It will do very well during falling inflation and terribly during rising inflation since it owns no assets biased to the latter economic climate (as indicated by zero arrows for that environment). This process can be continued until you have filled up all 100 boxes in (or 100 percent of) the portfolio.

You can follow the same philosophy when you include other asset classes and can continue with this approach until you end up with a balanced mix. In the next chapter, I will provide step-by-step instructions to complete the asset allocation process. Before proceeding, however, it is important that you grasp the conceptual framework of what it really means for a portfolio to be well balanced. Whatever the process, the end result needs to produce a portfolio that is not biased to do better or worse during any of the various economic outcomes.

## SUMMARY

This is a very simplistic, yet effective conceptual approach to identifying balance in a portfolio. It is clearly not an exact science, but it doesn't have to be. It is the logical connections that are critical. The bias of each asset class to the various environments is reliable. The impact of volatility to this bias is reasonable. Combining the asset classes from an economic bias perspective makes sense since we want the total portfolio to be economically balanced. It really is that easy.

CHAPTER **10**

# How to Build a Balanced Portfolio
## The Step-by-Step Process

To this point we have covered the conceptual framework for constructing a balanced asset allocation. In this chapter we roll up our sleeves and dive into a simple methodology for actually creating a balanced portfolio.

## THE LOGICAL SEQUENCE BEHIND EFFICIENTLY WEIGHTING ASSET CLASSES

There are two decisions you must make to create a balanced portfolio. First, you must determine which asset classes to include. This decision will be based on identifying the economic biases of various asset classes. The mix should include a variety that covers all the major potential economic outcomes: rising growth, falling growth, rising inflation, and falling inflation. Much of the book thus far has been dedicated to this topic.

After you have established which asset classes are appropriate for your portfolio, the second decision will be how much to allocate to each. An understanding of the volatility of each asset class will be an important factor in this decision. The goal of this chapter is to provide a step-by-step process to help you determine the right allocation to each asset class.

### The Ideal Portfolio for Each Economic Climate

The overall goal is to build a portfolio that is by and large indifferent to shifts in the economic environment. A helpful way to construct such an allocation is to first build the ideal portfolio *for each economic climate*. What is the best allocation for a rising growth environment? What is the ultimate mix for a falling growth period? What about rising inflation or falling inflation climates? What is the perfect mix during each of these economic outcomes?

**143**

Using the four basic asset classes we have covered, for the *rising growth* environment you would simply invest all your money in stocks and commodities. The reason is that these two asset classes are biased to outperform during such an economic environment. The other two assets covered in this book—Treasuries and TIPS—would likely underperform during rising growth. Note that you would own *both* stocks and commodities, as opposed to just stocks, because of the uncertainty about shifts in the inflation rate. Remember that we are isolating growth in this analysis and only considering the ideal portfolio during that climate. We would like to be agnostic to the direction of inflation, which can obviously rise or fall concurrently with a rising growth environment. If both growth and inflation were to rise, then commodities would probably do best. If growth rose and inflation fell, then stocks would be biased to outperform commodities. Given these conditions, you would own both stocks and commodities and feel relatively good that your portfolio would perform quite well regardless of the inflation outcome.

Conversely, during a falling growth environment, you would want to own Treasuries and TIPS for reasons opposite to those described above. Both of these asset classes benefit from falling growth, and regardless of which way inflation goes you are protected. The same analysis follows for a period of rising inflation (during which you'd own TIPS and commodities) and falling inflation (stocks and Treasuries). Table 10.1 summarizes the ideal portfolio in each economic environment.

**TABLE 10.1**  Ideal Portfolio for Various Economic Climates

| Economic Environment | Ideal Economic Portfolio |
| --- | --- |
| Rising Growth | Stocks and Commodities |
| Falling Growth | Treasuries and TIPS |
| Rising Inflation | Commodities and TIPS |
| Falling Inflation | Stocks and Treasuries |

## Combining Four Economic Portfolios into One

Since the odds of any of the four environments transpiring are about fifty-fifty (since it is relative to current market expectations), it makes sense that you should construct a portfolio that *balances your allocation among these four economic portfolios*. More specifically, the goal is to *achieve roughly similar exposure to each of the potential economic outcomes*. These are the four environments that you want to protect yourself from, and you know the assets that you should own in each of these four economic climates. Since your objective is to achieve a similar exposure (roughly, not exactly) from each of the four economic portfolios, you need to factor in the volatility

**TABLE 10.2**  Volatility of Asset Classes (1927–2013)

| Asset Class | Approximate Volatility |
|---|---|
| Equities | 15% |
| Long-Term Treasuries | 10% |
| Long-Term TIPS | 10% |
| Commodities | 15% |

when deciding how much to allocate to each. This means that you need to *own more of the lower-volatility asset classes and less of the higher-volatility asset classes.* Table 10.2 provides the approximate volatility of the four asset classes. Note: for simplicity I am rounding the historical volatility for this exercise. The key in this process is the relative volatility of each asset class, so even if you used precise data you would ultimately reach a similar conclusion.

The volatility of stocks and commodities has been similar from a long-term historical perspective. Likewise, long-term TIPS and Treasuries have fared alike over the long run. Furthermore, you should observe that the volatility of stocks and commodities is about 50 percent higher than that of long-term TIPS and Treasuries (again, precision is not required in this step).

In the previous chapter I shared a visual description of these relationships, which is repeated in Figure 10.1. The idea was to indicate the increased exposure to various economic environments by increasing the number of arrows in the economic boxes based on the volatility.

## Two Steps to Balancing the Portfolio

There are basically two steps to the balancing process. First, you need to ensure that there is balance *within* the four portfolios for each economic environment (which I will call the *economic portfolios*). Second, balance will be required *across* the economic portfolios, such that each portfolio has equal impact on the *total portfolio*. You should think of balance in terms of providing similar *exposure* to the various economic climates.

As described previously, exposure is merely a product of the volatility of each asset class and the allocation to each. I refer to this measure as *weighted volatility*. For each of the portfolios we have already defined two asset classes that perform best in that economic environment. The goal now is to identify a percentage allocation to the component asset classes within each economic portfolio, such that the weighted volatility of both asset classes is about the same. Table 10.3 demonstrates an appropriately balanced mix *within* the four economic portfolios.

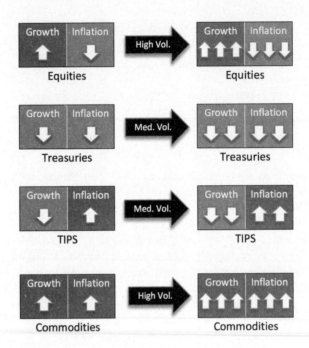

**FIGURE 10.1** Factoring in Volatility

**TABLE 10.3** Step 1: Balance *within* the Four Economic Portfolios

| Economic Portfolio | Asset Classes | Volatility | Allocation | Weighted Volatility |
|---|---|---|---|---|
| Rising Growth | Equities | 15% | 50% | 7.5% |
| | Commodities | 15% | 50% | 7.5% |
| Falling Growth | Treasuries | 10% | 50% | 5% |
| | TIPS | 10% | 50% | 5% |
| Rising Inflation | Commodities | 15% | 40% | 6% |
| | TIPS | 10% | 60% | 6% |
| Falling Inflation | Equities | 15% | 40% | 6% |
| | Treasuries | 10% | 60% | 6% |

The way to read Table 10.3 is to start from the far left and work your way right. Each of the four economic portfolios (one for each economic outcome) is listed in the first column. In the next column the ideal asset classes for each environment are displayed. Next, the approximate volatility of each asset class is provided. In the fourth column you will find the balanced asset allocation to each asset class *within* each of the four economic portfolios. For instance, in rising growth, there is a 50/50 split between equities and commodities because both asset classes have similar volatility. The fifth column provides the weighted volatility for equities and for commodities (50 percent of 15 percent volatility equals 7.5 percent weighted volatility). Thus, the rising growth economic portfolio is risk balanced since the weighted volatility of equities roughly matches that of commodities. Falling growth follows a similar logic because both Treasuries and TIPS have about the same volatility.

However, the other two environments—rising inflation and falling inflation—are a bit different. This is because the component asset classes within each portfolio exhibit different volatilities. In rising inflation, commodities are approximately 50 percent more volatile than TIPS. Thus, within this portfolio, *TIPS should receive about a 50 percent greater weight than commodities* in order to yield a similar weighted volatility between these two asset classes. Falling inflation follows a similar logic because of the mismatch in volatility between its component asset classes (equities and Treasuries).

The second step involves balancing *across* the four economic portfolios. Since you have already balanced *within* the four economic portfolios, you next need to do the same *across* each of the four segments. Using the same methodology of balancing by volatility, we determine the percentage allocation to each of the four economic portfolios that results in equal weighted volatility across the portfolios.

We begin by simply adding the weighted volatility of each asset class within each economic portfolio to come up with a total approximate volatility. For instance, in Table 10.3 the rising growth economic portfolio consists of 50 percent equities and 50 percent commodities, which yields a 7.5 percent weighted volatility to each asset class. By adding the two weighted volatilities we get about 15 percent total volatility in this economic portfolio (in reality, the total volatility is likely lower than a simple sum because of correlation benefits, but for the purposes of this exercise we are simplifying the process). Table 10.4 summarizes a well-balanced allocation breakdown *across* each of the four economic portfolios. You can tell the overall allocation across the portfolios is well balanced because the weighted volatility across economic portfolios (displayed in the far right column) is equal.

**TABLE 10.4**　Step 2: Balance *across* the Four Economic Portfolios

| Economic Portfolio | Volatility | Allocation | Weighted Volatility |
|---|---|---|---|
| Rising Growth | 15% | 20% | 3% |
| Falling Growth | 10% | 30% | 3% |
| Rising Inflation | 12% | 25% | 3% |
| Falling Inflation | 12% | 25% | 3% |

**TABLE 10.5**  Putting It Together

| Asset Class | Economic Portfolio | Step 1: Asset Class % in Economic Portfolio | Step 2: % in Total Portfolio | Step 1 X Step 2 | Total Portfolio Allocation |
|---|---|---|---|---|---|
| Equities | Rising Growth | 50% | 20% | 10% | 20% |
| | Falling Inflation | 40% | 25% | 10% | |
| Commodities | Rising Growth | 50% | 20% | 10% | 20% |
| | Rising Inflation | 40% | 25% | 10% | |
| Treasuries | Falling Growth | 50% | 30% | 15% | 30% |
| | Falling Inflation | 60% | 25% | 15% | |
| TIPS | Falling Growth | 50% | 30% | 15% | 30% |
| | Rising Inflation | 60% | 25% | 15% | |

To come up with the final allocation to each asset class, you simply take the allocation to each of the four economic portfolios (20 percent to rising growth, 30 percent to falling growth, 25 percent to rising inflation and 25 percent to falling inflation) and break it down by asset class. This essentially involves combining step one with step two as summarized in Table 10.5.

Table 10.5 should be read from left to right. The first two columns list each asset class and the economic environment in which they are biased to outperform. The third column lists the output of step one: balance *within* the four economic portfolios. For instance, equities, in step one received a 50 percent allocation in the rising growth portfolio and a 40 percent allocation in the falling inflation portfolio. The fourth column recaps the output from step two: balance *across* the economic portfolios. Rising growth got 20 percent in that step and falling inflation was allocated 25 percent. The fifth column in Table 10.5 is the product of step one times step two (50 percent times 20 percent equals 10 percent allocation to equities for the rising growth portfolio; the same output results for the falling inflation portfolio). The final column simply adds up the allocation in each asset class across the rising growth and falling growth buckets (10 percent plus 10 percent equals 20 percent total allocation to equities).

Using this methodology, we have constructed a balanced portfolio that consists of the following:

**The Balanced Portfolio**

20% Equities

20% Commodities

30% Long-Term Treasuries

30% Long-Term TIPS

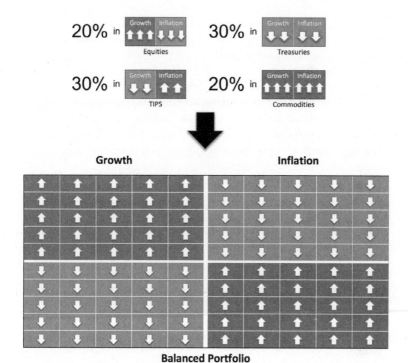

**FIGURE 10.2** The Balanced Portfolio

You can also view the balance that exists in this asset allocation through the box and arrows illustrations that we previously used. The total exposure to rising growth, falling growth, rising inflation, and falling inflation, as depicted in the boxes, is roughly balanced (see Figure 10.2).

Don't forget that the goal of this exercise is to build an allocation that has roughly similar exposure to the different environmental drivers. That allows you to achieve a return that holds up more consistently in the face of different economic outcomes because no matter what surprise happens, there is always a portion of the portfolio that has a meaningful positive outcome. There is no need to be overly precise in setting these weights since the main benefit comes in moving in the direction of improved balance.

## Not Exactly Risk-Parity

This general approach to weighting asset classes has come to be broadly known as *risk-parity*. The important distinction here is that risk-parity, as its name suggests, is merely focused on equalizing the risk of asset classes. Proponents of this strategy generally use many of the same asset classes as those used by more conventional asset allocation strategies and merely take the extra step of balancing the risk of each asset class. This is commonly accomplished by incorporating leverage for the lower-volatility asset classes and reducing the allocation to the higher-risk asset classes.

The missing element in many risk-parity strategies is an appreciation of the core reason to balance the volatility in asset classes in the first place. The focus should not be on balancing the risk, but on balancing the *economic exposure* of the portfolio. The reason is simple: It is the economic environment that is the fundamental driver of asset class returns and that is therefore the appropriate cause-effect relationship to emphasize.

For instance, it is common for a risk parity strategy to include a heavy allocation to equities and other credit sensitive asset classes such as corporate bonds. Since the asset classes used tend to perform similarly in various economic climates (most do well during rising growth and falling inflation and poorly during the opposite environments), the fact that the asset classes are risk balanced does not lead to strong portfolio balance.

## ANALYZING 60/40 THROUGH THE SAME LENS

In sum, the impact of an asset class on the portfolio's total return is simply a function of three factors:

1. Its economic bias
2. Its volatility
3. Its weighting in the portfolio

If all you did was invest in 10 different asset classes that shared exactly the same economic bias, you might feel that you are well diversified because of the large number of holdings. However, when you go through the steps I have described to build a balanced portfolio, you will discover that it cannot be done. They all fit into the same categories, and therefore, regardless of the other two factors (volatility and weight), you don't have enough tools in your kit to create a well-balanced asset allocation. Also, consider a situation in which you had selected four asset classes with different biases but one was much more volatile than the rest. Perhaps one had high volatility while the others were low-volatility assets. That scenario would also make it challenging to build good balance because of the significant volatility mismatch. Finally, even if you have the appropriate asset classes with comparable volatility, you have to ensure that the weighting is appropriate in order to obtain similarly weighted volatility for the four economic climate portfolios. All three factors are equally deserving of your attention in this process.

The balanced portfolio framework presented here can be applied to any portfolio. Once you have determined the bias, the volatility, and the weight, you can assess the balance of the portfolio to the various economic environments. By observing the imbalance in a portfolio from the balanced portfolio perspective, you will be able to predict fairly reliably in which environments it will outperform and underperform. You obviously do not have to guess *when* it will do well or poorly, just under what circumstances these results are likely. You can also be sure that the imbalanced portfolio will suffer through long episodes of significant underperformance.

Taking the framework described here and applying it to the traditional 60/40 allocation will reveal some vulnerabilities of that portfolio. Table 10.6 applies the same framework just described to a combined portfolio with a 60 percent allocation to equities and a 40 percent allocation to core bonds. Importantly, note that the core bond portfolio is about half as volatile as the long-term Treasuries portfolio due to its shorter duration. This lower volatility actually hurts the balance in the combined portfolio because of its smaller impact during falling growth environments, as you can observe in Table 10.6.

Table 10.6 considers the three key variables: economic bias, volatility, and allocation. Each portfolio (rising growth, falling growth, rising inflation, and falling inflation) is represented by one or both of the asset classes in the 60/40 portfolio. Each of these asset classes exhibits a certain volatility characteristic as summarized in the table. By combining the volatility and the allocation to that particular asset class, you can observe a weighted volatility for each portfolio. For instance, rising growth has a high weighted volatility relative to the rest because it is represented by equities, which have both high volatility and high allocation in the 60/40 mix. The only falling growth asset is core bonds, which have a low volatility. The medium allocation of 40 percent to this segment does not move the needle much in terms of weighted volatility because of the significantly lower volatility relative to equities. No rising inflation assets are included in this allocation so that portfolio has

**TABLE 10.6** Using the Balanced Framework to See That 60/40 Is Highly Imbalanced

| Portfolio | Asset Classes | Volatility | Allocation | Weighted Volatility |
|---|---|---|---|---|
| Rising Growth | Equities | 15% | 30% | 4.5% |
| Falling Growth | Core Bonds | 5% | 20% | 1% |
| Rising Inflation | None | None | None | None |
| Falling Inflation | Equities Core Bonds | 11% | 50% | 6% |

no representation. Finally, both equities and core bonds are biased to outperform during falling inflation periods so the entire 60/40 asset allocation
benefits from this environment.

By putting all this together and observing the column highlighted at the
far right you are able see how lopsided the 60/40 portfolio is. There is no
exposure to rising inflation and very little to falling growth. Essentially, the
portfolio should be reliably expected to perform well during rising growth
and falling inflationary periods and very poorly in the opposite environments. Unsurprisingly, the actual results are consistent with this expectation.
The wide range of historical returns during various economic climates was
presented in Chapter 2. Since half the time negative outcomes dominate the
environment, the 60/40 mix is biased to do poorly about half of the time.
Clearly, this is not well balanced, despite popular belief to the contrary.

Viewed in terms of the boxes and arrows figures, as displayed in
Figure 10.3, the imbalance in the 60/40 allocation is also easily observable.

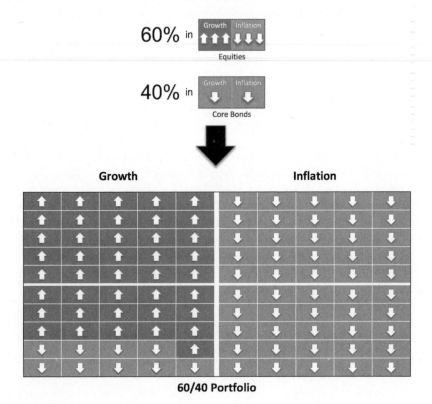

**FIGURE 10.3**   The Imbalance of 60/40

## SUMMARY

Minimal data has been used thus far in this book. This was intentional, as *my goal was to focus on the conceptual linkages rather than resort to a backfilled argument twisting historical results in favor of this approach*. It is the logic that is most compelling, endures over time, and creates confidence about the reliability of the approach going forward. You should consider whether the thought sequence is reasonable and makes more sense than alternative approaches to building your asset allocation. Think about all the possibilities of the future economic environment and whether your current portfolio can withstand the potential shocks. The vast majority of portfolios would fail this simple test.

# CHAPTER 11

# The Balanced Portfolio

## Historical Returns

The emphasis up to this point has been on establishing the conceptual framework for building a well-balanced portfolio. This makes sense because the fundamental principles rely on reasonable expectations of human and economic behavior that can be anticipated to persist through time. Therefore the concepts should be your focus. For this reason, little data has been used to support the cause-effect relationships.

Naturally, the goal has been to emphasize the logic behind the process rather than the exact outcome. Historical data is never perfect, so a portfolio strategy that is solely based on past returns is not as compelling and reliable as one that is dependent on reasonable cause-effect relationships. Moreover, since you have the flexibility to use different asset classes than the ones I have used, I did not want to present a specific portfolio as the only answer. If you believe in the concepts, you can apply them across various asset classes through time.

Notwithstanding the practicality of the framework presented, many people, perhaps including you, want to see the numbers. You may wish to ensure that the historical record supports the theories and conclusions I have presented. In this chapter, I will share the return series since 1927 for the simple balanced portfolio presented in the previous chapter. I use this allocation because of the long-term data that is available and because these four asset classes fit cleanly into the balanced portfolio framework and therefore help to reinforce the critical concepts.

The Balanced Portfolio
20% Equities
20% Commodities
30% Long-Term Treasuries
30% Long-Term TIPS

Three specific performance questions are addressed in this chapter. In essence, the conclusion I seek to support with data is that the balanced portfolio has historically delivered the main return objectives that were set out when we began this asset allocation process. All three questions relate to the success of the balanced portfolio's returns viewed from different dimensions.

1. Has the balanced portfolio earned *steady, attractive returns* over the *long run*?
2. Have there been *long-term periods* during which the balanced portfolio *underperformed*?
3. Over *shorter time frames*, are the occurrences of *significant downturns* small and infrequent or are they large and regular?

A comparison with the conventional 60/40 asset allocation will also be included in the historical analysis. The side-by-side contrast may help further emphasize the difference between a well-balanced mix and one that is imbalanced.

I attempt to present the data from multiple angles to give a full, objective picture of the results. The data series I use covers monthly returns from 1927 to 2013, a period during which reliable data on asset classes is available. Due to the extended history captured, the analysis is exhaustive. It covers a wide range of economic environments, including the Great Depression, the inflationary 1970s, the bull market of the 1990s, and the credit crisis of 2008. Periods of rising and falling interest rates and inflation are also part of the data set. Basically, anything that has happened in the financial markets and economy since 1927 is part of the analysis. The use of long-term data is important because it demonstrates that the concepts presented can be applied to various economic climates over a long period of time.

## THE BALANCED PORTFOLIO HAS ACHIEVED STEADY LONG-TERM RETURNS

Since 1927 the balanced portfolio has earned attractive and steady excess returns that are just as good as, if not better than, those of a 60/40 allocation. The historical results can be assessed from a couple of different perspectives. I will first examine *trailing returns* as of 2013 and compare them to the returns earned by the 60/40 portfolio. I will also look at the *growth of $1* since 1927 to assess the long-term stability of the return stream. Next, the long-term *volatility* of the balanced portfolio will be contrasted to that of a 60/40 allocation to further support the former's relative long-term stability. Finally, I will provide returns for the balanced portfolio for each calendar year since 1927.

## Solid Trailing Returns: The Tortoise and the Hare

The long-term trailing excess returns of the balanced portfolio as of 2013 are attractive from both an absolute perspective (versus cash) and from a relative perspective (versus 60/40). The data is summarized in Table 11.1.

These long-term returns may come as a surprise to you, considering that the balanced portfolio has only a 20 percent allocation to equities, the highest performing asset class among the four. How can a portfolio consisting of 20 percent equities match the returns of an allocation of 60 percent equities *over the long run*? Such a result defies conventional wisdom.

The main reason the returns of the two strategies are about the same is because the balanced portfolio's *superior stability* has helped it keep pace with the higher octane 60/40 mix. Think of the old story of the tortoise and the hare as a useful analogy. The hare (60/40) sprints ahead and then has to slow down to catch its breath. The tortoise (the balanced portfolio) maintains a steady pace, at times trailing the hare and at other times forging ahead. Most notably, the tortoise takes the lead not because he has started to sprint, but because his steady pace helps him *avoid major slowdowns*. Over the long run, the two approaches achieve roughly similar results, but the tortoise is able to be more consistent. If we begin the clock just after the hare has peaked, then it may take the hare many years (perhaps as long as a decade or more) to catch up.

The reason the balanced portfolio has kept up with 60/40 is because it has experienced smoother returns and—more significantly—*fewer major downturns*. It is the big losses that hurt long-term returns simply because of the way the math works. If you lose 50 percent, then you have to earn 100 percent just to break even. The greater the loss, the greater the required gain to get back to your original starting point. This is where lower range of returns comes into play. Some investors don't care about return fluctuations and feel that if you can hold on for the long run, then you should own more stocks because you don't care about risk. They fail to realize that the volatility matters! The lower volatility and downside risk of the balanced portfolio (as you will read shortly) has enabled it to achieve a similar return

**TABLE 11.1** Annualized Excess Returns of the Balanced Portfolio versus 60/40 (1927–2013)

| As of 12/31/2013 | 10 Years | 25 Years | 50 Years | 75 Years | Since 1927 |
|---|---|---|---|---|---|
| The Balanced Portfolio | 5.8% | 6.2% | 4.2% | 4.8% | 4.3% |
| 60/40 | 5.1% | 5.6% | 3.3% | 4.6% | 4.4% |
| Cash | 1.7% | 3.6% | 5.5% | 4.1% | 3.8% |

Total returns can be approximated by adding the return of cash to excess returns.

as 60/40 over the very long run. The lower risk, of course, comes from the better balance in the allocation.

Another reason the balanced portfolio has produced long-term returns similar to 60/40 is because of a *rebalancing advantage* that comes from maintaining an allocation of *highly diversified asset classes*. Since the four components of the balanced portfolio respond differently to various economic environments, and the weighted volatility has been evened out, the range of returns for each asset class in each environment varies considerably. For instance, stocks could be down by a lot but long-term Treasuries could post big gains during the same period (as was the case in 2008 when stocks had an excess return of *negative* 38.3 percent while long-term Treasuries produced a *positive* 39.2 percent excess return). Therefore, when the portfolio is rebalanced back to the target allocation each year (20 percent equities, 20 percent commodities, 30 percent long-term Treasuries, and 30 percent long-term TIPS in the case of the balanced portfolio), the repeated process of buying low and selling high generally prevails over time. Each time a particular environment plays out, each asset class responds differently. Predictably, some perform well while others underperform. By rebalancing back to the target allocation, you are forced to sell a portion of the segments that have done well and buy more of the underperforming asset classes because their current allocations would be below target (stocks rose 26.9 percent and long-term Treasuries fell 25.7 percent in 2009, immediately after you would have rebalanced by buying stocks and selling Treasuries). This process results in a positive impact to overall returns, because asset classes are cyclical and oftentimes strong returns follow periods of underperformance.

The net impact is that the *total return of the portfolio exceeds the weighted average return of each segment*. Normally, the total return of a portfolio is fairly close to the weighted average return of its component parts. For example, if you invest 50 percent in stocks that earned 10 percent and 50 percent in bonds that earned 6 percent, over time you would expect your portfolio to average out to an 8 percent return. In the case of the balanced portfolio, the actual return is about *1 percent better per year* than the weighted average. This fact has held true since 1927! In other words, if you took the average excess return of each asset class since 1927 and weighed it by its target allocation, you would get a total weighted return for the balanced portfolio that is about 1 percent less than the portfolio's actual return. Table 11.2 summarizes this outcome.

The powerful consequence of the process just described is that you can construct a portfolio of lower returning individual assets and still get a return similar to 60/40 over the long run. The extra boost shown in Table 11.2 is a premium that can be earned over time above and beyond any that are typically considered in portfolio construction. This premium is in addition to

**TABLE 11.2** Balanced Portfolio Average Actual Return versus Weighted Average Return for Components (1927–2013)

| Allocation | Asset Class | Average Excess Returns | |
|---|---|---|---|
| 20% | Equities | 5.6% | |
| 20% | Commodities | 2.0% | |
| 30% | Long-Term Treasuries | 1.4% | |
| 30% | Long-Term TIPS | 4.6% | |
| 100% | **Balanced Portfolio: Weighted Average** | 3.3% | +1.0% per year |
| 100% | **Balanced Portfolio: Actual Average Return** | 4.3% | |

any risk premium that is available, and it only exists because of the supreme diversification of the balanced portfolio.

## Stable Growth over the Long Run

The stability of the balanced portfolio's long-term returns can also be observed by following the growth of $1 invested in the portfolio from 1927 to 2013. Figure 11.1 demonstrates the actual experience you would have had through time. Over the long run the balanced portfolio's growth path closely resembles that of a straight upward sloping line.

Of course, there have been some detours along the relatively smooth path for balanced portfolio returns, but severe divergences have been

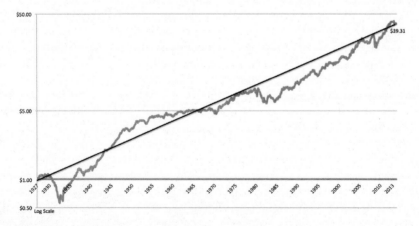

**FIGURE 11.1** The Balanced Portfolio: Growth of $1

relatively rare over this 86 year time frame. Ultimately reversion to the mean appears to hold over time as periods of underperformance have been followed by outperformance and returns get back to the long-term trend line. Later in this chapter I will take on the important topic of what causes these variances and why it is reasonable to expect future episodes to strike infrequently.

It would be beneficial if you are able to keep your focus on the long-term positive trend rather than on shorter-term time frames, which come later. By zooming out on the historical return chart and ignoring the shorter-term fluctuations you will observe a nearly straight path of excess returns. It makes sense that such a general trend would continue going forward. However, if you zoom in too much and, rather than having a 10+ year perspective, overreact to the experience from 1 or 2 years, then you may suffer longer-term underperformance by selling at the wrong time (just before a rebound). In looking at the chart too closely you may fail to see the upward sloping long-term line and instead mistakenly expect the line to become flatter or even downward sloping. For this reason I have emphasized the long-term trend here.

## Low Volatility

With the 60/40 asset allocation and most other mixes, the total portfolio volatility generally falls somewhere in between the volatility of its parts. Stocks have a high volatility and bonds low. The volatility of 60/40 is therefore higher than bonds and lower than stocks.

Since 1927 the balanced portfolio's returns have experienced relatively low volatility. In fact, the *total portfolio's volatility has been less than that of each of its components*. This outcome can only be achieved with great balance. The comparison is summarized in Table 11.3.

On a relative basis, the balanced portfolio's volatility is about 30 percent lower than that of the conventional 60/40 portfolio. After being introduced to the advantages of good balance, you may not be surprised by the difference in volatility. A well-balanced mix of asset classes should be expected to be less volatile than a poorly allocated portfolio. Since the balanced portfolio consists of asset classes that are biased to perform differently during various economic environments, then as one segment does poorly another is likely doing well. Another way to envision this dynamic is by comparing the balanced portfolio to a finely tuned car engine. If you take the cover off the engine, you will see multiple moving parts. Some are going up, while others are simultaneously shifting down, sliding sideways, or sitting still. From the outside, the engine and the car are running smoothly. All the ups and downs inside the engine offset each other to result in a steady product outside the

**TABLE 11.3** Volatility Comparison

| 1927–2013 | Volatility | |
|---|---|---|
| Equities | 19.2% | 11.7% total vol. is *in between* vol. |
| Core Bonds | 4.8% | of each component |
| 60/40 Portfolio | 11.7% | |
| | | |
| Equities | 19.2% | 8.2% vol. is *less than* vol. of each |
| Commodities | 17.1% | component |
| Long-Term Treasuries | 10.0% | |
| Long-Term TIPS | 10.6% | |
| **Balanced Portfolio** | **8.2%** | |

shell. The balanced portfolio works in the same way. Removing two of the key components because on their own they don't appear essential or beneficial is analogous to the 60/40 mix. The consequence is that the engine occasionally rattles, and it breaks down when the part that was removed is needed.

The difference in volatility between the balanced portfolio and 60/40 undermines conventional theories. The traditional assumption is that the higher the risk you take, the higher your long-term return should be. Another way to express this perspective is if the returns of the balanced portfolio and 60/40 are about the same, then the risk should also be about the same. This assumption is generally true in the investment world. However, when it comes to asset allocation there really is a free lunch, with proper diversification. In other words, by constructing *a well-balanced, appropriately diversified portfolio, you are able to earn the same return with less risk.* This holds true over the long run as well, contrary to popular investment belief. The core reason this opportunity exists is because the broad investment community fails to construct efficient portfolios. It just so happens that most investors simply do not take advantage of the free lunch, which is precisely what makes it free. The reason the inefficiency is available and the opportunity to take advantage of it exists is because the conventional approach is so flawed. *It is not that the balanced portfolio is so special, but that 60/40 is so inefficient.*

## Consistent Returns Year by Year

Another way to observe the stability of the balanced portfolio is to look at past returns year by year. This view of returns may more closely align with how most investors think about performance because of the focus on shorter time frames. It also helps show the variations that may exist for a given portfolio strategy during different environments. For example, seeing how a portfolio performed in 2008 or the late 1990s or the early 1970s may provide insight into its potential vulnerabilities and biases.

Calendar-year excess returns for the balanced portfolio from 1927 to 2013 are shown in Table 11.4. All calendar years that experienced excess return declines greater than 10 percent have been highlighted.

You will notice that there are only *three* cases of excess return declines greater than 10 percent in the past 86 years! The last such episode occurred over *30 years ago*. Note also that the returns in Table 11.4 are excess returns and therefore exclude the returns of cash. From a total return perspective, all of these numbers would have been better, particularly during the early 1980s when cash rates were unusually high. As an example, in 1981, when the balanced portfolio had one of its worst calendar years in terms of excess returns with a −16.7 percent outcome, cash earned 15.4 percent. This means the total return was −1.3 percent that year, which was one of the worst years in terms of excess returns.

Another interesting fact further highlights the stability of the balanced portfolio. There have only been three calendar years since 1927 in which equities, long-term Treasuries, long-term TIPS, and commodities all underperformed cash in the same year (1931, 1969, and 1981). Only in 1931—when nothing was safe as the Great Depression forced selling of every asset class to raise cash—was the *total* return (including cash return) negative for all *four asset classes*. In other words, *the only time in history that stocks, Treasuries, TIPS, and commodities all were negative in the same year on a total return basis was at the depths of the Great Depression*. This makes sense because whatever the economic climate, the negative influence on one asset class should concurrently positively impact another. History has demonstrated this undeniable fact time and again to quantitatively support the conceptual logic.

Due to the significant diversification benefits and downside protection of owning these four asset classes, overall calendar-year returns have been steady. In fact, *since the Great Depression the balanced portfolio's worst calendar-year total return (including cash) was −6.9 percent (in 2008)*. You hate to ever lose money, but most investors would have been thrilled with such a result, considering that the average portfolio was down 25 to 35 percent that year. Table 11.5 lists all the calendar-year returns since 1927 during which excess returns were worse than −5 percent. The cash rates and total returns are also included for reference. The balanced portfolio's downside protection has been compelling for a very long period of time!

Based on these numbers, the balanced portfolio clearly meets the return objective that was targeted. It has produced stable, attractive excess returns

**TABLE 11.4**  Balanced Portfolio Excess Returns (1927–2013)

| Calendar Year | Excess Return | Calendar Year | Excess Return |
|---|---|---|---|
| 1927 | 9.0% | 1971 | 7.2% |
| 1928 | 0.2% | 1972 | 10.3% |
| 1929 | −4.3% | 1973 | 6.8% |
| 1930 | −13.0% | 1974 | 6.5% |
| 1931 | −26.9% | 1975 | 2.2% |
| 1932 | −5.5% | 1976 | 7.1% |
| 1933 | 22.6% | 1977 | −2.3% |
| 1934 | 16.4% | 1978 | 1.9% |
| 1935 | 14.5% | 1979 | 3.9% |
| 1936 | 21.9% | 1980 | −5.1% |
| 1937 | −8.7% | 1981 | −16.7% |
| 1938 | 5.6% | 1982 | 10.9% |
| 1939 | 9.7% | 1983 | −5.0% |
| 1940 | 2.5% | 1984 | −1.5% |
| 1941 | 13.1% | 1985 | 15.7% |
| 1942 | 15.4% | 1986 | 9.5% |
| 1943 | 11.4% | 1987 | −1.3% |
| 1944 | 6.7% | 1988 | 4.7% |
| 1945 | 13.6% | 1989 | 15.3% |
| 1946 | 17.2% | 1990 | 4.7% |
| 1947 | 14.7% | 1991 | 9.5% |
| 1948 | 0.7% | 1992 | 4.0% |
| 1949 | 1.9% | 1993 | 7.0% |
| 1950 | 13.7% | 1994 | −9.9% |
| 1951 | 4.9% | 1995 | 22.6% |
| 1952 | 0.7% | 1996 | 5.5% |
| 1953 | −1.6% | 1997 | 5.3% |
| 1954 | 13.0% | 1998 | −0.4% |
| 1955 | 0.0% | 1999 | 3.3% |
| 1956 | −0.6% | 2000 | 13.5% |
| 1957 | 0.0% | 2001 | −6.7% |
| 1958 | 4.4% | 2002 | 14.5% |
| 1959 | −2.8% | 2003 | 14.0% |
| 1960 | 5.3% | 2004 | 12.6% |
| 1961 | 5.4% | 2005 | 6.5% |
| 1962 | −1.5% | 2006 | −6.2% |
| 1963 | 4.0% | 2007 | 12.1% |
| 1964 | −0.1% | 2008 | −8.8% |
| 1965 | 0.2% | 2009 | 8.3% |
| 1966 | −0.6% | 2010 | 11.9% |
| 1967 | −0.1% | 2011 | 22.0% |
| 1968 | 3.2% | 2012 | 9.0% |
| 1969 | −7.8% | 2013 | −4.9% |
| 1970 | 11.1% | Average | 4.3% |

**TABLE 11.5** Balanced Portfolio's Worst Calendar Years since 1927

| Calendar Year | Excess Return | Cash Return | Total Return |
|---|---|---|---|
| 1930 | −13.0% | 2.3% | −10.7% |
| 1931 | −26.9% | 1.2% | −25.8% |
| 1932 | −5.5% | 0.9% | −4.6% |
| 1937 | −8.7% | 0.3% | −8.4% |
| 1969 | −7.8% | 7.1% | −0.7% |
| 1981 | −16.7% | 15.4% | −1.3% |
| 1994 | −9.9% | 4.3% | −5.6% |
| 2001 | −6.7% | 3.8% | −2.9% |
| 2006 | −6.2% | 5.0% | −1.2% |
| 2008 | −8.8% | 1.9% | −6.9% |

(and total returns) since 1927. Next, I turn to how it has fared against the other two major portfolio goals: (1) avoiding extended stretches of poor results, and (2) minimizing drawdowns over shorter time frames.

## THE BALANCED PORTFOLIO HAS NOT UNDERPERFORMED FOR EXTENDED PERIODS

Long-term stability of returns is essential. Since the future is always uncertain and today's economic dynamics make the range of potential economic outcomes even more diverse and potentially outsized, you should focus on the need for stability. Even a normally stable mix may result in greater variability in today's climate: Imagine a poorly balanced mix and the extended period of underperformance it may experience.

When you have two strategies with similar long-term expected returns, the focus should then shift to risk. The reason risk analysis is important is because it will increase your confidence that *actual returns* will be close to *expected returns* over time. Expected returns represent the average you would anticipate over time, but the tighter the dispersion of actual returns to that average, the greater the likelihood that you will actually experience the attractive return. Thus, a steadier return stream over longer stretches is critical.

One way to measure sustained steadiness is to examine returns during various long-term historical cycles. What were the returns during the depressionary 1930s and 1940s? How about the war-dominated 1940s and 1950s? Given the high allocation to fixed income, would the balanced portfolio have performed well during the last rising interest rate environment, in the 1960s

**TABLE 11.6**   Annualized Excess Returns by Long-Term Market Cycles

| Period | Balanced Portfolio | 60/40 Portfolio | Cash |
|---|---|---|---|
| 1929–1948 (bear market) | 5.7% | 2.2% | 0.5% |
| 1948–1965 (bull market) | 2.8% | 8.4% | 2.3% |
| 1965–1982 (bear) | 1.1% | −2.3% | 7.5% |
| 1982–2000 (bull) | 6.1% | 9.2% | 6.5% |
| 2000–2013 (bear) | 6.1% | 2.7% | 2.1% |
| **Average All Periods** | **4.3%** | **4.1%** | **3.8%** |

and 1970s? What about the results during the greatest bull market in history, in the 1980s and 1990s? Did the returns of the balanced portfolio vary considerably among these divergent environments and how did it compare to the 60/40 mix?

Table 11.6 summarizes the returns of the balanced portfolio and the 60/40 allocation during the aforementioned historical periods. In sum, the balanced portfolio's results varied much less than those of 60/40. In fact, the variability of returns from period to period was about half as much for the balanced portfolio. In other words, regardless of the environment the overall return did not materially deviate from the balanced portfolio's long-run average as much as the 60/40 portfolio's results did.

These results are predictable. During the period from 1929 to 1948 the economy suffered its worst depression ever and was gripped by prolonged economic weakness. Stocks, as should be expected, performed terribly, but Treasuries did well. A very different climate dominated the 1982–2000 bull market as the economy enjoyed its greatest run in history. Stocks soared more than anyone could have predicted. Remarkably, the *excess returns of the balanced portfolio during these two completely different periods were almost identical* (5.7 percent versus 6.1 percent). Note that I am not talking about short time periods. These are 17- to 20-year runs! That's a long time to wait, and a huge timing risk to take with the 60/40 approach. The cycles may appear to alternate, but you don't know how long each cycle may last and the magnitude of the difference. Consider the simple fact that we have been in a secular bear market in equities since 2000—a long-term period during which equities only earned 1.2 percent per year excess returns—and few realize it.

The reason for the consistency of the balanced portfolio is because of the offsetting dynamics within the allocation. One part may not pay off, but another will benefit for the same reason. Weak growth hurts stocks, but helps bonds. Rising inflation is a negative for both stocks and bonds, but inflation hedges outperform in these environments. Most importantly, economic shifts can be long lasting, and if it turns out that you were betting on the wrong outcome, then the impact to your portfolio can be substantial. *Why take the risk, especially since you are not compensated with higher expected returns over the long term?*

Given the balanced portfolio's higher allocation to fixed income relative to 60/40, a common concern is how it may perform during a *rising interest rate environment*. This trepidation about the strategy is especially heightened because of the use of longer-duration fixed income assets. Your concern may be that not only is the allocation to bonds higher, but that the longer duration of the asset makes the portfolio doubly vulnerable. Thus the exposure to rising interest rates may seem too great at this point of the cycle, with historically low rates as the starting point. Perhaps you might argue that the strategy was fine when rates were falling, but is far too risky now that rates are so low.

All of these common concerns are misguided. Simply put, the portfolio is balanced by economic climate, so you need not worry excessively about whether interest rates are going to rise or fall. The *excess returns* should not vary too much between the two environments. That is the whole idea behind being balanced: Some portion of the portfolio will likely perform well to offset the segments that are doing poorly. Of course, cash rates may be low, *but that impacts all asset classes*. That is precisely why *excess returns* are emphasized in this book.

Ultimately, the results depend on *why* interest rates rise. Going back to the first chapter and how the economic machine works, the Fed controls short-term interest rates. Longer-term rates are merely a reflection of future expectations of short-term rates. Both shift in reaction to economic conditions in terms of changes in growth and inflation. Thus, rates will move based on how growth and inflation transpire relative to what has already been discounted.

This is the way to think about the benefits of being well balanced. You don't have to correctly anticipate what will cause interest rates to rise. If inflation increases force rates to rise, then the inflation hedges—TIPS and commodities—are biased to outperform and help offset underperformance in other segments of the portfolio. If stronger than expected growth puts upward pressure on interest rates, then rising growth assets—stocks and commodities—will probably contribute to overall results.

There is historical precedent for this dynamic. Between 1963 and 1981, 10-year Treasury interest rate rose from 3.8 percent to 15.3 percent. That surge represented the greatest increase in rates in U.S. history and it has never been matched to date. Out-of-control inflation caused this outsized

**TABLE 11.7** The Balanced Portfolio: Better than 60/40 with Rising
Interest Rates

| 1963–1981 | Excess Return | Risk | Return/Risk Ratio |
|---|---|---|---|
| Balanced Portfolio | 1.3% | 7.5% | 0.17 |
| 60/40 | −0.5% | 9.5% | −0.05 |
| Cash | 6.6% | | |

rise as the Fed continually elevated short-term rates to fight inflation. Consequently and unsurprisingly, the core asset classes of stocks and bonds vastly underperformed historical averages for nearly 20 years. Conversely, the inflation hedges of commodities and TIPS significantly outperformed their mean returns. The combination of these four asset classes delivered positive excess returns above cash during a time when cash was king. Table 11.7 provides the returns.

During this unprecedented run in inflation and interest rate hikes, stocks and Treasuries did not perform well since they are both falling-inflation biased assets. Equity returns barely beat cash by 0.3 percent per annum for 18 years and were clearly not worth the risk. Treasuries underperformed cash by 5.2 percent per year. However, commodities (+5.3 percent) and TIPS (+3.4 percent) more than made up for the weakness in stocks and bonds. The key, of course, was that the balanced portfolio had sufficient exposure to the winners to offset the underperformance of the core assets.

You may have noticed that the excess return of the balanced portfolio during the 1965 to 1982 period was the lowest of the long-term cycles presented in Table 11.6. The main reason for this, as will be more fully addressed shortly, is because cash rates rose far more than expected and therefore negatively impacted all asset class returns. Some asset classes, such as commodities and TIPS, still produced positive excess returns in the face of this headwind because of their bias to outperform during rising inflationary environments.

No one knows the reason that interest rates will rise in the future and whether rates will rise more than expected. If rates rise because of strong growth, then stocks might win. If it is due to inflation (as was the case last time), then the inflation hedges may carry the day. Given the current environment, do you really want to make a significant bet either way? What if rates stay low for a long period of time as they did during the 1930s and 1940s, when cash stayed near 0 percent for 15 years? It certainly seems more prudent to stay balanced and not be exposed to the risk of guessing wrong.

## THE BALANCED PORTFOLIO HAS HAD LIMITED MAJOR DRAWDOWNS

Earlier in the book I described three broad factors that influence asset class prices. They are unexpected shifts in

1. Future cash rates
2. Risk appetite
3. Economic environment (most importantly)

I further explained that two of these factors are not diversifiable and that one is (economic environment). The one that is diversifiable (meaning that you can take action to protect yourself against the risk) is also the one that produces the biggest impact to returns. Figure 11.2 reminds you of the relationships across these factors.

Another crucial distinction among these three factors involves the frequency and severity of their negative impact on asset class returns. Shifts in the economic climate occur all the time and can significantly impact asset class returns for a long period of time, whereas unexpected changes in the future cash rate and broad risk appetite only impact asset class returns negatively intermittently and for a relatively short period of time.

The focus of this book has been to explain a strategy that will largely neutralize unexpected shifts in the economic climate to minimize the risk of adverse consequences on the returns of your portfolio. Since the balanced portfolio is balanced by economic environment, we would not expect historical returns to vary considerably because of shifts in the economic backdrop. In the last section, this conclusion was verified. Returns did not fluctuate materially over long time frames despite substantial differences in economic

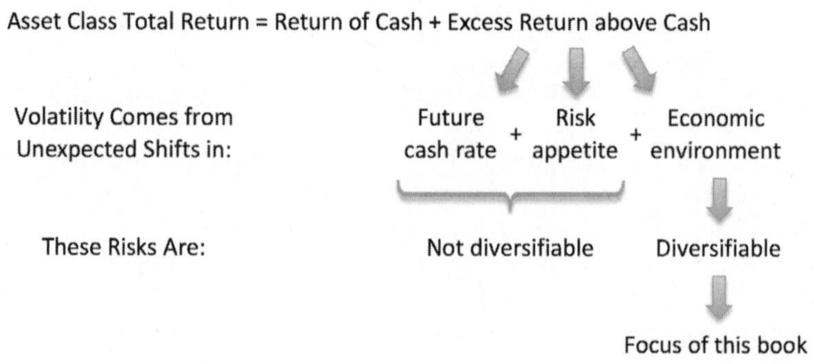

Asset Class Total Return = Return of Cash + Excess Return above Cash

| Volatility Comes from Unexpected Shifts in: | Future cash rate | + | Risk appetite | + | Economic environment |
|---|---|---|---|---|---|
| These Risks Are: | Not diversifiable | | | | Diversifiable |
| | | | | | Focus of this book |

**FIGURE 11.2**   Asset Class Volatility Framework

conditions. Perhaps most persuasive was the fact that the excess returns of the balanced portfolio during the 1930s and 1940s (one of the most challenging periods in our history) were nearly identical to the excess returns of the 1980s and 1990s (which saw the biggest economic boom ever). The balanced portfolio passed this true test of portfolio balance with flying colors.

Now that I turn to downside risks during *shorter time frames*, the other two factors come into play. Unexpected shifts in the future cash rate and general risk appetite impact asset class returns only in the short run. Furthermore, these factors do not negatively impact asset class returns frequently. Based on this understanding, *you should expect that a balanced mix of asset classes may also underperform infrequently and for short periods.* As we analyze the historical returns of the balanced portfolio in this chapter, we are essentially reviewing history to confirm that historical outcomes are consistent with what we would expect, given our understanding of what drives asset class returns.

### *Why* Unexpected Rising Cash Rates and Falling Risk Appetite Can Cause Short-Term Underperformance

Over shorter time frames, the balanced portfolio does not always outperform cash and you should not expect it to. If that were the case, it would not be considered a risky investment. The same tenet applies to every investment strategy and every asset class. Since the goal of a balanced portfolio is to capture the excess returns above cash offered by risky asset classes, such an approach would be expected to underperform when cash outperforms asset classes.

Most of the time cash does not simultaneously outperform all asset classes. This must be true because capitalism would fail if it weren't. If cash outperformed all asset classes for extended periods of time, then investors would not exchange cash for asset classes; the reason they do so is because of the expectation that over time they will earn more than cash returns. A prolonged period during which cash does better than all asset classes would certainly diminish the confidence that is required for investors to part with their cash for the promise of higher returns. Going back to the principles in the first chapter about how the economic machine functions, if investors did not give up their cash, then the normal functioning of the machine would be interrupted. Widespread hoarding of cash is a sure way for an economy to stagnate. Under these circumstances, the Fed—which is responsible for reacting to economic conditions with an appropriate policy response—would lower the rate of cash to entice investors to invest in something that promises higher returns. The lower hurdle of cash makes other investments relatively more attractive. We have seen this dynamic play out since 2009 when the Fed lowered cash rates to zero.

When current cash rates *rise* unexpectedly to a significant degree, then a yield of cash higher than what had been discounted makes it a suddenly more attractive investment. At the same time, this sudden increase in rates makes all other asset classes less appealing relative to cash. The previous price of the asset (before the unexpected big increase in cash yield) had discounted a premium above a certain level of cash. When cash rates increased more than expected, then unless the premium fell the price of each asset would have to decline to make up for this new reality. Think of the price of each asset class being a function of the rate of cash and an excess return above cash. The price is such that it is expected to roughly produce a long-term return of cash plus the excess return.

Return of asset class = Cash return + Excess return

If the cash yield suddenly and unexpectedly goes up, the price of the asset needs to go down if the expected excess return stays the same in order to readjust at the higher forward-looking return. A lower price results in better upside, all else being equal. Don't forget that cash would have to jump more than it is already discounted, since the expected increase is already factored into today's price. This type of situation may occur when the Fed unexpectedly raises interest rates (generally to stem risks of rising inflation). Note that the increase in the interest rate needs to be significant, because otherwise it would not materially impact investor behavior. It also must be unexpected. If everyone is anticipating rapidly rising interest rates and they do rise as expected, then there is no market surprise.

Two periods in history that provide helpful examples of this sort of dynamic occurred in 1994 and 1980. In 1994 the Fed shocked investors by rapidly hiking interest rates from 3 percent to 6 percent within a 12-month period because of a fear of rising inflation (which interestingly never materialized). A similar experience roiled asset class returns in 1980 as the Fed suddenly pushed interest rates to historic highs in an effort to finally end the inflation that had soared to unprecedented heights. Crucially, in both cases few investors were expecting interest rates to rise and it is the surprise that created the temporary conditions for asset classes to underperform cash. During these historical periods, all four asset classes simultaneously underperformed cash for a few months.

This dynamic may also exist when expectations of *future cash yields suddenly shift upwards*. Such an environment occurred as recently as 2013, when investors abruptly changed their expectations of future cash yields. With current cash yields at 0 percent and muted expectations of rising yields over the near term, a sudden shift in expectations to cash yields rising faster than discounted simultaneously hurt all asset class prices. That is, the current yield of cash did not change, but the future expectations of cash yields moved up significantly. And it was the change in expectations that negatively impacted all asset class prices concurrently. Note that this phenomenon lasted about a month.

The other general environment in which cash outperforms all asset classes is when *the appetite to take risk suddenly declines (or the premium required to take risk precipitously rises)*. This phenomenon is most pronounced during crisis periods. During these unique environments panic ensues and there is an overwhelming demand for liquidity and cash. No one really cares about the long run during these climates and most are willing to sell their assets for nearly any price just to have the peace of mind of holding risk-free cash. The general investor mentality abruptly swings from focusing on return *on* capital to return *of* capital. The mechanical consequence of widespread fear is rising risk premiums. Oftentimes the cash rate actually falls, which on its own would be a positive influence on asset prices. However, rapidly rising risk premiums—or the general level of excess returns demanded by investors for taking risk—abruptly and materially spikes because of the high demand for cash.

The years 2008–2009 and 1929–1932 are two vivid instances in U.S. history of this type of atmosphere. Both of these examples represented deleveraging periods, as described in the first chapter. During these times cash is king because the economic machine has literally frozen. This has only happened twice in U.S. history since 1927, but other countries have also experienced similar incidents in their history. Using the simple formula above (cash return + excess return = return of asset class), if the general risk premium for all asset classes spikes, then the price of all asset classes simultaneously drops. This occurs because the appetite for risk precipitously declines and much lower asset prices are required to attract new buyers.

Both of these environments—rapid, unexpected cash rate increases and deleveragings—are *rare events*. They simply do not occur very often. The infrequency of these events should not come as a surprise. The deleveraging process, as explained in the first chapter, may occur only once or twice in a century because of the self-reinforcing nature of the leveraging cycle. The mechanics of how the cycle runs results in protracted up-and-down cycles lasting decades. Similarly, rapid unexpected increases in interest rates are rare since the Fed normally manages the typical economic boom-bust cycle. It does this by raising rates when the economy is too strong, when inflation pressures start to build, or both—and it lowers rates when the economy is too weak, inflation is too low, or both conditions are present. These normal cycles cover most of history. For interest rate hikes to shock the market as described in this section, not only would the Fed need to make a big move, but that shift would also have to be completely unforeseen. Either occurrence is atypical on its own, based on history and rational Fed behavior. For both to occur concurrently is even more unusual.

More significant than the fact that these two events are rare, is the reality that they are *short-lived* even when they do occur. This characteristic should also be anticipated. When asset classes underperform cash, the overall economic environment is usually very weak. A deleveraging normally results in a depression, which is one of the worst economic outcomes. Rates rising rapidly beyond expectations produce a tightening of conditions because of the increased cost to borrow, which often results in a weakening economic climate. Both of these outcomes cause the Fed to react if conditions deteriorate too far, as they often do. The economic downturns are both exacerbated by and result from the decline in asset class values. If cash is outperforming asset classes, then the loss in value has a negative wealth effect because investors suddenly have less money (from declining asset values) than they had previously. Feeling less wealthy causes a natural response of less spending, which further feeds into weakening economic growth and inflation. The declining conditions result in a policy response of greater stimulus, which in turn pushes asset prices higher once again. In other words, the reason these negative environments are transitory is because the Fed won't let them last too long. Note that a period of deleveraging may last longer than a period of rapidly rising interest rates because the quickly deteriorating and drastic conditions associated with the former are generally more difficult to swiftly overcome with stimulus.

Another factor to consider is that immediately after these rare periods, asset classes typically tend to do very well because they are positioned to take advantage of higher risk premiums (due to recently falling prices) from that point forward. Thus, even if you are caught in the middle of the downturn, you have the option of waiting it out and taking advantage of higher prospective returns. This is another reason why the downturns are short lived and reversion to the mean is typical after big declines.

Now that we have covered *theoretically* when the balanced portfolio may underperform versus cash, we can now turn to the data. Is our understanding of the key drivers of asset class returns borne out in historical returns? We will analyze underperformance within two dimensions. First, we will address the *frequency* of declines in the past. Second, an examination of the *severity* of downturns will be scrutinized.

### Major Drawdowns Have Infrequently Occurred

An extremely comprehensive analysis of historical drawdowns involves the use of *rolling returns*. A rolling period refers to a snapshot of returns that are based on all the available starting and ending points rather than a more arbitrary time frame. Since you can't assume when in history you would have bought an investment and sold it, a review of rolling returns considers all the possibilities. Rather than starting in January and ending in December of each year, you can analyze returns starting in January, February, March, and so on. By slicing the data as short as rolling 3-month returns since 1927, nearly every possible historical scenario will be captured. I will also compare rolling 1-, 3-, 5-, 7-, and 10-year historical returns to offer longer rolling measurement periods. This summary covers a total of 5,955 data points! There is no hiding when utilizing rolling returns in this manner. If the portfolio contains a flaw, it will certainly surface when magnified under this level of scrutiny.

Table 11.8 summarizes how often the balanced portfolio has underperformed cash since 1927 using various rolling time periods. The same results are listed for the traditional 60/40 allocation as a point of comparison. The final column provides the percentage of time that all four asset classes (stocks, Treasuries, TIPS, and commodities) simultaneously underperformed cash over the rolling period. This data is shown because one of the core concepts of the balanced portfolio is the notion that it is rare for all four asset classes to do poorly at the same time, because the environment that causes one to underachieve is usually the same that results in a positive environment for another.

You should draw three main conclusions from Table 11.8. First, for both the balanced portfolio and 60/40, you have historically been more likely to beat cash the longer your time frame. That is, if you randomly selected any three-month period in history, you would have a 36 percent chance of doing worse than cash with the balanced portfolio and a 36 percent chance with 60/40. If you instead checked over a five-year measurement period, the odds decrease meaningfully for both. This is why investing is a long-term venture. *The longer your time horizon, the more likely you are to be successful. Importantly, in order to achieve this type of consistency, you must hold on*

**TABLE 11.8** Underperformance versus Cash (1927–2013)

| Rolling Periods | Percentage of Time Underperformed Cash | | |
|---|---|---|---|
| | Balanced | 60/40 | All Four Asset Classes* |
| 3 months | 36% | 36% | 5% |
| 1 year | 28% | 33% | 4% |
| 3 years | 13% | 24% | 1% |
| 5 years | 13% | 23% | 1% |
| 7 years | 10% | 15% | 1% |
| 10 years | 2% | 15% | Never |

*Asset classes are stocks, long-term Treasuries, long-term TIPS, and commodities.

*for the duration of the ride. If you change course along the way, you nega-tively impact your odds. This is true because you are most likely to change your strategy after your portfolio has underperformed (and just before it is about to outperform) and not vice versa.*

The second important point this data highlights is the fact that the balanced portfolio is much more consistent than 60/40 in outperforming cash over time. This result should not be a surprise because of the superior balance. The problem with the imbalance of the 60/40 allocation is that individual asset classes can underperform for very long stretches of time. If the success of the asset allocation is overly dependent on the outperformance of just one segment, then prolonged periods of underperformance should be expected. The data clearly reveals this reality.

Finally, Table 11.8 further helps explain why the balanced portfolio has beat cash much more consistently over the long run than 60/40. Even over short periods such as three months or one year, it is quite rare for all four asset classes to concurrently return less than cash. The logic should be straightforward at this point. Each asset class is expected to beat cash over the long run. Additionally, each asset class contains different biases to various economic environments. As economic conditions shift, these changes impact asset classes differently causing them to perform better or worse than average. Since economic shifts occur at the same time for all asset classes, what causes one to underperform simultaneously drives another to outperform. The reason that 95 percent of rolling three-month periods since 1927 (this represents a lot of data points!) have resulted in at least one of the four asset classes doing better than cash is because of this core understanding of what fundamentally drives asset class returns.

If you were to dive deeper into the data, you would discover that the only periods during which all four asset classes underperformed cash on a rolling three-year basis were during the Great Depression (1929–1932) and during a period of rapidly rising cash rates (1981–1982). Over 10-year rolling periods (still a lot of data points), not once in history have all four underperformed cash. Never! If you are building a portfolio using these asset classes and efficiently weighting them in the process, then you stand to have a high probability of beating cash over time. Of course, all of this assumes you do not sell at a low point and you are able to emotionally survive the trough (which admittedly is far easier said than done).

As you would expect with the balanced portfolio, the rolling periods during which it underperformed cash generally involved times in which cash rates suddenly rose, or during deleveraging periods. The early 1970s and early 1980s are examples of times in history when cash rates unexpected increased materially. The early 1930s and the years 2008–2009 were periods in which we lived through a deleveraging process. *These events explain all the underperformance for every rolling 5-, 7-, and 10-year period since 1927!* In other words, the only times in history that the balanced portfolio underperformed cash for more than a few years was during these unique, short-lived events.

## Drawdowns Have Not Been Severe or Long Lasting

I have established that the balanced portfolio historically has not underperformed cash very often, particularly over longer time horizons. That observation only provides a part of the picture. Frequency is good to know, but what about degree? It is one thing to rarely fall behind cash, but what if those periods resulted in devastating losses that took years to recover?

A good way to assess the downside risks of a strategy is to calculate the returns had you bought the investment at the worst possible time and sold it at the absolute low. The measurement of the *peak-to-trough drawdown* provides a helpful glimpse of the maximum a strategy has underperformed cash historically. By comparing the results from the balanced portfolio with 60/40, you can gain additional useful context into the differences between the two approaches. Also relevant in this analysis is the *recovery time*. If you lose 20 percent but make it right back in three months, then that is far more acceptable than if it takes you five years to come back. Table 11.9 lists the peak-to-trough periods for both allocations as well as the number of months it took to get back to the prior peak. Every excess return drawdown of at least 10 percent since 1927 is listed.

Notice the time periods for the biggest peak-to-trough drawdowns for the balanced portfolio. From 1930 to 1932, we felt the most severe consequences of the Great Depression. The years 1980–1982 were impacted by rapidly rising cash rates that surprised almost everyone. Finally, the more recent deleveraging episode of 2008–2009 caused severe losses across most markets. You would expect the balanced portfolio to underperform cash during these rare, short-lived events.

When compared to 60/40, the balanced portfolio's performance is clearly superior during these rare periods. It has only experienced three peak-to-trough drawdowns greater than 15 percent in history (versus eight for 60/40), and the recovery time has been much more palatable. Over any rolling time period it has had a total of only eight periods in history in which it underperformed cash by more than 10 percent. In contrast, 60/40

**TABLE 11.9** Worst Absolute Periods versus Cash (Excess Returns)

| | Balanced | | | 60/40 | |
|---|---|---|---|---|---|
| Period | Cumulative Underperformance | Months to Recover | Period | Cumulative Underperformance | Months to Recover |
| 1929–1932 | −50% | 49 | 1929–1932 | −64% | 53 |
| 1937–1938 | −15% | 20 | 1937–1938 | −32% | 58 |
| 1968–1970 | −13% | 8 | 1968–1970 | −27% | 188 |
| 1980–1982 | −31% | 50 | 1972–1974 | −33% | 132 |
| 1983–1984 | −15% | 17 | 1980–1982 | −22% | 8 |
| 1993–1994 | −14% | 10 | 1987–1987 | −21% | 20 |
| 2005–2007 | −11% | 6 | 2000–2002 | −29% | 50 |
| 2008–2009 | −26% | 19 | 2007–2009 | −32% | 22 |
| | | | 11 More Periods | −10% to −15% | 18 (Average) |

List represents all periods in which each portfolio experienced at least a 10 percent drawdown from peak to trough.

failed on nineteen separate occasions, with far longer recovery times to get back to the old peak.

Note also that the returns shown in Table 11.9 are excess returns above cash (or below cash in this case, since they are negative). The total return you would have earned would have been the figures shown plus the return of cash. Thus, in reality, even though you should think of returns relative to cash, your actual experience would have been better than that represented here. By way of example, cash earned 5.6 percent between 1929 and 1932, 30 percent between 1980 and 1982, and 0.8 percent between 2008 and 2009. Of these periods, the years from 1980 to 1982 predictably benefited the most from the high yield of cash because it was an environment in which cash outperformed because the yield rose so quickly. The other two climates were deleveraging phases during which cash yields actually fell to zero to stimulate the economy. Note also that during these devastating deleveraging periods the balanced portfolio outperformed 60/40 because of the greater balance in the portfolio and the lower allocation to equities (which get nearly wiped out during deleveragings).

Finally, Table 11.10 summarizes the returns of the two strategies during the most notable bear markets in history. *The balanced portfolio outperformed 60/40 in every single major bear market!*

**TABLE 11.10** The Balanced Portfolio: Better Downside Protection than 60/40 during the Worst Bear Markets

| 1927–2013 | 2011 Downturn | 2008 Credit Crisis | 2000–2002 Bear Market | October 1987 Crash | 1973–1974 Bear Market | 1939–1941 Downturn | 1937 Recession | 1929–1932 Depression |
|---|---|---|---|---|---|---|---|---|
| Balanced Portfolio | +5.5% | −17.6% | +21.2% | −5.7% | +13.7% | +30.5% | −15.1% | −49.8% |
| 60/40 | −8.3% | −32.3% | −26.6% | −20.5% | −33.3% | −13.7% | −31.7% | −63.6% |
| Cash | 0.0% | 2.6% | 10.9% | 1.6% | 16.5% | 0.3% | 0.3% | 5.6% |

All returns are *cumulative excess returns*.
2011 downturn: 4/30/11–9/30/11 (S&P 500 declined 16.4% versus cash); 2008 credit crisis: 10/31/07–2/28/09 (S&P −51.9%); 2000–2002 bear market: 3/31/00–2/28/03 (S&P −49.4%); October 1987 crash: 8/31/87–11/30/87 (S&P −30.7%); 1973–1974 bear market: 12/31/72–12/31/74 (S&P −48.2%); 1939–1941 downturn: 12/31/38–4/30/42 (S&P −29.0%); 1937 recession: 2/28/1937–3/31/1938 (S&P −50.0%); 1929–1932 depression: 8/31/29–6/30/32 (S&P −84.4%).

Note that the time periods used in Table 11.10 are not based on calendar years, but on a measurement clock that starts at the peak and stops at the trough of each bear market (e.g., the 2008 credit crisis includes returns from October 2007 to March 2009). Therefore, this data provides good insight into performance during the entire span of a bear market.

## SUMMARY

Overall, the balanced portfolio has earned attractive, stable excess returns above cash since 1927, a period that covers a very wide range of economic outcomes. During no long-term period within that time frame did the balanced portfolio significantly underperform. Although it did experience drawdowns at times, as is inevitable in any risky strategy, the occurrence of such periods was scarce and not severe.

The historical results of the balanced portfolio versus 60/40 are also compelling. The balanced portfolio has achieved a similar return with less risk since 1927. The volatility has been lower, the downside protection better, and the consistency of returns during various economic environments far superior. Thinking of the benefits of the balanced portfolio versus 60/40 from this perspective makes the virtues of true balance even more compelling.

Although the data may sound persuasive, you should consider the often overlooked caveat that should accompany any analysis of historical results. I'm not referring to the ubiquitous "past performance is no guarantee of future results" warning. The data that you will see in this chapter only reflects what actually happened in the past. The major shortcoming of an analysis of historical results is its failure to adequately address *all the events that could have occurred but failed to do so*. What did not happen should at least be as important as what did transpire. This is because the actual history represents just one outcome, while all the other possibilities combined had a higher probability of playing out. Imagine if the path taken by history is one of a hundred sequences that could have occurred. If we reran history a hundred times, the odds that we would get a completely different result would be relatively high. We should learn just as much from those other instances as we do from the actual experience.

Of course, we don't really know what could have happened; we can only relate to history as it actually materialized. Nonetheless, this line of thinking is a critical step in preventing you from making unwarranted assumptions based just on what you've seen in the past. I also make this point to further emphasize that you should not overly rely on the data that I have presented in this chapter. Although you may find it compelling, the concepts survive through time and are what truly make this investment approach most persuasive. In sum, *focus on the process rather than the historical data*. In the next chapter, I turn to how you might think about *implementing* in practice the balanced portfolio concepts that you have learned.

CHAPTER **12**

# Implementation Strategies

## Putting Theory into Practice

I have described the conceptual logic behind how to efficiently build a balanced portfolio. You have also learned the details of how to construct a balanced allocation by analyzing the economic exposure of various asset classes and appropriately weighting them. It is now time to take the theories that you have studied and apply them in practice.

If you are like most investors to whom I have described the balanced portfolio, your initial reaction may be that the allocation looks highly unconventional. Some of you may even go as far as to say that the logical sequence has been intuitive up to a point, but you are surprised by the unusual allocation and are not sure it makes sense. You may conclude that given historically low interest rates, it is crazy to maintain a portfolio with 60 percent allocated to fixed income strategies. If these concerns are on your mind (or if I just made you think of them), there are two main reasons you should not be overly apprehensive.

First, if one asset class looks unattractive for whatever reason, it is better to think of hedging yourself by *adding* offsetting asset classes rather than *removing* the asset class you don't like. For instance, instead of reducing Treasuries because you think yields are too low, you should simply own enough of the asset classes that do well in the environment in which Treasuries do poorly. If you cut the allocation to Treasuries, then you actually increase your risk because you are leaving yourself more exposed. This topic has been covered at length throughout this book.

A second reason you should not be alarmed by the makeup of the balanced portfolio is because you can think of this allocation as the *efficient starting point*. Consider it as the asset allocation you might want to hold if every asset class were fairly valued, interest rates were normal, and you had no opinion about the relative attractiveness of any market segment. You might also decide to hold this neutral portfolio if you felt that the odds of accurately predicting tomorrow's economic climate relative to expectations were too low.

## THE BALANCED PORTFOLIO AS THE EFFICIENT STARTING POINT

You should always start with the portfolio that logically represents the neutral allocation. This is useful in establishing a solid foundation for investing in risky assets. The 20-20-30-30 asset allocation can be used, or some other mix that includes additional asset classes can serve as the efficient neutral allocation. So long as the methodology utilized to come up with the neutral asset allocation is that which was described in this book, you can use whatever asset classes you like to construct your balanced portfolio. With this efficient mix you have the opportunity to stay balanced, rebalance to the target allocation once per year, and forget the rest. You won't really need to worry about the economy's ups and downs or various market fluctuations.

Another way to view this is by saying that this is the allocation that you can hold if you have no opinion or views about which market might outperform next. By holding this mix you are essentially stating that you don't want to guess how the future economic environment will play out relative to consensus expectations. If the market is discounting 2 percent GDP growth and 2 percent inflation, by holding this balanced allocation you are indifferent to whether growth, inflation, or both underperform or outperform these expectations. You recognize the low odds of consistently outguessing everyone else about what the future holds. You realize that it is not enough to predict correctly whether growth or inflation will be strong or weak if your views merely match everyone else's, since those views are likely already discounted in today's price.

## IMPLEMENTING THE BALANCED PORTFOLIO

Should you wish to proceed with the approach of investing in the balanced portfolio, you can easily implement the strategy by buying *index funds*. You can use index funds that track as closely as possible each of the asset classes that are included in your balanced asset allocation (again, it doesn't have to be the 20-20-30-30 mix presented here since that was an oversimplification to emphasize the key concepts). The advantage of index funds is they provide exposure to various markets at extremely low costs, far below what active managers typically charge to attempt to beat the market. The number of low cost index funds continues to grow, helping investors achieve market returns extremely efficiently.

Index funds are also generally appealing from a tax standpoint. Since they typically do not trade frequently (often just once per year), minimal capital gains are normally generated. Taxes and fees add up quickly, particularly when overall expected returns may be lower due to the interest rate on cash being exceptionally low.

Putting it all together, you are able to implement the balanced portfolio strategy relatively easily by using index funds. The result will be a very low cost, tax efficient way to gain exposure to the various markets in your efficient allocation. Most portfolios are far less efficient in all three respects. The allocation is imbalanced, the costs are more expensive (since an all-index fund portfolio is uncommon), and the taxes higher (for the same reason). Moreover, another advantage of implementing using index funds is that the portfolio will be completely liquid, transparent, and simple to follow. Few portfolios share similar appealing characteristics.

## TRYING TO IMPROVE UPON THE BALANCED PORTFOLIO

Practically speaking, however, much of the marketplace and media, and many research pieces, are focused on predicting the next trend. Prognostication is commonplace. You hardly hear anyone profess to have no idea of where to invest and that every asset class is fairly valued. Perhaps it is because such a conclusion is not interesting, or people actually think they possess great insight into the future. Holding an efficient market portfolio is fairly rare in today's world of information overload. People all seem to think that they have an inside track on tomorrow's winners. Unfortunately for most, the reality is that their long-term records do not support the high confidence they have in their purported expertise to accurately and consistently predict the future. Note also that if it seems that your market views generally follow the consensus perspective, then you most likely do not possess great insight, since what you think you know is probably already priced into the market. To hold true insight by definition requires a view that is *different* from the majority of investors.

Of course, despite these warnings, you can try to do better than the balanced portfolio. Before I proceed to various approaches that you can take to try to outperform the balanced portfolio, there is an important distinction that warrants explanation. Up to this point of the book, I have described a thought process that had the goal of efficiently capturing the excess returns that various asset classes offer. Over the long run, an approach that involves the simple assumption that an efficiently allocated portfolio of asset classes should be expected to outperform cash is sensible. History bears this out and the logic behind its construction makes sense. Thus, *no skill is needed in order to attain these returns.* You can simply hold an efficiently balanced portfolio and collect the excess returns above cash when asset classes out-perform cash over the long run. This is why the balanced portfolio can be considered the neutral asset allocation. *You don't have to successfully predict the future in order to earn a profit.* This is *not a zero sum game* because every-one can hold the balanced portfolio and earn a positive return in relation to cash over time, since this is not a trading strategy or some other sophisticated construct to try to earn excess returns above what is readily available in the market. The only reason the balanced portfolio strategy may stand out and appear to be too good to be true is because the conventional approach is so inefficient.

If you wish to achieve a return potentially greater than that offered by a balanced asset allocation, you will have to take on a *new risk*. As a reminder, the risk you take with the balanced portfolio is that cash will out-perform asset classes. I explained that this rarely occurs over longer time periods because the causes of such an outcome infrequently transpire. It is uncommon for the Fed to surprise the market by rashly raising cash rates. For similar reasons, markets generally don't suddenly discount future cash rates to materially increase. Finally, precipitous drops in risk appetite are unusual and normally short-lived. Of course, with the balanced portfolio you are essentially avoiding the biggest risk that investors face by owning asset classes, because you have largely neutralized the impact of unexpected shifts in the economic environment.

By moving away from the balanced asset allocation in the ways that I will explain in the rest of this chapter, you would be introducing a risk that I have yet to address in this book. By investing differently from the neutral efficient allocation as represented by the balanced portfolio, you will be taking what can be called *active risk*. To be successful against this risk, you need to *possess exceptional skill*. The balanced portfolio requires no skill for success because this is an *efficient passive portfolio*. However, any shift from this efficient mix does require skill to add value over time.

I will describe three major ways that you can *try* to outperform the balanced portfolio. First, you can tactically hold an asset allocation that deviates from the efficient allocation. For instance, you may feel confi-dent that, looking ahead, growth is likely to disappoint (versus what is discounted in the market), and therefore you can opt to overweight assets that would benefit from this outcome and underweight those that would do poorly under these circumstances. Another approach that you might take to try to beat the balanced portfolio is by implementing the allocation using active managers rather than passive index funds. The active managers may be able to outperform their market segments and therefore add incremental returns to your portfolio. Finally, you can use a combination of these two approaches. That is, you can simultaneously tilt from neutral *and* use active managers.

Importantly, as I will describe in detail, each of these tactics for adding value above the balanced portfolio requires exceptional skill in order to prove successful over time. This is because *active risk is a zero sum game.* For every winner there is a loser. This must be correct because all of the stocks, bonds, and other asset classes combine to make up the total market. There exists an efficient allocation to the total market (i.e., the balanced portfolio). If you veer away from this allocation, then in order to earn more than the market you will need to possess greater skill than the average investor (who is pretty smart). Adding up all the winners and losers versus the efficient market portfolio results in zero net gains. This is the risk you take. You are risking that your bets versus the neutral portfolio will pay off and that whoever is taking the other side of your trade will lose relative to the efficient allocation. This applies both to tilts away from the neutral asset mix and to active management within asset classes.

You might guess right in the beginning or even several times in a row. However, to be successful over the long run you must be right more than you are wrong *net of any costs associated with active risk.* Some costs may include higher fees, more taxes, and greater transaction costs from trading more actively. I now discuss each of the three tactics you can adopt to try to outperform the balanced portfolio.

## Tactic #1: Tilt from the Neutral, Efficient Starting Allocation

If you feel that you have superior insight to try to outguess the consensus view, then you can try to profit from your prescience. In other words, you can attempt to do better than the balanced asset allocation by expressing your market views. You can do this by overweighting and underweighting asset classes *relative to the neutral allocation.* Recall the neutral mix is what you would hold if you did not want to try to outguess the market. There may be times when you feel strongly that the market is wrong. During these periods you can express this view by tilting your allocation away from the neutral mix.

For instance, you might want to increase your allocation to equities versus Treasuries. If the neutral mix is 20 percent equities and 30 percent Treasuries, then you might increase the equities to 25 percent and decrease the Treasuries to 25 percent in order to express this sentiment. Each of these moves relative to the balanced portfolio can be considered a bet. You are making a bet that you know better than the market because you are moving away from the truly balanced allocation, which is agnostic to future economic conditions. Since both equities and Treasuries are falling inflation assets, you would only make this shift if you were confident that growth would be increasing more than consensus expectations. If this prediction comes true, then it would make sense that stocks would outperform their average return relative to bonds against their average return. In other words, *you can express this market view by shifting the allocation from the neutral mix*. The bigger the bet, the more significant your economic positioning. You can tilt more if you are more confident that you know the future. If you guess right, then you would likely outperform the balanced portfolio allocation; if you are incorrect in your forecast, then you will underperform the balanced mix.

A reasonable question you may be asking is the potential negative impact of rising interest rates on a portfolio that has a majority invested in fixed income investments. In general, rising interest rates pose a headwind for fixed income because the higher yield makes existing bonds less attractive and therefore results in principal loss. You might therefore argue that today a lower allocation to Treasuries and TIPS is warranted.

This simple logic, although seemingly intuitive, completely misses the point of having a well-balanced asset allocation. Because the portfolio is balanced, it is actually expected to perform about the same whether interest rates rise or fall. The same question should be asked when stocks rise or fall. Rather than be worried about the *outcome*, the key is to understand what kind of economic environment would *cause* interest rates to rise. You can diversify against the cause by owning asset classes that are biased to outperform during the same environment. If you focus on the *outcome* instead and try to protect yourself against that scenario, then you risk exposing yourself to another outcome because this approach will take you away from good balance. *The protection comes in being balanced, not in avoiding the asset class you expect will perform poorly.*

Following this logic, if interest rates rise due to strong growth, then Treasuries and TIPS would both likely underperform, but stocks and commodities would be biased to provide above-average results. If, however, interest rates rise due to rising inflation, then the outperformance of TIPS and commodities would likely offset the downside of Treasuries. Note that TIPS bonds may actually be a positive contributor if it were inflation that caused rates to rise because of the inflation component of these securities. These inflation hedges make up half of the fixed income holdings of the balanced portfolio. It may look like Treasuries lose in either case. However, if rates do not rise as much as priced in or if they actually fall, then Treasuries would provide a much-needed boost. This is precisely what happened from 2007 to 2013, when most investors had assumed interest rates were going to rise because they were so low relative to historical levels. Since the portfolio is well-balanced, then the losses from Treasuries, TIPS, or both would be offset by the outperforming asset classes to roughly net out at the average excess return from all asset classes, just as would be the case if interest rates fell.

Consider also that imbalanced portfolios (such as 60/40) may actually do worse than the balanced portfolio during rising interest rate periods because they are underweight inflation hedges. If inflation rises, then both the 60 percent and 40 percent components would likely underperform. This is exactly what happened during the 1970s as stocks and bonds underperformed inflation. The 60/40 portfolio suffered devastating negative excess returns for over a decade with severe drawdowns and extended recovery times. In contrast, the balanced portfolio (as summarized in the chapter on Treasuries) outperformed 60/40 by a meaningful amount. The 60/40 portfolio may do well if interest rates rise due to strong growth because of the overweight to equities. However, the results will depend on how inflation plays out. If inflation also rises, then that would pose a headwind because neither stocks nor bonds are great inflation hedges.

Another common concern with the balanced portfolio relates to the specific asset classes that I have used. Some experts have argued against the assumption that all of these asset classes offer a risk premium. In other words, some think that even though there is risk of loss from investing in an asset class, it does not guarantee that there is an excess return available to investors. *If this were true*, then there would be no benefit from investing in the asset class, since the main objective of the balanced portfolio framework is to capture risk premiums as efficiently as possible. If there were no risk premium to capture, then allocating to that asset class in the portfolio would not be advantageous.

In particular, there are concerns that commodities may not offer a risk premium looking ahead, even though this is a very risky and volatile asset class. The argument is that the number of speculators has vastly increased over the near term, effectively eliminating all the future excess returns of this asset class. Commodities are a unique asset class because this real asset is normally accessed using financial instruments, which can arguably be considered a zero sum game. For every winner there is a loser, because each transaction is technically a contract.

There is no clear answer to this question. The data still supports the existence of a risk premium because commodities have produced excess returns above cash over the near term. Furthermore, there is nothing unusual in the return patterns of late given the *economic conditions that have transpired* (falling growth and falling inflation—both of which are negatives for commodities) and the types of returns you would expect during such environments. It is very possible that opponents of commodities have simply mistaken poor recent returns as a flaw in the asset class rather than the more plausible explanation that it has predictably underperformed because of the occurrence of an unfavorable economic climate. Finally, the long-term excess returns above cash are relatively small to begin with. Despite the relatively low returns, the benefits of diversification and the fact that the positive returns come when you really need them still provide a benefit to including this asset class.

Throughout this book I have reinforced that the key takeaways are the concepts, not the specific investments provided or historical returns. Whether you agree with the argument that commodities, or any of the asset classes for that matter, no longer offer a risk premium is immaterial. If you don't like an asset class, then don't include it in your balanced portfolio. However, you will need to *find another asset class* that you think will cover the economic environments covered by the asset class you are excluding. *It is the exposures that are key*. If you can't find another reliable inflation hedge like commodities, then you may need to include it in your portfolio even if you don't favor it at present because it at least is biased to benefit you *when you really need the protection*.

Even with these caveats, should you decide to proceed with tilting away from the efficient allocation you can efficiently implement any active bet with the use of *index funds*. Since you are trying to add value by shifting the asset allocation, the application of this gamble comes from the difference in allocation. Thus, you are able to maintain a low cost, tax efficient portfolio and still try to add value over time by opportunistically shifting the asset allocation.

One notable implication of this analysis is that any asset allocation that is different from the efficient neutral allocation is effectively making a bet on a certain economic outcome. This is true even if the portfolio holder is unaware of it. For instance, if you think you are invested in a balanced portfolio and your allocation is the conventional 60/40 mix, then you are misinformed. The 60/40 allocation is a clear bet that economic growth will outperform expectations and that inflation will come in less than what is discounted. This fact can easily be observed by studying the environments in which 60/40 has outperformed historically.

### Observe the Golden Rule: Diversification Always Trumps Conviction

One critical point should be made about shifting the allocation away from the balanced portfolio. The benefits of diversification are intuitive, reliable, and time-tested. It is not a zero sum game to hold a well-balanced portfolio because this concept only relates to capturing the excess returns of asset classes that are dependably and easily available. Everyone can do it and everyone can similarly invest in the balanced portfolio without detracting from anyone else. There does not need to be one loser for every winner. Due to these virtuous attributes, you should always observe the golden rule of investing: *Diversification always trumps conviction.* You should have greater confidence in the benefits of diversification than in your individual investment convictions. You might be convinced that Treasuries are the worst investment you can make. Notwithstanding this conviction, you should not underweight Treasuries relative to the efficient, neutral starting point *too much.* Your conviction that Treasuries are going to perform poorly is another way of saying that you don't expect growth to fall less than or inflation to rise more than discounted. Since you know that these outcomes occur about half the time, it appears foolhardy to feel so confident. *Moving away from neutral is fine, but you should not veer too far away.* How much is too much? There are no clear answers; however, moving your allocation to zero is certainly too far. Arguably, cutting the allocation in half may even represent too large a bet. As obvious as this may sound, most investors take active positions that are much more significant than what I am suggesting here. Not only is their starting point imbalanced, but they often take even bigger positions relative to this inefficient starting point than proposed here and are surprised when their portfolios experience excess volatility and underperformance.

Some professionals approach the asset allocation decision from a very different framework. They choose to invest in undervalued asset classes and avoid unattractive market segments. This approach may sound intuitive to those not trained to think in balanced portfolio terms. The problem, as you know, is that the asset allocation is most likely going to end up *highly imbalanced.* One way to reconcile these approaches is to start with a balanced portfolio as the neutral starting point. If you conclude that every asset class is fairly valued, then you would simply hold the balanced mix. If you have viewpoints that you would like to express in the allocation, then you can over- and underallocate *from the neutral mix.* And, of course, you should never allow your conviction in any area to trump the diversification of the asset allocation by significantly overweighting one or two market segments. Again, you should think about the *economic bets you are making rather than the attractiveness of each individual asset you are buying. This is because of the appreciation that fundamentally each asset class is merely a bundle of economic biases and it is the cause-effect relationships that are most reliable through time.* And, most critically, each asset class plays a *role in the total balanced portfolio.*

## Tactic #2: Use Active Managers to Try to Outperform the Market

Another approach that you can adopt to try to do better than the balanced asset allocation is by using *active managers* to implement your portfolio. This is in contrast to using passive index funds to gain exposure to the various asset classes. A passive strategy typically refers to index funds. They are passive because of the lack of trading in the fund. The objective of index funds is merely to match the market, be it the stock market, bond market, commodities market, or some other market. Since the constituents of these markets do not change often, the index funds that track them buy and sell positions infrequently. Therefore, index funds are typically low cost and tax efficient.

Active funds, on the other hand, move around because they are vying to repeatedly buy low and sell high. Some funds do this by focusing on which holdings are in the indexes they are trying to beat and how their portfolios relate to these holdings. Others ignore the index and attempt to outperform over time by buying assets that they deem attractive and avoiding those that appear unappealing. Because of all the movement, these funds tend to charge higher fees and be less tax efficient than index funds. Additionally, the underperforming active managers eventually go out of business, leaving the ones with promising track records from which you must choose. This survivorship bias may make it seem that picking tomorrow's winners is easier than is really the case. In truth, a large percentage of the survivors owe much of their success to luck rather than skill and therefore may not achieve similar outperformance in the future (after you hire them).

If you choose to try to add value by using active strategies, then you would simply take your balanced allocation and implement each asset class using an active manager. For instance, if you have 20 percent allocated to global equities, then you might select one or two global equity managers or funds in which to invest this segment. With this approach you are taking the risk that the managers will do worse than the low-cost, tax-efficient index fund you could have used to nearly guarantee a market-like return. If after fees and taxes your active strategies do better than their respective markets, then you will outperform the balanced portfolio, even though you maintained the exact same allocation as the neutral mix. In other words, you can simultaneously hold a balanced mix of asset classes and use active strategies. Thus, your asset allocation may be balanced, but you may achieve an implementation advantage if you successfully select managers who possess skill in outperforming their respective markets. Conversely, you may still underperform the balanced portfolio because of an implementation shortfall.

As was the case with an active asset allocation decision, the use of active managers is also a *zero sum game*. For every manager that outperforms their market, there is another that underperforms. Adding up all the active strategies and funds results in a net negative, net of fees and taxes. This is because all the holdings make up the market, and since fees and taxes are taken off the top, the net result is less than the market by the amount of the fees and taxes. Since this is a zero (or negative) sum game, you should recognize the risk of using active managers to implement your balanced asset allocation. To be successful you need to have *skill in finding managers who, in turn, possess skill.* About half of the managers outperform the market over time. To add value to the balanced asset allocation, you need to find the half that will outperform *in the future.* Just because they outperformed in the past does not guarantee forward-looking success.

## Tactic #3: Use a Combination of the Two Approaches

A combination of the two strategies just described may also be utilized. You may shift from the neutral mix *and* implement the portfolio using active managers. You may also combine the use of active funds with passive funds in implementing your portfolio. That is, some market segments may be more efficient (such as large capitalization stocks and TIPS) and therefore warrant the use of index funds along with their low fees and tax efficiency. Others may be less efficient (perhaps small capitalization stocks and commodities), which provides the manager with greater opportunities to outperform net of all added costs.

Note, however, that since you are combining two forms of value-added strategies, you stand a chance of either really doing well or falling significantly below the neutral mix's results. This is because both value-added approaches may not work simultaneously and detract value. Consequently, if you take this tack, you might want to temper your bets on both sides. In other words, you might take smaller active bets on the allocation and use fewer active funds in order to observe the golden rule of investing: *Diversification always trumps conviction.*

## OTHER IMPLEMENTATION CONSIDERATIONS

There is indeed a growing trend in the investment community in favor of the balanced portfolio philosophy as this line of thinking gains popularity. Many of the largest pools of assets have shifted their strategy in this direction, and some of the most sophisticated investors are recognizing the inefficiency of their existing portfolios and are being drawn to the rationality of the balanced portfolio approach.

Despite these facts, *the simple truth is that to an uninformed investor the balanced portfolio is unconventional.* The vast majority of portfolios today still follow a 60/40 discipline, and investors have not fully adopted the balanced portfolio mind-set. Consequently, those who fully support this philosophy are likely to hold portfolios that are markedly different from their peers. For individual investors, peers may include friends and neighbors; for those fiduciaries responsible for institutional portfolios, co-trustees and representatives will be in that group. Either way, being different can be highly rewarding over the long run, but may occasionally pose challenges over short periods of time because of the dissimilar return pattern from the conventional portfolio.

Underperformance is an inescapable part of any strategy, so the key is not to sell at the lows and thereby lock in underperformance. Hence, complete buy-in is crucial (as it is with any approach to investing). You must know what you are doing and, most critically, *why* you are doing it. What you own and why it is there are two questions to which you should always know the answer. The risk of being different will decline over time as you gain confidence in your new approach and others gradually realize the benefits of the balanced portfolio strategy. Confidence comes from surviving downturns and experiencing the bouncebacks. It can also be generated from living through the consistency while traditional portfolios go through their usual roller coaster ups and downs. Moreover, as these concepts become more and more widely understood and adopted, your early acceptance of the approach will further reinforce your conviction.

The risk of being different is a true obstacle in implementing the strategy and should not be hastily dismissed. One suggestion to help minimize the impact is to *think of the balanced portfolio as being on one end of the spectrum and the traditional portfolio at the other end.* The spectrum covers the possibilities from well-balanced asset allocations to poorly balanced mixes. The balanced portfolio sits at one extreme, while a portfolio dominated by one asset class (perhaps equities) would fall at the other extreme. Since the traditional 60/40 allocation is highly correlated to equities because of its great imbalance, the conventional portfolio is also near the opposite end of the spectrum from the balanced portfolio. Picture yourself gradually moving across the spectrum from imbalance toward balance. *You do not have to immediately shift from one extreme to the other. Any move in the direction of the balanced portfolio end of the spectrum would be beneficial since it would obviously entail improving the balance in your portfolio.*

Perhaps you can make some shifts in that direction and test the results. The key is not the returns, but the cause-effect relationship along the way. In other words, don't add Treasuries to move toward balance and then be discouraged if Treasuries don't perform well over the short-run. Doing so would be analogous to buying fire insurance for your house and getting upset if you don't have a fire. The cause-effect relationship to observe is *why* the asset class you added performed as it did. If you bought Treasuries and they fell in value, then ask yourself *why* that occurred and whether that response makes sense given the shifts in the economic environment. For instance, if the economy strengthened more than discounted and Treasuries fell, then that would be something you should have expected, *given those sets of conditions that actually transpired.* The fact that it could have gone the other way should not be neglected. You obviously did not know which way it was going to turn out, and that is precisely why you moved in the direction of enhanced balance in your portfolio. If the economy had weakened, then Treasuries would have likely outperformed, as is their normal mechanical response to such an economic outcome. Step-by-step you can add asset classes and analyze their responses to shifting conditions to gain comfort with the cause-effect relationships and the logic. It is perfectly acceptable to take baby steps over time toward improved balance as a way to slowly introduce and become comfortable with this new way of thinking.

## SUMMARY

The bottom line is that you have options in how you implement the balanced portfolio. The most important thing, however, is that you first embrace the concepts and framework for how to establish the neutral mix. You should try to fully recognize *why* you are moving toward good balance before proceeding, so that you will be better able to appreciate and anticipate the patterns of returns you are likely to live through. The critical aspect of actually implementing the portfolio is to emphasize the fact that simply holding the balanced asset allocation over the long run is probably the safest and most reliable way to earn good, stable returns. Whenever you steer away from this approach, either by shifting the allocation to express your market views or by hiring active managers, you run the risk of underperforming. Consider the obvious fact that of all the people who try to outperform, at least half will be worse off over time. Therefore, if you choose to try to add value above the balanced mix, make sure to temper your bets.

# CHAPTER 13

# Conclusion

The conventional portfolio is conventional for a reason. This has been the common approach for many years. It is easy to cling to the way people have approached investing for a long time. This is true even if the strategy has not worked well for over a decade. There may be a certain level of comfort that comes from following the herd. My goal in this book was to share with you what I have learned over the past 15 years. As an institutional consultant advising clients with a total of $14 billion in assets, including several portfolios in excess of $1 billion, I have been fortunate to have the opportunity to interact with some of the smartest investment minds in the world. I have been exposed to a wide variety of investment strategies from the most forward-thinking investors in the industry.

This book provides a synthesis of what I have learned. I feel that the insight that I have gleaned from the brightest investment professionals should be shared. For this reason I chose to write this book, with the hope that I can at least introduce you to other perspectives that you should consider before making the crucial asset allocation decision for your portfolio. I hope I have been able to effectively present a balanced portfolio viewpoint that helps you see asset classes and the portfolio construction process in a deeper, more thoughtful way. The decision is completely yours. My goal is to help you make a well-informed one. In that aim I hope I have succeeded.

# About the Website

**B**alanced Asset Allocation: How to Profit in Any Economic Climate has a companion website at www.wiley.com/go/balancedassetallocation (passcode: wiley15). The website contains the following resources:

- FAQs. Frequently asked questions and answers on asset allocation and other topics covered in the book.
- Updated returns. Annual updates to the returns of the balanced portfolio.
- Links to additional resources.

Active funds and active
   management, 182, 184–191
Active risk, 184–191
All Weather approach, 29, 129.
   *See also* Risk parity
Alternative investments, 124
Asset allocation
   about, 2, 3
   balanced portfolio. *See* Balanced
      portfolio
   and economic outcomes, 14–17
   neutral, 128–130, 134, 140, 141,
      168
   60/40 conventional mix of stocks
      and bonds. *See* 60/40
      conventional portfolio
Asset classes
   analyzing, method for, 115–126
   bonds. *See* Bonds
   cash. *See* Cash
   commodities. *See* Commodities
   customizing, 56
   cyclical nature of, 158
   economic bias, 25–27, 47, 67,
      115–117, 125, 130–133,
      150. *See also* specific asset
      classes
   economic growth, impact of,
      14–16, 40. *See also*
      Economic growth
   and economic machine, need for
      understanding, 5
   excess returns above cash. *See*
      Excess returns above cash

inflation, impact of, 14–16, 40.
   *See also* Inflation
private equity, 124–126
real estate. *See* Real estate
return of cash, 30–32, 45, 47
returns versus exposure to
   varying economic climates,
   26, 27, 132
stocks. *See* Stocks
total returns, 21–23, 31, 45, 72,
   74–77, 150, 158, 162, 164,
   168
Treasuries. *See* Treasuries
Treasury Inflation-Protected
   Securities (TIPS). *See*
   Treasury Inflation-Protected
   Securities (TIPS)
volatility, 29, 30, 45, 50, 116,
   117, 126, 150, 168. *See also*
   Volatility

Balance. *See also* Balanced portfolio
   conventional portfolios (60/40
      stocks/bonds), 21–27,
      51–58, 63, 150–152
   good balance, 19–21
   imbalance, 1, 22–25, 27,
      150–152, 189
   importance of, 5, 14–17, 27
   new perspective on, 26, 27.
      *See also* Balanced portfolio
      lens (balanced portfolio
      perspective)
   stable returns, 19–22

Balance  (*Continued*)
  true portfolio balance, 1, 3, 47,
    61, 62, 65–67, 89, 113, 141
  and volatility, 20–27, 150.
    *See also* Volatility
Balanced portfolio
  active managers, use of, 190, 191
  active risk, 184–191
  asset classes, selecting, 129–133,
    137–141, 143
  asset classes, weighting, 129,
    133–141, 143–150
  cause-effect relationships.
    *See* Cause-effect
    relationships
  commodities, role of, 112, 113
  conceptual framework, 128–141
  confidence in investing strategy,
    192
  economic portfolios, 145–149
  as efficient starting point, 181,
    182
  excess returns above cash, 134,
    156–171, 175, 176, 178
  future cash rate, shifts in,
    168–172
  gradual shift to, 192, 193
  historical returns, 155–179
  implementing, 182, 183,
    191–193
  index funds, use of, 182–184,
    188, 190, 191
  and interest rates, 186, 187
  long-term returns, 156–164, 172,
    173, 178
  neutral asset allocation,
    128–130, 134, 140, 141,
    168, 181, 182, 185
  outperforming, 183–191
  process for balancing, 145–150
  purpose of, 127
  rebalancing advantage, 158
  returns compared to 60/40
    portfolio, 156–161,
    165–167, 173–178
  risk appetite, shifts in, 168, 171,
    172
  rolling returns, 32, 172–174
  and shifts in economic
    environment. *See* Economic
    environment, shifts in
  stable growth, 19–22, 159, 160
  stocks, role of, 65, 66
  total return, factors impacting,
    150. *See also* Economic bias;
    Volatility
  Treasuries, role of, 84–87
  Treasury Inflation-Protected
    Securities (TIPS), role of,
    97–99
  true portfolio balance, 1, 3, 47,
    61, 62, 65–67, 89, 113,
    141
  underperformance periods, 160,
    164–178, 192
  volatility, 135–139, 144, 145,
    157, 158, 160, 161. *See also*
    Volatility
Balanced portfolio lens (balanced
    portfolio perspective)
  commodities, 108–113
  60/40 portfolio analysis, 26, 27,
    150–152
  stocks, 58–67
  Treasuries, 80–84, 87
  Treasury Inflation-Protected
    Securities (TIPS), 93–97
  use of, 26, 27, 47, 48, 50, 67, 70
Bear markets, 21, 53–55, 66, 78,
    79, 86, 165, 176–178
Bonds
  corporate, 119, 120, 125, 126
  credit ratings, 77, 119
  economic bias, 66, 77–87

emerging markets, 120, 121, 125, 126

excess returns above cash, 33, 72–75, 83

foreign sovereign bonds, 77, 119, 120, 125, 126

global, 117, 125, 126

municipal, 121, 122, 125, 126

Treasuries. *See* Treasuries

volatility, 21, 23–26, 56, 77, 83, 84

Bridgewater Associates, 1, 5, 29, 95, 127, 129

Bull markets, 21, 38, 39, 53, 55, 60, 78, 79, 156, 165

Business cycles, 6–11

Buy and hold approach to investing, 2

Cash

excess returns. *See* Excess returns above cash

excluded in balanced portfolio, 133

future cash returns. *See* Future cash rates, shifts in expectations of

return of, 21, 30–34, 45, 72, 75, 94, 170

Cause-effect relationships

between economic shifts and asset class returns, 40, 41, 60, 61, 64, 65, 83, 93, 105, 115, 128, 130, 150, 155, 189, 192, 193. *See also* Economic environment, shifts in

between unexpected shifts in growth and inflation, 60, 61, 64, 65

Central banks, 7. *See also* Federal Reserve (the Fed)

Commercial real estate. *See* Real estate

Commodities

about, 101, 102

balanced portfolio perspective, 108–113

conventional thinking, flaws in, 105–108

conventional view, 104, 105, 113

economic bias, 47, 105–106, 109–113, 116, 125, 131

and economic growth, 109–112, 125, 144, 166, 187

excess returns above cash, 31, 33–34, 36, 104–107, 110–112, 187, 188

futures contracts, 102, 103, 107, 187

futures price, 103, 105–110

index funds, 103, 104

and inflation, 101–103, 106, 109–112, 125, 144, 166–167, 187

and interest rates, 186

investing in, 102, 103

percentage of in balanced portfolio, 148, 155, 159

return-to-risk ratio, 104

and rising economic growth, 109–112

risk, 102, 104, 105, 111, 112

risk premium, 187, 188

role of in balanced portfolio, 112, 113

and shifts in economic environment, 40, 47

spot price, 103, 105–108

types of, 101

volatility, 14, 104, 105, 110–112, 116, 126, 145, 146

Conventional thinking on asset allocation
commodities, 104, 105, 113
stocks, 21–23, 49–58, 66
Treasuries, 21–23, 69–72, 84
Treasury Inflation-Protected
Securities (TIPS), 91–93
Conventional thinking on asset allocation, flaws in
commodities, 105–108
60/40 asset allocation, 25, 26, 51–58, 66, 67, 71–79, 105–108
stocks, 25, 26, 51–58, 66, 67
Treasuries, 25, 26, 71–79
Treasury Inflation-Protected
Securities (TIPS), 91–93
Core bond index, 56
Corporate bonds, 119, 120, 125, 126
Correlation of conventional
portfolio performance to stock market, 24, 25, 57, 58, 192
Credit
deleveraging process, 6, 9–16, 171–176
long-term debt cycle, 8–14
and short-term business cycle, 6–9, 11
as source of spending, 6, 9, 10, 13
Credit crisis of 2008, 10, 12, 13, 39–42, 158, 162, 164, 171, 174–178
Credit ratings, 77, 119
Credit risk, 77

Dalio, Ray, 1, 29, 127–129
Debt
deleveraging process, 6, 9–16, 171–176
long-term debt cycle, 8–14
United States, 11–13

Deflation, 13, 14, 39, 81–83, 86, 94, 95, 119–120, 133
Deleveraging process, 6, 9–16, 171–176
Depressions, 10–13, 39, 40, 42, 73, 74, 82, 156, 162, 164, 165, 172, 174–177
Diversification, 2, 3, 78, 79, 127, 128, 188, 189, 191, 3637

Economic bias. *See also* Economic
growth; Inflation
and balanced portfolio, 67, 130–133
bonds, 66, 77–87
commodities, 47, 105–106, 109–110, 112–113, 116, 125, 131
and conventional thinking, 25–27
corporate bonds, 119, 120, 125
emerging markets, 117, 118, 120–121, 125
global bonds, 117, 125
global stocks, 117, 125
hedge funds, 124–125
municipal bonds, 122, 125
private equity, 124, 125
real estate, 122–123, 125
stocks, 25, 47, 59–64, 67, 116, 118, 119, 131
Treasuries, 25, 47, 66, 77–87, 116, 119, 131
Treasury Inflation-Protected
Securities (TIPS), 47, 93–98, 116, 131
Economic environment, shifts in.
*See also* Economic growth;
Inflation
about, 36–41, 127, 128
asset classes, impact on, 40, 41, 115, 116, 132, 133, 165,

166. *See also* specific asset classes

cash, impact on, 32

and cause-effect relationship with asset class returns, 40, 41, 60, 64, 65, 83, 93, 105, 115, 128, 130, 150, 155, 189, 192, 193

and commodities, 40, 47

and corporate bonds, 120

and diversifiable risk, 30, 36, 45, 46, 67, 128, 168

and excess returns above cash, 36

growth, unexpected changes in. *See* Economic growth

inflation, unexpected changes in. *See* Inflation

and interest rates, 76. *See also* Interest rates

neutralizing, 168. *See also* Neutral asset allocation (strategic asset allocation)

and return of cash, 32

returns, reasons for impact on, 40, 41

and 60/40 conventional portfolio, 174

and stocks, 38–40, 47, 59–67

and Treasuries, 37, 38, 48, 76

and Treasury Inflation-Protected Securities (TIPS), 47, 94–96

unexpected, 14

and volatility of returns, 29–41

and weighting asset classes in balanced portfolio, 129, 130, 133–141, 143–150

Economic growth

and asset allocation, 14–16, 130, 131, 143, 144, 165, 166. *See also* Balanced portfolio

and commodities, 109–112, 125, 144, 166, 187

and corporate bonds, 120, 125

diversifiable risk, 36, 37

and economic bias, 47

and emerging market bonds, 125

and global bonds, 125

and global stocks, 125

and hedge funds, 124–125

and private equity, 125

and real estate investment, 122, 123, 125

and 60/40 asset allocation, 24, 25, 150–152, 188

and stocks, 15, 38–40, 59–67, 144, 166

and Treasuries, 37, 38, 80–86, 144

and Treasury Inflation-Protected Securities (TIPS), 89, 94–99, 144

Economic machine

about, 16, 17

and balance, importance of, 14–17

Bridgewater Associates research on, 5

deleveraging process, 6, 9–16, 171–176

economic outcomes and asset allocation, 14–16

economy as machine, 6

long-term debt cycle, 8–14

money, effect of printing, 12–16

short-term business cycles, 6–9, 11

template for, 5

Emerging market bonds, 121, 125, 126

Emerging markets, 117, 118, 120–121, 125, 126

Equities. *See* Stocks

Excess returns above cash
  and asset class returns, 21–23,
    30, 31, 33–47, 130, 132.
    *See also* specific asset classes
  balanced portfolio, 134
  bonds, 33, 72–75, 83
  commodities, 31, 33–34, 36,
    104–107, 110–112, 187,
    188
  and economic environment, shifts
    in, 36. *See also* Economic
    environment, shifts in
  factors impacting, 36
  and future cash rates, shifts in
    expectations of, 36, 46.
    *See also* Future cash rates,
    shifts in expectations of
  and risk appetite, shifts in, 36,
    46. *See also* Risk appetite,
    shifts in
  risk premium, 31, 40, 42, 128,
    159, 171, 172, 187, 188
  stocks, 33–35, 50, 51, 54, 61, 62
  Treasuries, 33–35, 51, 70–76,
    79, 83, 84
  Treasury Inflation-Protected
    Securities (TIPS), 33–35
  and volatility, 30, 33, 34, 45–47,
    168
Extreme outcomes, 12, 15, 16, 41, 42

Fear and greed, 10, 41, 42, 55, 78
Federal Reserve (the Fed)
  and inflation, 7, 8
  and interest rates, 7–13, 31, 32,
    37, 43, 44, 72, 166, 167
  money, printing, 12–16, 19, 74
  role of, 7, 12
  Treasuries, purchase of, 74–76
Financial assets, 102
Foreign sovereign bonds, 77, 119,
  120, 125, 126

Future cash rates, shifts in
  expectations of, 29, 30, 34, 36,
    42–46, 92, 127, 168–171
Futures contracts, 102, 103, 107,
    187
Futures price, 103, 105–110

Global bonds, 117, 125, 126
Global stocks, 117, 118, 125, 126
Great Depression, 10, 12, 13, 39,
    42, 73, 74, 82, 162, 164, 165,
    174–177
Gross domestic product (GDP),
    11–13, 182

Hedge funds, 124–126
Hyperinflation, 13

Index funds, 56, 103, 104,
    182–184, 188, 190, 191
Inflation
  and asset allocation, 14–16, 130,
    131, 143, 144. *See also*
    Balanced portfolio
  and commodities, 101–103, 106,
    109–112, 125, 144,
    166–167, 187
  and corporate bonds, 120, 125
  diversifiable risk, 36, 37
  and economic bias, 47, 166
  and emerging market bonds, 121,
    125
  and global bonds, 125
  and global stocks, 125
  and hedge funds, 124–125
  hyperinflation, 13
  and interest rates, 32, 166, 167,
    187
  and printing money, 13–16
  and private equity, 125
  and real estate investment, 123,
    125

risk, 14, 39, 91, 94, 103
and 60/40 asset allocation, 25,
150–152, 188
and stocks, 25, 38–40, 59–62,
64–67, 144, 186
and Treasuries, 25, 37, 38,
76–78, 81–86, 144, 186
and Treasury Inflation-Protected
Securities (TIPS), 89–99,
144, 166, 167
Interest rates
and balanced portfolio
performance, 166, 186, 187
bonds, 71–78, 80–83, 85–87
cash, 31, 32
and commodities, 186
Federal Reserve setting of, 7–13,
31, 32, 166, 167
future cash rates, shifts in
expectations of, 42–45.
*See also* Future cash rates,
shifts in expectations of
and inflation, 32, 166, 167, 187
and stocks, 167, 186
and Treasuries, 70–78, 80–83,
85–87, 186, 187
and Treasury Inflation-Protected
Securities (TIPS), 186, 187
Intermediate-term bonds (core
bonds), 56
Investors
common mistakes made by, 1, 2,
24, 25, 31, 71
confidence, 2, 3, 17, 192
fear and greed, 10, 41, 42, 55, 78
portfolio objective, 2

Leverage and deleveraging process,
6–16, 171–176
Long-term debt cycle, 8–14
Long-term Treasuries, 75, 76, 78,
83–85. *See also* Treasuries

Market predictions, 2, 3, 17
Market prices, 2, 15
Market timing, 2
Money, printing, 12–16, 19, 74
Municipal bonds, 121, 122, 125,
126

Neutral asset allocation (strategic
asset allocation), 128–130,
134, 140, 141, 168

Private equity, 124–126

Real assets, 102. *See also*
Commodities; Real estate
Real estate, 31, 122–123, 125, 126
Recessions, 11, 108, 177
Recovery time, 175, 187
Return-to-risk ratio, 50, 56, 104,
117
Returns
cash, 21, 30–32, 34, 45, 72, 75,
94, 170
excess returns above cash. *See*
Excess returns above cash
and future cash rates, unexpected
changes in. *See* Future cash
rates, shifts in expectations
of
per unit of risk, 50, 104
and risk appetite. *See* Risk
appetite, shifts in
total returns, 21–23, 31, 45, 72,
74–77, 150, 158, 162, 164
volatility. *See* Volatility
Risk. *See also* Volatility
active risk, 184
appetite. *See* Risk appetite,
shifts in
balance, 150
commodities, 102, 104, 105,
111, 112

Risk  (*Continued*)
  corporate bonds, 119, 120
  currency risk, 121
  diversifiable, 30, 36, 37, 45, 46,
      67, 128, 168. *See also*
      Economic environment,
      shifts in
  emerging market bonds, 121
  future cash rates. *See* Future
      cash rates, shifts in
      expectations of
  inflation, 14, 36, 37, 39, 91, 94,
      103
  and investment strategies, 2
  nondiversifiable, 34, 36, 41–46,
      128, 168
  and return, 33, 161
  return-to-risk ratio, 50, 56
  shifts in economic environment.
      *See* Economic environment,
      shifts in
  stocks, 51
  Treasuries, 69, 71, 72, 75,
      77–79, 83, 84, 87
  Treasury Inflation-Protected
      Securities (TIPS), 90, 91
  of underperformance, 1
Risk appetite, shifts in, 29, 30, 34,
      36, 40–42, 45, 46, 127,
      168–171, 184
Risk parity, 29, 129, 149, 150
Risk premium, 31, 40, 42, 128,
      159, 171, 172, 187–188. *See
      also* Excess returns above cash

Short-term Treasuries, 83–85.
      *See also* Treasuries
60/40 conventional portfolio
  analysis of through balanced
      portfolio lens, 26, 27,
      150–152
  asset allocation, 21–27, 150–152

  correlation to stock market
      performance, 24, 25, 57, 58,
      192
  and economic bias, 25–27
  and economic environment, shifts
      in, 174
  and economic growth, 24, 25,
      150–152, 188
  excess returns above cash, 21–23
  flaws in thinking about, 25, 26,
      51–58, 66, 67, 71–79,
      105–108
  imbalance, 21–27, 51–58, 63,
      150–152
  and inflation, 25, 150–152, 187,
      188
  and interest rates, 187
  returns, historical, 21, 22, 25
  returns compared to balanced
      portfolio, 156–161,
      165–167, 173–178
  stocks, 21, 22
  Treasuries, 21, 22
Spending, 6–13, 81, 82
Spot price, 103, 105–108
Stagflation, 39
Stock market
  attention paid to, 49
  bear markets, 21, 53–55, 66, 78,
      79, 86, 165, 176–178
  bull markets, 21, 38, 39, 53, 55,
      60, 78, 79, 156, 165
  correlation of conventional
      portfolio performance to
      stock market, 24, 25, 57, 58,
      192
  cycles, 52–55
Stocks
  balanced portfolio perspective,
      58–67
  cause-effect relationship between
      unexpected shifts in growth
      and inflation, 60, 61, 64, 65

conventional thinking, flaws in, 25, 26, 51–58, 66, 67
conventional view on portfolio allocation, 21–23, 49–58, 66
correlation of conventional portfolio performance to stock market, 24, 25, 57, 58, 192
and deflation, 82
economic bias, 25, 47, 59–64, 67, 116, 118, 119, 131
and economic growth, 15, 38–40, 59–67, 144, 166
excess returns above cash, 33–35, 50, 51, 54, 61, 62
global, 117, 118, 126
inclusion of in most portfolios, 49, 50
index funds. *See* Index funds
and inflation, 25, 38–40, 59–62, 64–67, 144, 186
and interest rates, 167, 186
and investor emotions, 55
percentage of in balanced portfolio, 148, 155, 159
private equity, 124
return-to-risk ratio, 50, 56
risk, 51
role of in balanced portfolio, 65, 66
and shifts in economic environment, 38–40, 47. *See also* Economic environment, shifts in
and shifts in risk appetite, 46
in 60/40 portfolio. *See* 60/40 conventional portfolio
stock market cycles, 52–55
subsets, 118, 119

underperformance, 24, 25, 50–55, 57, 58, 61, 66
volatility, 21–26, 50–51, 58–59, 61–64, 66, 116–118, 145, 146

Tax consequences
active management, 191
index funds, 183
municipal bonds, 121, 122
TIPS. *See* Treasury Inflation-Protected Securities (TIPS)
Total returns, 21–23, 31, 45, 72, 74–77, 150, 158, 162, 164
Treasuries
balanced portfolio perspective, 80–84, 87
conventional perspective on, 21–23, 69–72, 84
conventional thinking, flaws in, 25, 26, 71–79
credit risk, 77
and deflation, 81–83, 86, 120, 133
diversification benefits of, 78, 79
duration, 72, 73, 75–79, 83–87
economic bias, 25, 47, 66, 77–87, 116, 119, 131
and economic growth, 37, 38, 80–86, 144
excess returns above cash, 33–35, 51, 70–76, 79, 83, 84
Federal Reserve purchase of, 74–76
and inflation, 25, 37, 38, 76–78, 81–86, 144, 186
interest rates, 70–78, 80–83, 85–87
intermediate-term (core bonds), 56
long-term, 75, 76, 78, 83–85

Treasuries (*Continued*)
  maturity, holding to, 37, 62, 69,
    75, 136, 139
  percentage of in balanced
    portfolio, 148, 155, 159
  restructuring, 56
  returns, 56, 70, 71, 73, 76, 79,
    83, 84
  risk, 69, 71–72, 75, 77–79,
    83–84, 87
  role of in balanced portfolio,
    84–87
  and shifts in economic
    environment, 37, 38, 47.
    *See also* Economic
    environment, shifts in
  and shifts in risk appetite, 46
  short-term, 83–85
  in 60/40 portfolio. *See* 60/40
    conventional portfolio
  TIPS compared, 90, 91
  volatility, 21, 23–26, 56, 69, 77,
    83, 84, 116, 145, 146
  yields, 69–76, 82, 83
Treasury Inflation-Protected
    Securities (TIPS)
  balanced portfolio perspective,
    93–97
  conventional thinking on,
    91–93
  and decreasing economic growth,
    89, 94–99
  and deflation, 94, 95
  described, 90, 91
  economic bias, 47, 93–98, 116,
    131
  and economic growth, 89,
    94–99, 144
  excess returns above cash, 33–35
  and inflation, 89–99, 144, 166,
    167
  maturity, holding to, 90, 92

percentage of in balanced
    portfolio, 148, 155, 159
  risk, 90, 91
  role of in balanced portfolio,
    97–99
  and shifts in economic
    environment, 47
  Treasuries compared, 90, 91
  use of, 89
  volatility, 93, 96, 97, 116, 145,
    146

Underperformance
  balanced portfolio, 160,
    164–178, 192
  risk of, 1
  stocks, 24, 25, 50–55, 57, 58,
    61, 66
United States debt ratios, 11–13

Volatility
  asset classes, 45, 50, 126, 150,
    168
  and balance, 20–27
  balanced portfolio, 135–139,
    144, 145
  bonds, 21, 23–26, 56, 77, 83, 84
  commodities, 14, 104, 105,
    110–112, 116, 126, 145,
    146
  corporate bonds, 120, 126
  emerging market bonds, 121, 126
  and excess returns above cash,
    30, 33, 34, 45–47, 168.
    *See also* Excess returns
    above cash
  global bonds, 117, 126
  global stocks, 117, 118, 126
  hedge funds, 125, 126
  municipal bonds, 122, 126
  private equity, 124, 126
  real estate, 123, 126

reasons for, 29, 30. *See also*
  Economic environment,
  shifts in; Future cash rates,
  shifts in expectations of;
  Risk appetite, shifts in
stocks, 21–26, 50, 51, 58, 59,
  61–64, 66, 116–118, 145,
  146
Treasuries, 21, 23–26, 56, 69,
  77, 83, 84, 116, 145, 146

Treasury Inflation-Protected
  Securities (TIPS), 93, 96, 97,
  116, 145, 146
weighted, 145–147

Zero sum game
  active management, 190, 191
  active risk, 185
  commodity futures, 103, 187
  trading securities as, 2